The Recipes that made a Million

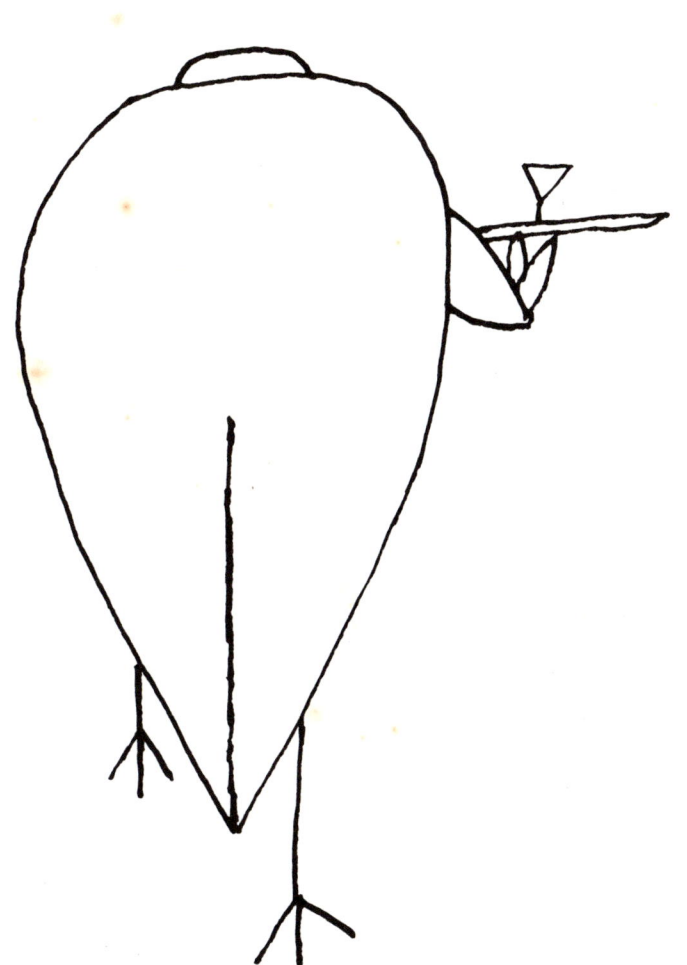

The Recipes that made a Million

Franco Lagattolla

With drawings by Enzo Apicella

© Franco Lagattolla 1978
Published by Orbis Publishing Limited, London
Printed in England by The Pitman Press

ISBN 0 85613 489 9

To my dear mother Luisa who first showed me what good food was all about, Sara my beautiful wife, Nicolas and Fabio my two sons, our labrador Bruna and to my hardworking typewriter which never once answered back.

CONTENTS

FOREWORD	7
INTRODUCTION	9
ANTIPASTI	11
ZUPPE *Soups*	39
UOVA *Egg dishes*	49
FARINACEI *Pasta & Rice*	53
PESCE *Fish*	77
CARNE, POLLAME E CACCIAGIONE *Meat, Poultry & Game*	95
LEGUMI E VERDURE *Vegetables & Salads*	133
DOLCI *Desserts*	151
SAUCES, STOCKS, ODDS & ENDS	159
FORMAGGI *Cheese*	166
GLOSSARY	170
WEIGHTS & MEASURES	171
INDEX	172

FOREWORD

I was fourteen. I had asked the Savoy Hotel's Head Hall Porter for a job as a pageboy – the lowest possible rung of the hotel ladder. He sent me up to the Housekeeper for a uniform. I was always too big for my age and she couldn't find one large enough to fit me. So I was sent back to the Hall Porter, who was sorry for me but couldn't do any more to help. He suggested that I go round to the left, past the marble pillars, and speak to the Head Waiter.

I did. He interviewed me briefly. Did I have any black shoes? No? Then I could dye those I was wearing. I was told to go out and buy myself a short 'cafe-jacket', black dinner trousers, a washable celluloid shirt-front, some wing-collars and an apprentice's white bow tie. I had been given my first job in the restaurant business. My friends told me I was nuts! All that work, that humping, carting, serving other people, those ridiculously long hours? I was told quite clearly that I would live to regret it. Well, I'd give it a try anyway.

And, despite the tough going and the hard years things went remarkably well. It was not an easy life. I had to learn everything from scratch. Jobs were hard to find and had to be held on to grimly with willingness and professional ability. I was lucky to work at some of the finest restaurants in London, under the most marvellous directors. I watched, observed and stored as much experience as I could.

In 1959 I put down £800 (plus £200 more soon after) and threw in my £600 car, too. A colleague matched this with £1000. A partnership was formed, a site located and exciting plans for the first small restaurant were made. But the dream was short-lived. The meagre funds were not enough to warrant the bank loan that was needed to cover the conversion costs. My own faithful, ever trusting parents came to the rescue, pledging their home. The bank agreed, the deeds were placed in the vault and the vital overdraft was authorized. To help matters along, I took a night job and shared my wages with my partner who had decided to stay on-site to supervise the workmen.

Eventually a small Italian restaurant with seating for 30 people, a colourful mural of the Bay of Naples and an indoor vine laden with real grapes (to be presented to the customers at the end of their meal) was opened. And, in the basement, a small private club was, literally, launched on a wave of drinks and did such fantastic business that it financed the upstairs restaurant which did not go so well at the start.

With a lot of hard work, a lot of new dishes and ideas, friendly service, the best food the markets offered, good honest wines, easy pricing, and an atmosphere that was original and vibrant, its reputation spread far and wide. A second, very exclusive restaurant, designed by Enzo Apicella, was opened in 1962. It was a rave from the beginning. For the first time an Italian restaurant was accepted by the French élite as a worthy contender.

Despite some trip-ups and a couple of headlong pitfalls, which placed my parents' house in extreme peril, there was no stopping the restaurants' fantastic progress. A third and then fourth restaurant were added to the popular, personally run chain. In 1968 the group was making such large profits that it was successfully floated as a public company on the London Stock Exchange with a quoted issuing share value approaching £1½ million. And all this from a first year loss of £350, inside nine years, and with only four restaurants.

The group continued with the same successful expansionist programme. The restaurants were soon increased to ten and more were planned. Profits were more than doubled. Then, in 1973, after a majority vote, the group was taken over by a large British food manufacturing concern. I left quite soon afterwards of my own accord.

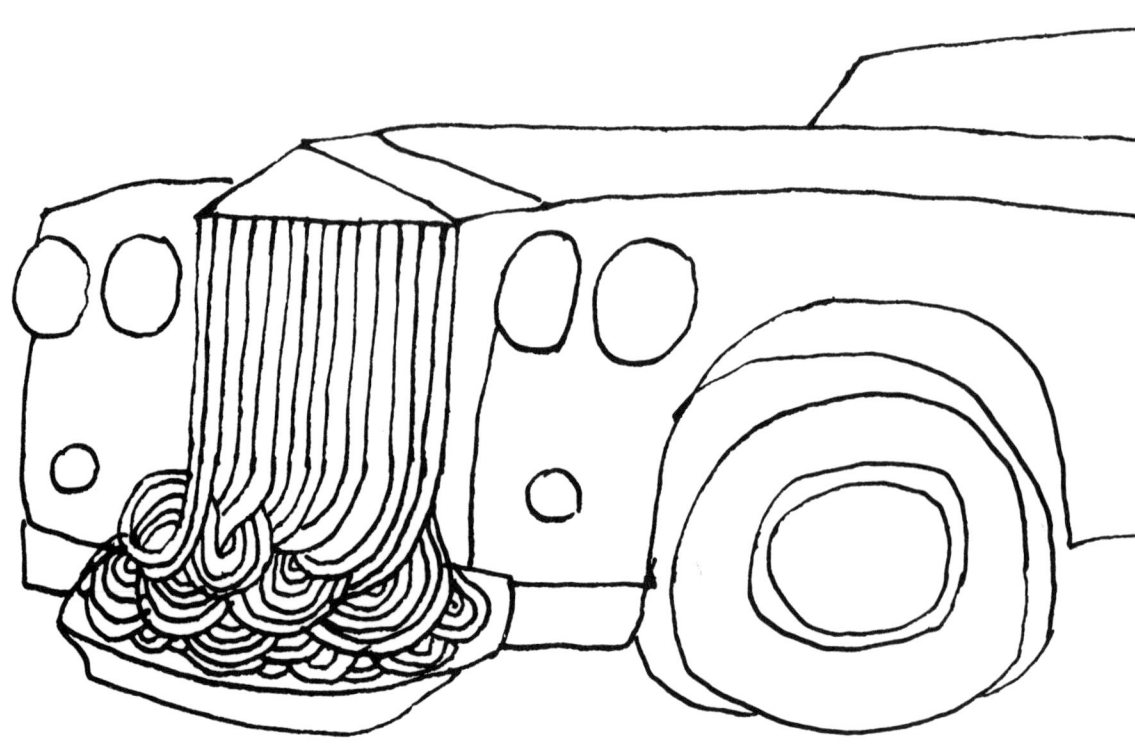

INTRODUCTION

Someone once said that the best cookery books are those that may be enjoyed on a train journey. I hope you will find this such a book. For personal reasons my old restaurants are not mentioned by name. The observations and comments I make are strictly my own. Whether for or against, they are always impartial. They are meant to be constructive and are made with a professional eye, with the practical experience of one who has spent many years in the restaurant business.

I do not intend to go into a long preamble about the origins of Italian cooking – Catherine de'Medici and all that – it has all been done so many times before. Nor am I going to tell you that the following recipes are the sacrosanct originals. No one could ever do that. Italians are so independent that they have changed or adapted recipes over the centuries to suit individual tastes, their pockets and more

especially, their families. There are definitely no hard and fast rules to be rigidly adhered to such as exist for French haute cuisine.

The recipes are, in the main, for those dishes which regularly appeared on my restaurants' menus. There are some exceptions, but most are of Italian origin. A lot of them are simple southern (Neapolitan or Amalfitan) ones which my mother used to prepare. Many of them are specialities which I liked to recommend and serve while working in some of London's exclusive West End restaurants so many years ago. Some I invented or devised myself. Others I borrowed from other countries' cuisines for, fortunately, my gastronomic philosophy is flexible enough to embrace the fact that other nations have splendid cuisines of their own. The result is, I suppose, a combination of food and ideas that became known as typical of the group of famous restaurants that I ran.

One thing is certain about these recipes. They, together with a lot of hard work, brought me much good fortune. I hope that they will be lucky for you too.

I am assuming that your enthusiasm and culinary experience will permit you to take it from here. This is not a cookery book for beginners. You may think at first glance that in some recipes, especially the pastas, I have stipulated an excessive amount of garlic: not so! Those really are the quantities necessary for successful southern Italian cooking. Always crush the garlic cloves and discard the tiny, strongly flavoured, centre core. Remember that raw spring onion or scallion, so well loved by the British and Americans, is infinitely more overpowering than properly cooked garlic.

In many recipes I also suggest that butter or pure lard be used. I believe that, if the correct flavour is to be savoured, you should use them. But if you are worried about cholesterol content use olive, vegetable or seed oil or a good vegetable margarine.

Except where stated, all the recipes are for four people. The measurements are as specific as possible. You will find that Italian cooking is very adaptable. It provides a chance to correct many mistakes as you go along. Don't worry about precise ounces, grammes, gills, pints and decilitres. If wine is stipulated, pour out a little extra and share it between yourself and the pot. Use only the finest ingredients, and the freshest of everything. The best results depend on those two factors perhaps more than any other. Work with a smile. Italian food is just great. It is fun to eat. It should be just as much fun to prepare.

ANTIPASTI
Hors d'oeuvres

The word antipasto means exactly what it says: *anti* (before) *pasto* (the meal). Unless there are guests, or it is Sunday or a special occasion, antipasti are not usually served as part of an everyday Italian home meal which will generally start with a soup, rice or pasta dish. In hot weather, however, starchy dishes are often dispensed with and the meal may start with an antipasto.

Regretfully it is true to say that surprisingly few restaurateurs in Italy use their imagination and offer, by way of antipasti, much more than a simple selection of regional hams, salami or cold seafoods (usually garnished with sharp-tasting vegetables pickled in awful commercial vinegar) or, on a good day, a pale, often amateurish, imitation of a French hors d'oeuvre. There are, of course, exceptions.

When planning for my first small London restaurant I was already certain, from past experience, that the average restaurant customer would seldom order more than three courses. Knowing the British love of desserts, I decided to widen the choice of first courses by including many tempting non-Italian dishes. Necessarily, most of them are not of the Italian antipasto type at all, but are 'starters' or first-course dishes.

In some cases a dish could be allocated to another section of the book. This is because of the versatility of Italian cooking which makes it more than possible for some dishes to be served not only as first courses, but also as very good vegetable or even main courses. So check the index if in doubt.

ALICI IN TORTIERA
Baked savoury anchovies
You may be lucky enough to buy, at certain times of the year, some small, fresh, Mediterranean anchovies. They are absolutely delicious, especially when cooked in this very simple way. Do not, on any account, try to make this dish by using small sardines or sprats: they taste too strongly of oil.

Split 900g (2 lb) of fresh anchovies with your thumb and slide out the tiny backbone and head. Leave the tails. Wash and drain well. Close them back to their original shape and arrange them side by side in a large baking dish. Sprinkle with two tablespoons of coarsley chopped parsley, two finely sliced garlic cloves, salt and milled black pepper. Douse liberally with olive oil and sprinkle evenly with a tablespoon of mild vinegar. Cover. Place in a hot oven for ten minutes, then uncover and cook for a further five minutes. These delicious anchovies may be eaten hot, warm or cold, either as an hors d'oeuvre or as a light main course.

ANTIPASTO PASQUALE
An Easter hors d'oeuvre
In New York when the talk is of Italian antipasti, those served at Mamma Leone's immediately spring to mind. Mamma Leone's, the largest Italian restaurant in the city, possibly in the world, serves more than 3000 meals a day. I've never seen anything like it. In a word, Mamma Leone's is unbelievable. It has all the

romantic touches and ingredients which Italy, even Hollywood, was glad to forget years ago. The food is not up to much (how could it be with all those customers to serve) but, in fairness, neither are the prices. The atmosphere is cheerful and happy-go-lucky; the wine is all right; the service pleasant and, as I was saying, the special Mamma Leone antipasto is really very good indeed. It's almost worth going there just for that!

Here is a typically Neapolitan antipasto which traditionally precedes the Easter Sunday lunch. The inclusion of the tomatoes is my own idea: they do not clash, and add colour. It is very simply composed of attractively arranged slices of coarse-cut Italian salami or coppa, sliced Ricotta (Greek Feta cheese will do), sliced hard-boiled eggs, ripe black olives with fennel seeds and thinly sliced tomatoes dressed with olive oil, salt, milled black pepper and chopped fresh basil leaves or the merest pinch of oregano.

ARINGHE ALL'UBRIACA
Soused herrings

Place eight very fresh, cleaned herrings in a deep, flat dish. Bring to the boil 280ml (10 fl oz) each of dry white wine and light malt vinegar together with one thinly sliced onion, one thinly sliced carrot, one bay leaf, some torn-up parsley, a small sprig of thyme, a few black peppercorns and salt. Pour over the herrings and simmer them gently for 15 minutes. Let them cool in the cooking liquor. Serve cold. Do not serve wine, just good beer will do.

ASPARAGI FRESCHI
Fresh asparagus

Fresh asparagus is one of the most distinguished of all vegetables. So much so that it should always be accorded a course to itself: an hors d'oeuvre, light main course or salad course, but it should never be served as a vegetable accompaniment. That would be an extravagant waste, for apart from being expensive, its delicately fresh individual taste would be completely lost with the other flavours.

Always try to buy the green asparagus and make sure that it is not the very thin sort which is really only fit for soup. The fat white kind, to my mind, is rather tasteless and should be avoided. Asparagus should be trimmed to uniform length and the stalk ends lightly scraped with a sharp knife. They have to be washed very carefully in lots of running water to rid them of all sand or grit. Tie them into bundles of eight, stand them in a deep pan, wedging them so that the points are upright, and pour in boiling, salted water up to (but not covering) the tips. Cook for 15 minutes or more according to the thickness of the asparagus. Drain well on a cloth. Serve either hot, cold or warm with melted clarified butter, hollandaise sauce, olive oil and salt, olive oil and vinegar, or lemon or a vinaigrette. But please, whatever you do, do not destroy good asparagus the way the Milanese do, with gooey undercooked fried eggs, black butter and grated Parmesan cheese.

BARCHETTINE DI SCAMPI
Zucchini stuffed with scampi

Cook two medium-sized zucchini in a little salted water until firmly tender. Drain and cool. Cut them in half lengthways and hollow the centres. Fill them with finely chopped, hard-boiled eggs mixed with chopped chives or spring onions. Moisten with olive oil and vinegar. Range six medium-sized, cooked, shelled scampi on top of each one. Mask with a thick Cocktail sauce (page 161) to which a little chopped dill has been added. Serve chilled.

BEIGNETS DI COZZE
Mussel fritters

Wash and scrub 24 large mussels. Put them into a saucepan and cover tightly. Shake them over a high flame until the mussels open – discard any that don't. Shell and let them cool. Make a Beer batter (page 160) and leave to stand for an hour. Dip the mussels in flour and then in the batter. Deep-fry until they are golden and crisp. Serve with lemon wedges and tartare sauce.

BIGOS ALLA POLACCA
Pork and cabbage, Polish style
Those two smart, internationally known, London restaurant-clubs, Les Ambassadeurs and the Twenty-One, specialize in this Polish dish. It faintly resembles Casseola, an Italian pork and cabbage casserole which is essentially a hearty main course.

In a heavy casserole, cook a medium-sized, chopped onion in butter until soft together with one chopped, medium-sized cooking-apple and three crushed garlic cloves. Discard the garlic. Add 900g (2 lb) of sliced and blanched white cabbage, four sliced mushrooms and four roughly chopped tomatoes. In a separate pan, brown 225g (8 oz) of cubed pork and 225g (8 oz) of thickly sliced, smoked Polish sausage in a little lard and add to the casserole. Deglaze the pan with a cup of vegetable stock and add to the pork and vegetables. Season with salt and black pepper. Cover. Simmer for an hour and a half, then uncover and cook for a further ten minutes. If the pan should run dry add a little hot water. The end result should not be too liquid. Serve hot with a plainly boiled rice-potato to each portion, a lot of fresh, crusty bread and many glasses of red wine.

BOTTARGA
Salted, dried tuna or grey mullet roe
My old friend Tony Harris, who seems to live on a long lease in the right-hand corner of Gaston's London French Pub in Soho, introduced me to Avgotarago, a Greek speciality. I had never heard of it before. I found it to be so delicious that I served it occasionally to parties I knew would appreciate it. The Greeks must have brought it over to Sardinia for it is also well known there as Bottarga.

Bottarga is salted, pressed and dried tuna fish or grey mullet roe. It is sausage- or block-shaped and often has the most marvellous amber colour. It is merely sliced very, very thinly and left to macerate in olive oil and lemon juice and then eaten with brown bread or toast. This very good, difficult to obtain, rather expensive delicacy is, however, probably best passed round at informal gatherings, or to impatiently waiting restaurant customers – it quietens them in a flash!

BRESAOLA DELLA VALTELLINA
Salted, smoke-cured beef
This delicacy comes from the Valtellina area of Lombardy. They call it simply *carne secca* or dried meat. Bresaola is salted, smoke-cured and dried beef and is the pride of local gastronomy. It is supposed to make a very good hors d'oeuvre and it does make a welcome change from the eternally offered prosciutto.

Bresaola must always be sliced paper-thin and is usually dressed with olive oil, lemon juice and plenty of milled black pepper. A little chopped spring onion or chive will improve this speciality no end.

CALZONCINI AL CURRY
Curry puffs
Sauté a crushed clove of garlic and a small, finely chopped onion in oil. Discard the garlic when golden. Add 225g (8 oz) of minced beef, a grated celery stalk, half a cup of beef stock, one dessertspoon of curry powder and season with salt and milled black pepper. Cook for 20 minutes.

Roll out some good, light, Flaky pastry (page 162) quite thinly. Cut out circles about the diameter of a cup. Place a little of the curried meat mixture in the centre of each and sprinkle with a little raw, grated apple. Fold the pastry over. Seal and flute the edges firmly. Stand them upright on a baking tray and brush with milk. Bake in a fairly hot oven for the first ten minutes, then reduce the heat and cook for another 20 minutes.

These curry puffs are not a first course at all, but they are delicious and go particularly well with some soups and consommés.

CAPONATA ALLA SICILIANA
Piquant-sweet egg-plants

An intriguing and exotic way of preparing egg-plant – when cold it is good either as an hors d'oeuvre, as an accompaniment, or even as a light main course.

Fry four ripe, cubed, unskinned egg-plants in olive oil until golden. Drain well and set aside. In the same oil (add more if needed) sweat one thinly sliced, large onion. Add 450g (1 lb) of roughly chopped, drained, canned tomatoes and four sliced, tender celery stalks. Season with salt and milled black pepper. Cook gently until the celery is soft. Now add one heaped tablespoon of rinsed capers, two tablespoons of stoned, chopped, green olives, one tablespoon of pine nuts, four tablespoons of malt vinegar and one level dessertspoon of sugar. Return the egg-plants to the pan and carefully mix together. Cook gently for a further ten minutes. Check the seasoning and cool before serving.

CARCIOFI ALLA CONTADINA
Artichokes country style

Remove the tough, outer leaves and cut the stalks and points from the remaining leaves of four large, young artichokes. Prise the leaves apart and gouge out the choke with a spoon. Soak the artichokes for ten minutes in cold, salted water to which you have added the juice of a lemon. Drain well.

Meanwhile, scrub 450g (1 lb) of new potatoes the size of table-tennis balls (or cut larger ones to size). Mix together three heaped tablespoons of coarsely chopped parsley with four finely chopped cloves of garlic and place some in the centre between the artichokes' leaves, working the mixture down as far as possible. Stand the artichokes in a heavy saucepan, surround with the potatoes and place one in the centre of each artichoke. Sprinkle inside and out with salt and milled black pepper. Douse the potatoes with olive oil and drizzle some inside the artichokes. Pour in one cup of water. Cover the pan, bring to the boil and simmer for 45 to 60 minutes, depending on the size of the artichokes. If the liquid should run dry, add a little olive oil and hot water. When the leaves pull out easily they are ready.

You may serve them either hot or cold, as a first course or together with the potatoes as a marvellous vegetarian main course. The potatoes, on their own, make great partners to any plain meat, fish or egg dish as they will have acquired by now a unique flavour.

CAROTE ALL'OLIO
Carrots dressed with olive oil

These may be served alone as an hors d'oeuvre or as part of a composite first course or a salad course.

Scrape 450g (1 lb) of young carrots and quarter lengthways. Cook in salted water until barely tender. Drain well. Put them into a shallow dish and, while still hot, add four tablespoons of light malt vinegar and two crushed cloves of garlic. Turn the carrots over now and then. When cool, add two small roughly chopped chillies, six tablespoons of olive oil, one teaspoon of oregano, salt and milled black pepper. Turn them over until they glisten. Serve cold but not chilled. Should they seem too sharp, then sprinkle them with a little sugar.

CARPACCIO
Raw, dressed fillet of beef

Fully cover an hors d'oeuvre plate with the thinnest possible (and I do mean tissue-thin) slices of raw, lean fillet steak. You will have to use a mallet to beat them even thinner. Simply dress each portion with olive oil, salt, plenty of milled black pepper, chopped parsley, a little lemon juice and the merest touch of finely chopped spring onion or a mustardy mayonnaise. Scatter sliced baby artichokes, mushrooms, very thin shavings of good Parmesan cheese or, if at all possible, some thinly sliced white Piedmontese truffles. Hot toast accompanies this.

CARROZZELLA ALLA LUCANIA
Fried Mozzarella with anchovies

Cut eight, 8mm ($\frac{1}{3}$ in) thick slices of stale sandwich bread. Trim them into rounds. Prepare four slices of fresh Mozzarella cheese of the same thickness. Make four sandwiches and press them down firmly. Dust with flour and soak them in a mixture of two seasoned, beaten eggs and grated Parmesan cheese for a few minutes. Fry the sandwiches gently in olive oil until golden on both sides. Drain well.

Meanwhile, in another pan, heat a little

butter and one tablespoon of olive oil with four chopped anchovies, one dessertspoon of chopped parsley and one finely chopped garlic clove. When frizzling pour it over the Mozzarella sandwiches. Serve very hot. The Mozzarella will ooze out when the crispy covering is cut. This can either be a first course, a snack or a light main course.

CAVIALE
Caviar
Caviar is the *non plus ultra* of hors d'oeuvre. Although Beluga caviar is more commonly available, it is often possible to obtain, from the bigger importers, quantities of Sevruga and Ocietrova. The latter, tiny, dark-green to black grains, is considered by some to be the best. All caviar tins should be marked with the word 'Mallosol', which indicates that the eggs have been particularly well selected and only very slightly salted.

Caviar should always be served chilled – in crystal bowls or straight from the tin. It must be eaten very simply. No chopped egg, onion or parsley nonsense! Just with slightly buttered, plain or toasted dark or rye bread, and highlighted with a few drops of lemon juice. The only other permitted juices are iced Russian Vodka or a good, chilled champagne.

CAVIALE DE MELANZANE
Egg-plant caviar
If you can't afford to eat caviar, then try this amazingly delicious spread on your slice of toasted rye bread or plain, fresh, crusty loaf. And maybe you'll never miss the real thing.

Slash the skin of four ripe egg-plants. Place them in a hot oven or under a grill for 40 minutes or until they are soft and tender inside. Scoop out all the pulp. Discard the skin. Pound two garlic cloves to a paste, add to the pulp and rub through a sieve. Now, in a thin, steady stream, add five tablespoons of olive oil and blend smoothly. Stir in a finely chopped shallot or some spring onions. Season to taste with salt and milled black pepper and sharpen lightly with lemon juice. Pot and chill well.

CAVOLFIORE ALL'OLIO
Cauliflower dressed with olive oil
Wash a cauliflower well. Tear off the florets whole. Now proceed in the same manner as for Carote all'olio (page 14). Serve in the same way.

CIPOLLINE AL CURRY
Glazed, curried button onions
Clean 20 button onions, cross-cut the bottoms and sauté them in butter and oil. Stir in one teaspoon of good curry powder, keeping the onions continually on the move. Season with salt and pepper. Lower the flame and add half a cup of light stock or water, together with a dessertspoon each of sultanas and pine nuts. Simmer until the stock is consumed and the onions glazed and tender. These may be served either hot or cold as part of an hors d'oeuvre or as a vegetable accompaniment to a suitable main course.

COCKTAIL ALL'AMALFITANA
Seafood cocktail, Amalfi style
Scrub 450g (1 lb) of live clams and 12 large mussels. Place them in a large saucepan. Cover tightly, shake briskly over a high flame until they open and discard any that don't. Add a little water to the liquor and cook a medium-sized squid (cut into rings), its tentacles, four medium-sized scampi and eight large shrimps. Add two sliced scallops for the last few minutes. Let them cool in the cooking liquor. Drain and chill slightly.

Cut a crisp lettuce heart into julienne strips and mix with some chopped celery. Season lightly with salt and sprinkle with a few drops of olive oil and malt vinegar. Divide into four parts and place in coupes or glasses. Top with the seafood mixture.

Mask with Cocktail sauce (page 161) to which a little chopped dill has been added. Sprinkle with cayenne pepper and chopped parsley. Serve chilled.

COPPA DI ASTACO
Lobster cocktail
The famous Twenty-One Club, New York, is not really a club at all. It is the most expensive restaurant in the world, a very exclusive association indeed, formed not by a members' selection committee, but by a natural process of drastic financial elimination and, of course, by one's personal standing in the diplomatic, business, theatrical and social world.

The Twenty-One, where all the tables have to be reserved, has an unbelievable atmosphere. It is always jammed, but there are just occasionally unoccupied tables here and there. These belong to regular clients who, although away on trips or overseas business, have tables kept vacant for them on the off-chance that they might pop in!

Twenty-One's food, by an Italian chef, is remarkable in its excellence. The wines are expertly chosen and handled (they are interestingly racked and cellared in the original 'speakeasy, hide-away' cellar of prohibition days), and the service is always smooth and professional. If you are lucky enough to have a table reservation there, and have passed the friendly welcoming scrutiny of Chuck Anderson, the suave Head Receptionist, and of Twenty-One's Directors, Pete Kriendler and Messrs Sheldon and Berns, walk past the impressive cigar stand, down a couple of Ballantine Scotch sours at the long bar and then order a first course of a Twenty-One lobster cocktail. It will amaze you in size, imagination and presentation.

But here's how I used to like them made at my restaurants. Simpler, but just as tasty, I'll guarantee! Half-fill a cocktail coupe or glass with a crispy julienne of lettuce hearts mixed with a little chopped cucumber, celery and slivers of black Umbrian (canned) truffles. Season with salt and cayenne pepper, moisten with olive oil and a dash of malt vinegar. Top generously with cooked, sliced lobster tails. Cover with Cocktail sauce (page 161). Decorate with a whole, shelled lobster claw and sprinkle with chopped hard-boiled egg, parsley and cayenne pepper. Serve chilled.

COPPA ALLA CAPRESE
Crabmeat cocktail
Half-fill a cocktail coupe or glass with a crispy julienne of lettuce hearts mixed with chopped celery and cucumber. Season with salt, moisten with olive oil and a few drops of vinegar. Top generously with cooked, cubed or flaked crabmeat. Mask with Cocktail sauce (page 161). Decorate with chopped hard-boiled egg and parsley and dust with cayenne pepper. Serve chilled.

COSTE DI MAIALE 'MARCO POLO'
Barbecued spare ribs
I fought with my conscience and selfish instincts before deciding to set out what was once my own very jealously guarded secret recipe. A Chinese neighbour once gave my wife the recipes for several succulent Chinese and Malay dishes. The spare rib recipe was particularly good, so I introduced it to the Italian chefs at my restaurants and the tasty news spread like wildfire. The pork rib-cuts were difficult to obtain which meant that I could not always satisfy the demand.

As time passed and some of the cooks left, as they are inclined to do, so did the recipe. Other restaurants jumped on the spare rib wagon and they, too, introduced the dish to their own customers. The Chinese clientele who frequented my restaurants had restricted themselves to consuming large quantities of their favourite Linguine alle vongole (page 61) and piles of crisply fried scampi and squid, but they too tried them, and liked them, so much that they actually began to ask for the recipe!

One reason which helped banish any qualms I might have had in so barefacedly introducing this Chinese dish was the fact that the recently bought corner building (to be part of the restaurant's vast extension) had been for many years a small exclusive French restaurant called Le Lyric. Its main claim to fame was not, as might be expected, its food or wines. Rather the fact that King Edward VII had been a regular patron of the establishment, but he had avoided the restaurant altogether by using the discreet side entrance and going straight up to one of the well-furnished hotel rooms above, where his dinner, of a particularly piquant flavour, would be sent up to him by a most efficient room service. I like to think that he would have appreciated the thought of the crispy, succulent spare ribs appearing on the site of the old Lyric.

This is how they are prepared. First do not buy so-called spare ribs cut from the shoulder—they will not do at all. Allow four long, meaty ribs per portion as an antipasto and more for a main course. Cut them lengthways along the bone, leaving equal amounts of meat on each rib. Make a marinade with seven tablespoons of liquid soy sauce, three tablespoons of brown sugar, three tablespoons of olive oil, three crushed garlic cloves, a little black pepper, two bay leaves, one large crumbled chilli, a level teaspoon of dried fennel seeds and a little salt.

Coat each rib well and leave to marinate for three hours. Turn them over regularly. Range them side by side in a flat oven dish and bake very, very slowly in a moderate oven for at least one and a half hours. Watch them carefully. Should they seem to be darkening too much, add a little hot water and turn them over. When ready, they should be a dark, golden colour and glisten with the rich, sticky glaze. Serve very hot with Barbecue sauce (page 159).

COUPE 'PACIFICO'
Pacific seafood cocktail

I used to serve this appetizer in half a coconut shell, but of course any cocktail coupe or glass will do as well, although the effect will be more subdued.

Lightly mix together three tablespoons of flaked crabmeat, four whole, shelled crab claws, eight shelled, cooked scampi, 12 small, fresh pineapple balls, 12 sweet melon balls, two dessertspoons of diced white chicken meat, one dessertspoon of sliced almonds and a crisp julienne lettuce heart. Place in the chosen container.

Dress with a mixture of two teaspoons of Dijon mustard, one teaspoon each of curry powder and castor sugar, eight tablespoons of heavy cream, one dessertspoon of chopped, fresh dill, salt and white pepper. Decorate with the crab claws. Sprinkle with chopped, hard-boiled egg and parsley. Dust with cayenne pepper. Serve chilled.

CROCCHETTE DI GRANCHIO
Crabmeat croquettes

To 450g (1 lb) of crabmeat (or indeed any finely chopped, cooked shellfish) add enough thick Béchamel sauce (page 159) to make a moist, but not runny, mixture. Add a little dry English mustard, two tablespoons of tomato ketchup, two egg yolks, some Worcester sauce, salt and cayenne pepper. Mix well and heat thoroughly through. Spread out onto a flat tray and chill in the refrigerator for two hours. Roll into cork shapes or round patties. Flour, egg and breadcrumb them. Deep-fry in oil until they are a golden colour. Drain well. Serve with a light Tomato sauce (page 164), Barbecue sauce (page 159) or Tartare sauce (page 164).

CROSTONE DI SCAMPI 'ROTHSCHILD'
Scampi-filled croûte

I abhorred the often haughty reception areas of some smart restaurants and preferred them to be regarded more as 'welcome' areas. In time the reception-welcome became very practised. The welcome was habitually courteous, even when a very inebriated gentleman, despite his squiffy-eyed concentration, missed the last steps altogether and landed in a crumpled heap at the feet of the unruffled head waiters. Their enquiry, with ever so slightly raised eyebrows, 'Did you reserve a table, this evening, sir?' was still sympathetically put.

Their smiles a little fixed, the elegant receptionists remained just as unflappable, holding their ground and resisting all temptation to turn and flee, when a chic young lady once came down the wide, brass-railed staircase preceded by a full-grown, quietly snarling leopard held back by a bejewelled leash.

Reception patience grew a trifle thin, but even then triumphed, when Harry Saltzman, the movie producer, arrived unexpectedly one evening, led his party of nine straight past the 'welcoming committee', sat his guests at the largest and best table (reserved for someone else), demanded menus and his regular bottle of Malvern water as though nothing out of the ordinary had occurred. From that evening, a table was kept for him until a reasonable hour (Twenty-One-Club style) as a precaution against further unexpected appropriation of tables for ten.

Harry Saltzman likes tasty fish dishes as savoury starters to his meals. This is one that I am sure he enjoyed more than once. Cut four 37mm ($1\frac{1}{2}$ in) thick slices of stale sandwich bread. Trim off the crusts. Carefully hollow out the centres with a sharp knife leaving the sides and bases about 6mm ($\frac{1}{4}$ in) thick. They should look rather like open boxes. Drench them with melted butter and bake them in a hot oven until they are golden and crispy. Or you may fry them. Keep them hot.

Sauté 20 medium-sized, floured scampi in butter. Season with salt and cayenne pepper. Flame them and deglaze the pan with half a wine glass of good brandy. Add one and a half cups of Lobster or Aurore sauce (pages 162 and 159). Stir well. Fill the croûtes with the scampi mixture and sprinkle with grated Gruyère cheese. Brown them quickly under a hot grill.

CROÛTE LANDAISE
Foie gras au gratin
This dish is a speciality of M. Raymond Olivier, the famous French gourmet, Maître Chef de cuisine, cookery writer, television personality and truly fantastic

restaurateur, also the owner of the fabulous Grand Vefour in Paris.

I first served this dish many years ago when M. Olivier came to London's Mirabelle Restaurant with his chef in order to demonstrate the art of his fine cooking. The customers went into raptures over it. I had no scruples at all about including Croûte Landaise on some of my menus. Indeed, it was a compliment to one of the great men of the gastronomic world. The dish, of course, is rather expensive but then so is the Grand Vefour restaurant. However, if it is any consolation, it is extremely simple to make.

To make the croûtes cut four slices of day-old sandwich bread about 12mm ($\frac{1}{2}$ in) thick and trim off the crusts. Fry them gently in butter until golden and crisp. Cut four slices of the finest foie gras about 8mm ($\frac{1}{3}$ in) thick (you could, of course, use a cheaper parfait de foie gras), carefully heat them through in butter and set them on the fried croûtes. Cover them completely with mornay sauce. Sprinkle them with mixed grated Gruyère and Parmesan cheese. Glaze under a hot grill. Serve very hot.

FOIE GRAS
Preserved, truffled goose liver
What can anyone say about foie gras except that, after caviar, it is the most ambrosial of hors d'oeuvre and that the mind stops, glands quiver and one's spirit is sublimely lifted when eating it? Spread it on hot, crispy, thick toast, with the creamiest of butter and simply eat it without any further discussion.

FUNGHI FRITTI TARTARE
Mushrooms fried in batter
Make a smooth Beer batter (page 160) and let it stand for an hour. Carefully wipe and clean 450g (1 lb) of mushrooms and cut off their stalks. Dip the mushroom caps in flour and then into the batter. Deep-fry them until they are golden. Drain well. Serve them very hot and crispy with tartare sauce which makes them delicious.

FUNGHI SOTT'OLIO
Mushrooms in olive oil
The quantities, as for all of the recipes in this book, are for four people. So, if you wish to set aside some of these mushrooms (they keep very well in the oil), then adjust the ingredient quantities accordingly – but go easy on the spices! Serve these on their own or as part of a varied hors d'oeuvre.

Bring 570ml (20 fl oz) of water, and the same quantity of malt vinegar with two bay leaves, 12 black peppercorns, two cloves and one finely sliced onion to the boil. Plunge in 900g (2 lb) of cleaned and stalked button mushrooms. Boil them for no more than three minutes. Drain. Spread the mushrooms and the sliced onions on a dry cloth and leave them in a dry place for 24 hours. Put them into an airtight jar with roughly chopped chillies, two sliced garlic cloves, a sprinkling of oregano, a little salt and black pepper and cover with olive oil.

They will be ready to eat 12 hours later, if you can wait that long! See how good the olive oil is when you dunk a piece of bread in it. The remaining oil can, of course, be used over again for the same purpose or for dressing similarly prepared carrots, cauliflowers or egg-plants.

GAMBE DI RANE PONTINA
Sautéed frogs' legs
Some people, almost understandably, look impressively distressed, indeed alarmed, at the thought of eating frogs! But, as you've no doubt been told many times before, they taste just like chicken. If you want to try them do give your fishmonger a little warning, for he may well have some difficulty in obtaining them.

Allow six pairs of frogs' legs per portion. Marinate them for an hour in olive oil, a bay leaf, lemon juice, a few peppercorns, a little thyme and some salt. Pat dry and roll them in flour. Rub a frying pan well with garlic and sauté the legs in butter and oil until they are golden. Remove and keep them warm. Clean out the frying pan. Put in 50g (2 oz) of butter, a little chopped parsley, chervil and tarragon and a good amount of lemon juice. When the butter frizzles browns and foams, pour it over the frogs' legs. Serve immediately.

INSALATA ALLA NIZZARDA
Salade Niçoise

Nice, that beautiful town on the French Riviera, was Italian territory until the middle of the last century when, along with other chunks of Italy, it was literally handed over to France in payment for having (only partially) cleared the Austrians out of northern Italy. What on earth would they have demanded had they done the job properly? Rome? It was, in any event, a very high price to pay.

Along with the territories, northern Italy also ceded many of her *provenzale* recipes and dishes to the French gastronomic treasury. I suppose that we can at least be grateful to Napoleon's batman for having left to Italy that superb dish Poulet à la Marengo. The French can have that back with pleasure though! What we really want back is our Insalata alla nizzarda. And while they are about it we wouldn't complain if Nice and the rest were handed back too!

Quartered ripe, unskinned tomatoes, crisply cooked French beans, ripe black olives, anchovy fillets, tuna fish, sliced green peppers, quartered hard-boiled eggs and cold new potatoes. All carefully proportioned and dressed with a slightly garlic-flavoured vinaigrette. Served only very lightly chilled, with lots of cool, clear white wine.

INSALATA DI RISO ALL'AMALFITANA
Seafood and rice salad

Cook 225g (8 oz) of Italian arborio rice in plenty of boiling, salted water until tender but still with a fraction of a bite to it. Drain well. Rinse with cold water to stop it from cooking in its own heat. Now add anything colourful, tasty and savoury that will mix well, such as chopped peppers, cooked mushrooms, capers, green or black olives, gherkins, crispy, chopped celery, shredded celeriac, peas, cooked zucchini, cubed, firm tomatoes. Then mix in seafood such as tuna fish, anchovies, cooked mussels, squid rings and tentacles, clams, peeled shrimps, crabmeat and sliced cooked scampi.

Mix a dressing with olive oil, malt vinegar, English mustard, Tabasco sauce, salt and milled black pepper. Dress the rice salad lightly and sprinkle with some shredded basil leaves. Turn the rice into an oval dish. Shape and decorate it. Serve chilled.

INSALATA DI SCAMPI
Scampi salad

Gently cook 24 unshelled, large Dublin Bay prawns. Let them cool, and then shell and de-vein them. You may, of course, use frozen shrimp or prawns (which will need gentle thawing, cooking and cooling in the same way). Prepare a dressing by mixing together four tablespoons of creamed horseradish, two tablespoons of Mayonnaise (page 162), two tablespoons of heavy cream, two teaspoons of chopped dill, a few drops of Tabasco sauce and a little seasoning. Mix the cooked scampi well with the dressing and pile onto crispy lettuce hearts. Decorate with sliced hard-boiled eggs, sliced cucumber and radishes and sprinkle with chopped parsley and cayenne pepper.

INSALATA ALLA SINATRA
Sinatra's seafood salad

Joni James, the Italo-American singer, had enjoyed many a meal at my first small restaurant while in London recording an album. When she went back to New York, after having given a lively going-away party, she vowed that she would tell Frank all about the great food.

Jimmy Van Heusen and Sammy Cahn, those brilliant songwriters, said the place and atmosphere reminded them of their favourite Los Angeles restaurant, La Scala. And they, too said that they would make sure that Frank heard of 'this great little joint!'

Irrepressible, dynamic Sammy Davis Jnr, after a wild dinner-party the night before flying back to the coast, said exactly the same thing. I often wondered whether this was not some sort of gag – that maybe someone called Frank J. Smith might not turn up and say 'Joni, Sammy, Jimmy and Sammy told me to come!'

But no – one fine, unforgettable evening the real Frank, the one and only man with the golden voice, arrived. He was in town to record his now famous 'London' album. I was at home at the time taking a night off when I was hurriedly called out to organize the meal.

When 'Ole Blue Eyes' arrived, a long table was ready for him. It was laden with southern Italian specialities which I knew he would enjoy: garlic- and chilli-spiked octopus salad, shrimp and scallop vinaigrette, tomato salad with basil, anchovies, Black olives with fennel seeds (page 37), Peperonata (page 30), egg-plant al funghetto, spicy coarse-cut salami, prosciutto, sun-dried tomatoes with olive oil, and wedges of tangy Caciocavallo cheese.

Many, many bottles of Caruso Bianco di Ravello were ready chilled and waiting in the wine coolers.

Frank and his guests tucked in with gusto. When the party left the restaurant on the way to a night recording-session, Frank shook hands with all the staff and asked someone in the group to make sure that they were all well looked after. The next evening there was a repeat performance. Both times the waiters received more by way of a tip than did the cashier from the table checks!

After those happy evenings I devised a mixed seafood salad that I was proud to name after Frank Sinatra. Gently cook two small squid (cut into ringlets) and their tentacles, eight shelled scampi, 16 shelled shrimps and two halved scallops. Let them cool in the cooking liquor. Meanwhile, place 450g (1 lb) each of well-scrubbed clams and mussels in a saucepan. Cover tightly and shake it over a brisk flame until they open. Discard those that don't. Drain all the fish well. Leave the clams and the mussels in their shells.

Mix everything together with two large tablespoons of diced, cooked crabmeat and lobster. Dress with a sauce made of six tablespoons of olive oil, three crushed garlic cloves, two roughly chopped chillies, one heaped tablespoon of chopped parsley, lemon juice, salt and milled black pepper. Marinate for two hours in a cool place. Turn the seafood over now and again. Remove the garlic. Serve slightly chilled on crisp lettuce hearts, with lots of fresh, country-style, crusty bread.

INSALATA DI SPIGOLA
Sea bass salad
Cut 675g (1½ lb) of raw, filleted sea bass into finger-width strips. Lay them flat in a dish. Barely cover with salted water. Add a bay leaf, a few torn sprigs of parsley and a dash of vinegar. Bring to the boil. Remove immediately. Do not let the fish overcook. Leave to cool in the cooking liquor. Drain well and arrange the fish on crisp lettuce hearts. Sprinkle abundantly with finely chopped shallots, parsley and a level dessertspoon of chopped fresh tarragon. Dress with a light vinaigrette.

INSALATA 'TIZIANA'
Mozzarella salad
We were witnessing the blossoming of London's fabulous Swinging Sixties. The youngsters of those days, the restless ones with the new ideas, were bored. They felt hemmed in. Prime Minister Macmillan's famous 'wind of change' had barely been a draught to them! So they decided to get to work. They made things happen.

All sorts of new places, restaurants, clubs, discos, boutiques, markets, galleries, studios, theatres and journals sprouted. Some, of course, withered and died. I clearly remember a place with a definite style of its own. It was a restaurant called the Black Diamond. In it everything was black. Floors, walls, ceilings, tablecloths, furniture, plates, food and staff. Even when they turned the lights on, no one could see a thing!

But the new wave was with us. The moribund, rich establishment looked over its shoulder with alarm. There were no hang-ups any more, no self-consciousness. After all, what were rich people but poor ones with money! And the whole scene was light-hearted – with hair long, miniskirts, bell-bottomed pants and even wider brimmed hats. And what about the girls of those days? They all looked so beautiful, serene, relaxed and uninhibited – doing their own thing!

Some say that London's Swinging Sixties never really existed, that it was all a gigantic hoax by courtesy of *Time* magazine's famous article. But they were great days. No one can ever take them away. The whole world came to London, and London, with newly found flair, rose brilliantly to the occasion.

The girls of that time grew very fond of

this low-calorie antipasto dish, which they used to order as a main course. Thinly slice two very fresh and soft Mozzarella cheeses, four large, ripe, unskinned tomatoes and a peeled cucumber. Moisten four hard rusk biscuits or bagels with a little garlic-flavoured oil and lemon dressing. Arrange the sliced ingredients in an overlapping circle. Season with salt and milled black pepper. Sprinkle with finely shredded, fresh basil leaves or the merest suggestion of fresh oregano. Provide more olive oil and lemon if required.

LUMACHE FARCITE AL FORNO
Baked stuffed snails

The service of snails has always held a peculiar fascination for me. I like to watch customers' deep concentration as they fiddle around with the thin snail forks, intent on extracting the reluctant morsels out into the open. Some disdainfully ignore the thoughtfully provided snail tongs and choose to pick up the unexpectedly red-hot shells in their fingers, barely able to smile nonchalantly while trying manfully to disguise the look of acute anguish on their faces. It can be interesting to follow the progress of a somewhat apprehensive customer who, having studied the mechanical function of the tongs, is now satisfied that he can manipulate them. Gingerly pincered and held tentatively at a distance, he lifts the shell cautiously higher and closer to his probing fork. Then, at the last minute, he panics and grips it too tightly. To his alarm (and to that of the others sitting, spellbound, at his table) the now live and slippery shell shoots across the table with a speed that it no doubt wished it had possessed in life, landing with a splash in someone's soup.

I have toyed with many ideas on how to relieve customers of the tedious snail-evicting chore. I even wondered whether a confectionery or pasta company could not make a crunchy, edible snail shell, one that could stand up to the rude treatment snails are inclined to receive in kitchens. After all, they do make macaroni pasta-shells.

The nearest I ever came to solving the problem was in the early years, when I asked a chef to bake tiny profiteroles a little crisper than usual. These, being hollow, were easy to fill with the snails and the hot garlic-butter mixture. The customers delighted in being able to pop the whole morsel, now with an unusually crispy-soft covering that absorbed much of the flavour, into their mouths. The result was satisfaction all round. No more scorched fingers, troublesome tongs, embarrassed looks, stained tablecloths or spotted ties.

I am sorry to say that my bright idea eventually fizzled out. Mostly because of blind resistance by some staff to progress of any sort! It was never brought back to life. So, today, my recipe for snails is exactly the same as all the others. I just used to add some finely chopped walnuts and a whole lot more parsley. I liked to insist that my snail butter was always fresher and greener.

MELANZANE 'IMMAM BAYELDI'
Baked savoury egg-plant

Here is a Turkish way of preparing eggplants. It is so sensuous and tasty that its very name explains that 'the Sultan swooned with pleasure' on tasting it for the first time.

Cut four large, ripe egg-plants lengthways. Snick a little off each bottom so that they will stand firmly. Scoop out and reserve most of the pulp. Sprinkle with salt. Leave for an hour in a slanted dish so that the bitter juices will run off. Wash and pat dry. Brown them quickly in olive oil. Drain them on absorbent paper.

In the same frying oil, gently sauté two crushed garlic cloves until golden. Add a sliced medium-sized onion and the egg-plant pulp and cook until soft. Remove the garlic. Mix in 450g (1 lb) of undrained, roughly chopped, canned tomatoes, six bruised basil leaves, one dessertspoon of sultanas, one dessertspoon of pine nuts or pine kernels, salt and milled black pepper. Cook briskly for five minutes. Fill the egg-plants with the stuffing and place them in a baking tray. Spread any surplus sauce on the bottom. Bake in a moderate oven for 25 minutes. Cool. Serve as a first or light main course. I will not guarantee that you will swoon, but I'm sure you are going to like them!

MELANZANE ALLA PARMIGIANA ALLA MINORESE
Egg-plants 'Parmigiana', Minori style
This is the local Amalfitan coast version of the Neapolitan dish, which, strangely enough, bears the name of Parma. Try it this way, you'll find that it is far more subtle and refined than the coarser Neapolitan method. This is another of those dishes that is more than suitable, hot or cold, as an antipasto, a light but rich main course, as a tasty garnish to a plain dish or even very good in sandwiches!

For this dish you will need a double quantity of Simple tomato sauce (page 164). Cut four medium-sized egg-plants lengthways into slices 6mm ($\frac{1}{4}$ in) thick. Fry these in olive oil until golden. Drain them well on absorbent paper. Dip in flour and then into a mixture of two seasoned eggs beaten with two tablespoons of grated Parmesan cheese. Fry them again in oil until golden.

Spread the bottom of a deep baking dish with some of the tomato sauce. Cover this with a layer of egg-plant. Spread with more sauce. Sprinkle liberally with grated Parmesan cheese. Continue building up layers until the egg-plants are used up. Top with tomato sauce and grated Parmesan cheese. Bake in a moderate to hot oven for 20 minutes or until well heated through. Serve hot or cold.

MELANZANE SOTT'OLIO
Egg-plants in olive oil
Cut four large, ripe egg-plants lengthways into slices 6mm ($\frac{1}{4}$ in) thick. Bring to the boil 570ml (20 fl oz) of water and the same quantity of malt vinegar together with two bay leaves, 12 black peppercorns and two cloves. Plunge in the sliced egg-plants. Let them boil for a minute or two or until they become translucent. Drain them well. Spread out the egg-plants on a towel. Leave for at least 12 hours in a dry place. Put them into an airtight jar with two large, roughly chopped chillies, three sliced garlic cloves, a slight sprinkling of oregano, salt and milled black pepper. Cover with olive oil. After 12 hours they will have absorbed enough flavour and will be ready to eat. These will keep for a long time in oil.

MELONE DI STAGIONE
Seasonal melon
Ripe sweet melons of any variety, except water-melon, are delightful when served as a first course. The most acceptable to my mind are the green and delicately sweet Spanish honeydews, the lush, moist and delectable Israeli ogens, and the most superb of them all, that fragrant burst of sun, perfume and sweetness, the small French Charentais.

Melons must be served well-chilled or not at all. They should always be presented on crushed ice. Powdered ginger should be offered. Some customers prefer to bring out the flavour of their melons by sprinkling either salt or pepper or both over them. Occasionally, a little port can be poured to extremely good effect into the hollows of Charentais or ogens.

Sweet melon balls served cold in a mild curry sauce is certainly an intriguing and different method, and very good, too. I was once served with an ogen melon which had been filled with shrimp in cocktail sauce and which I found disgusting! On the other hand, I have been served with ogen melon filled with sweetly sugared blackcurrants—absolutely delicious!

Ripe melon slices served with moist San

Daniele or Parma ham have now become almost an automatic way of starting many Italian meals. I have tired of it and find it rather boring. If you do wish to serve it though, never place the melon underneath the thin slices of prosciutto—it imparts a disagreeable flavour.

One of the most glorious sights I have ever seen was a bright, colourful mound of locally grown cantaloups piled high in the vegetable markets of Southern California. Unfortunately this delicious strain of melon seems to have all but died out in Europe.

MOULES 'RAVIGOTE'
Piquant mussel salad
Wash and scrub 48 large mussels. Place them in a large saucepan. Cover tightly. Toss the saucepan around over a brisk flame until they open up. Discard any that don't. Shell the mussels and let them cool. Arrange them in the centres of crisp lettuce hearts. Cover with Ravigote sauce (page 163) to which you should add a little of the mussel liquor. Dust with cayenne pepper and serve slightly chilled.

MOUSSE DI PERA AVOCADO E SALMONE AFFUMICATO
Avocado and smoked salmon mousse
Mash the pulp of three large, ripe avocado pears and blend with 140ml (5 fl oz) of heavy cream, 140ml (5 fl oz) of béchamel sauce, one dessertspoon of lemon juice, two tablespoons of home-made mayonnaise, salt and white pepper. Pass this through a fine sieve. Add four heaped tablespoons of julienne smoked salmon and fold in. Mix one tablespoon of powdered gelatine in two tablespoons of water, dissolve over a gentle heat and work smoothly into the avocado-salmon mixture. Pour into an oiled mould. Chill until set firmly. Slice into portions and serve on thinly cut smoked salmon. Garnish with lemon wedges and serve with buttered brown bread.

MOZZARELLA IN CARROZZA
Fried Mozzarella sandwich
Cut eight, 8mm ($\frac{1}{3}$ in) thick slices of stale sandwich bread. Trim them into rounds. Prepare four slices of fresh Mozzarella cheese of the same thickness. Make four tidy sandwiches and press them down firmly. Dust with flour and leave them to soak for a few minutes in a mixture of two seasoned, beaten eggs and a little grated Parmesan cheese. Fry the sandwiches gently in olive oil on both sides until golden. Drain well. Serve very hot with lemon wedges.

NERVETTI ALL'INSALATA
Calves' feet salad
In a saucepan, cover three calves' feet with cold, salted water containing two bay

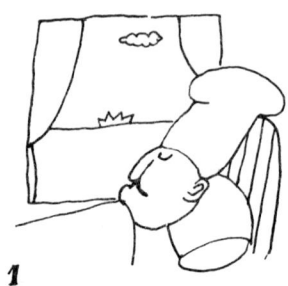
1

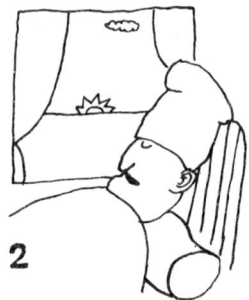
2

3

leaves, one onion, two sliced carrots, two cloves and a cut-up celery stalk. Bring to the boil. Skim off the froth. Simmer for at least two and a half hours or until the calves' feet are tender. Leave them to cool in their own cooking liquor. Drain well. Slice all the meaty, jelly-like and gristly parts thinly. Put them in a bowl and dress them with chopped shallots, chopped parsley, capers, olive oil, malt vinegar, salt and plenty of milled black pepper. Serve them heaped in the centre of crisp lettuce hearts. Don't forget lots of crusty French bread and carafes of hearty red wine, too.

OSTRICHE
Oysters

The ancient Greeks adored oysters. They not only ate them but also used the pearly shells as ballot cards for voting purposes. Greek elections must have been happy occasions indeed – gastronomically always successful, if not politically.

The ancient Romans, who were also bivalve fanatics, went to extraordinary lengths to ensure that Rome and its colonies were constantly supplied with oysters. Indeed those clever Romans of old left, in their conquered territories, a grand legacy in the form of beautifully cultivated oyster beds.

Although the Chinese knew about oysters long before the Romans, it does not seem that the Chinese handed down any very remarkable oyster recipes for us to enjoy and appreciate, except of course their oyster sauce, which I am sure does not contain any oysters at all.

Until late in Victorian times oysters were regarded somewhat disdainfully by the English as being food for the poor and the working classes. Today, at current prices, few can afford to eat them. How times have changed! When in peak condition there are no finer oysters in the whole of Europe than those plump, succulent ones from Colchester or the flatter, superbly flavoursome natives of Whitstable.

Many restaurant customers regularly perform the ritual of eating straight from the shell and then proceed to comment knowledgeably on the qualities of the natural juices. Little do these oyster-fanciers know that in 99·9 per cent of restaurants those same oysters have been thoroughly washed and rinsed under tap-water. I used to insist, however, that the oyster juices should be meticulously collected and then strained through fine muslin. A tedious chore, maybe, but not many other restaurateurs can swear to that. The only other person who could have commented on the subject was my oyster-man – especially on busy evenings!

Purists will say that oysters should only be eaten raw. Not true. As long as they are treated with the respect they merit, with

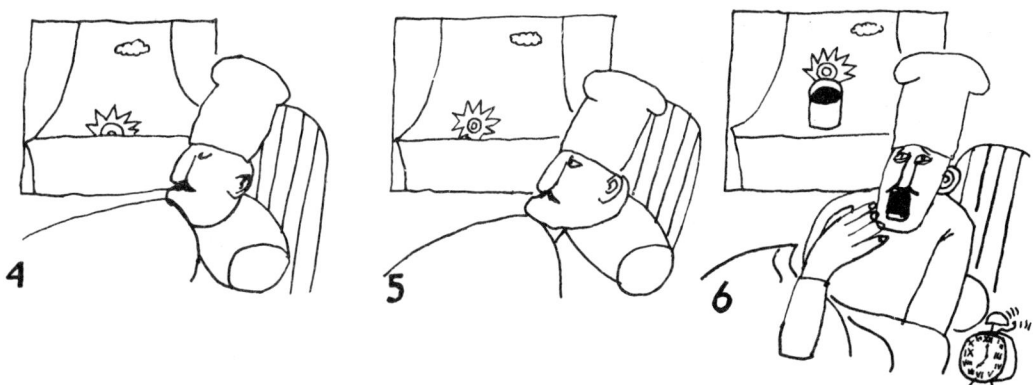

lemon juice, chilli vinegar, shallot dressing, Tabasco, horseradish, cayenne, *mignonette* pepper, or cocktail sauce; or stewed, sautéed, creamed, fried, baked, gratinéed, broiled; or included in puddings, in pies or even in sandwiches, oysters are the greatest! If you fancy raw oysters straight from the shell at any time in London, then the only place worth considering is Wheelers, the established Soho fish restaurant. Not because they are any better there than anywhere else, but because the atmosphere is always just right. Sit up at the long ground-floor bar and eat them with lots of buttered brown bread and tankards of rich, dark Guinness or some of the chilled house white wine.

Oysters that have disappointed? I am sorry to say – because this restaurant is probably one of the most fascinating anywhere in the world – that these were the Oysters Rockefeller de rigueur so beautifully served and of such insipid taste, at Antoine's in New Orleans.

Oysters I have loved? And remember with enchantment? The beautifully selected, juicy, freshly opened ones (I almost expected to find a Tiffany pearl) that started off a memorable meal at the luxurious Hotel Carlyle, New York. And those, so superbly stuffed, baked to perfection and consumed with such gusto at Mosca's, a modest, quite remarkable Italian restaurant a few miles out of New Orleans.

OSTRICHE 'CHABLIS'
Oysters in white wine sauce
British writer Quentin Crewe once gave my new Mayfair restaurant what he felt was a merited write-up in *Queen* magazine. That article did three things. It provided a lot of useful publicity, raised the sales of oysters, and cost the restaurant a couple of thousand pounds. Apart from lauding the quality of the oyster dishes (amongst others), he loudly lamented the fact that the restaurant's attractive vaulted ceilings clearly redirected all the different conversations from table to table. And so the ceilings were duly treated with special, absorbent plaster so as to deaden the sound and protect customers' secrets, maintain oyster sales and get some better, less costly, magazine write-ups. I could have charged, come to think of it, ceiling prices after that!

Quentin Crewe enjoys his oysters any fashion, but especially this way. Open and remove 24 large oysters from their shells. Poach them gently in their own strained liquor together with a glass of Chablis or similar dry white wine. Drain and set them aside. Meanwhile, gently sweat two finely chopped shallots in butter until soft. Add the wine-liquor and reduce. Blend in a cup of heavy cream and heat well. Whisk 75g (3 oz) of soft butter and a few drops of lemon juice smoothly into the sauce. Season with salt and cayenne pepper. Replace the oysters in their heated half-shells. Coat them with the sauce. Dust with cayenne pepper and serve hot.

OSTRICHE ALLA NEW ORLEANS
Oysters baked with spinach
Open and detach 24 large oysters but do not remove them from their shells. Cook six tablespoons of finely chopped spinach and three tablespoons each of sorrel (or lettuce) and shallots in three tablespoons of butter until soft. Add four tablespoons of soft breadcrumbs, two tablespoons of heavy cream, a few drops of Tabasco, a little Worcester sauce and salt. Mix well. Cover each oyster with some of the mixture. Sprinkle with some soft, butter-moistened breadcrumbs. Heat well in a hot oven, and then brown them quickly under a hot grill. Sprinkle with a julienne of crisply fried bacon. Serve hot.

PADELLE REALI 'DONNA LUISA'
Sautéed scallops, my Mother's way
Place 12 shelled, fresh scallops (with the sweet orange part) in a large frying pan together with eight tablespoons of olive

oil, four large crushed garlic cloves, two tablespoons of coarsely chopped parsley, one roughly chopped chilli, two tablespoons of plain water, salt and milled black pepper. Cover the pan. Cook until the oil and the juices have amalgamated and thickened. Serve them very hot in warmed scallop shells with lots of crusty bread to mop up the sauce. This can be either a first course or a main dish.

PÂTÉ DI ARINGHE AFFUMICATE
Kipper pâté

Simmer three large, meaty kippers in the normal way until cooked. Skin and bone the fillets carefully. Flake the fish while it is still warm, mix it with two tablespoons of lemon juice and a lot of freshly milled black pepper. Add 100g (4 oz) of butter and eight tablespoons of heavy cream. Work the mixture thoroughly with a wooden spoon until well blended. Put it into an earthenware pot. Serve well chilled, with plenty of hot, toasted brown bread.

This type of quick pâté is also good if made with smoked brislings, sprats or buckling, which require no cooking.

PÂTÉ ALLA CAMPAGNOLA
Country-style pâté

Sauté two large, chopped garlic cloves, one large, finely chopped onion and 100g (4 oz) of chopped bacon in butter until golden. Add 100g (4 oz) each of cubed belly of pork, pie veal, pigs' liver, chuck steak, two bay leaves, one tablespoon of chopped parsley, salt and milled black pepper. Cook briskly over a high flame to seal the meats.

Flame with two measures of brandy. Add a small wine glass of dry Marsala and a cup of stock to which a little gelatine has been added. Cook gently for 20 minutes. Remove the bay leaves, mince the mixture coarsely and add all the pan juices. Check the seasoning. Rub a loaf tin with lard and smooth the mixture into the tin gently. Dot with lard. Cover with foil and stand the tin in a shallow pan containing hot water. Place in a moderate oven and cook for one and a half hours. Remove the foil for the last 15 minutes. Cool. Serve slightly chilled with thick, toasted farmhouse bread, butter, some radishes, gherkins and much red wine.

PÂTÉ DI FEGATINI DI POLLO
Chicken-liver pâté

Sauté one finely chopped, medium-sized onion with two crushed garlic cloves in two tablespoons of butter until soft. Add 225g (8 oz) of chicken livers, a bay leaf and a small sprig of thyme. Cook until the chicken livers are pink inside. Flame with a small wine glass of brandy. Discard the bay leaf, the thyme and garlic. Cool. Season with salt and plenty of milled black pepper. Mince finely. Blend in two tablespoons of heavy cream. Put into a small pot and chill well. Sprinkle the top liberally with finely chopped spring onion and hard-boiled egg. Serve with fresh crusty bread or thick hot toast.

PÂTÉ DI MERLUZZO AFFUMICATO
Smoked haddock mousse

In a bowl, mix 280ml (10 fl oz) of béchamel sauce with 450g (1 lb) of cooked, boned and flaked smoked haddock, 50g (2 oz) of butter, two tablespoons of stiffly whipped cream, a few drops of Tabasco, salt and milled black pepper. Work well with a wooden spoon. Rub through a fine sieve. Dissolve one tablespoon of powdered gelatine in four tablespoons of water over a gentle heat and blend into the mixture. Turn it into a buttered mould. Chill well.

Serve sliced with a mustardy mayonnaise which has been thinned with a little light cream and flavoured with a small amount of chopped dill. Thin, hot toast should accompany this delicate pâté.

PEPERONATA
Sautéed spicy peppers

Whenever a dish of these superb, piquant-tasting peppers is put on our table at home, it is a struggle to keep everyone from impulsively dunking pieces of bread into the marvellous sauce. This dish makes a wonderful hors d'oeuvre or a grand accompaniment to a plain meat, fish or egg dish.

Wash, seed and cut into finger-width strips six large, red, yellow or green peppers (or all three). Place in a large frying pan with four sliced garlic cloves, four drained and chopped canned tomatoes, six tablespoons of olive oil, one level dessertspoon of oregano, salt and milled black pepper. Cover the pan. Simmer gently for 40 minutes. Stir fairly often. If too liquid (and this dish shouldn't be) remove the cover for the last ten minutes. Add a little sugar if too sharp. Remove the garlic pieces before serving, if you can find them! Serve hot or cold.

PEPERONI ARROSTITI
Grilled peppers

Place four large and very fleshy yellow or red, but not green, peppers fairly close to a hot grill until their skins begin to bubble and burn slightly. Keep turning them so that this happens evenly all round. Peel off

the thin skin while still hot. Remove the seeds. Cut the peppers into long finger-width strips and dress them with olive oil, one finely sliced garlic clove, a teaspoon of oregano, salt and milled black pepper. Let them stand for an hour or so or until they have absorbed enough of the flavours to become piquant and savoury.

Eat them cold. They make a good hors d'oeuvre on their own or an even better one served with not too salty anchovy fillets. These peppers are also good as an accompaniment to any plain dish. Their presence lifts ordinary cold meat to new heights and they are also good as sandwich filling.

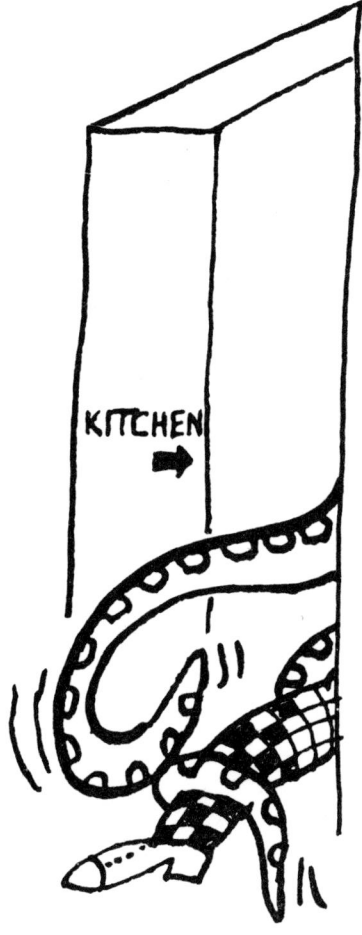

PEPERONI RIPIENI ALL'AMALFITANA
Peppers with savoury stuffing

Make incisions around the stems of four large, fleshy, red, yellow or even green peppers, remove the core and all the seeds. Wash and dry them. Sauté two finely chopped garlic cloves in olive oil until nearly golden. Add four tablespoons of soft, white breadcrumbs and let them take on a little colour. Remove the pan from the stove. Add one dessertspoon of chopped capers, 12 stoned, halved black olives, two large, skinned, chopped tomatoes, one small (previously diced and fried with garlic) egg-plant, a pinch of oregano, a tablespoon of coarsely chopped parsley, four cut-up anchovies, salt and milled black pepper. Mix lightly and add, if necessary, a little warm water to bind.

Stuff the peppers and replace the tops. Lay them in an oven dish, douse with olive oil and cover with foil. Bake in a moderate oven for 40 minutes. Uncover for the last ten minutes. These peppers may be eaten warm or cold, as an hors d'oeuvre or as a light main course.

PERA AVOCADO 'CAPRICCIOSA'
Avocado stuffed with shrimp and ham

Cut two large, ripe avocado pears in half and remove the stones. Fill the centres with a balanced mixture of small shrimps, julienne strips of Parma ham, finely sliced spring onion, chopped celery and chopped hard-boiled egg. Dress with a mustardy vinaigrette sauce and serve in individual bowls filled with crushed ice.

PERA AVOCADO 'FAVORITA'
Avocado stuffed with tuna fish

Cut two large, ripe avocado pears in half and remove the stones. Stuff them with a filling of moist tuna fish, chopped celery, thinly sliced raw apple, soaked sultanas and pine nuts. Dress with a mustardy vinaigrette sauce. Serve on crushed ice.

PERA AVOCADO 'MERIDIANA'
Avocado stuffed with chicken and crabmeat

I had this delicious dish served to me at Walter and Enzo's buzzing Meridiana Restaurant in London's Fulham Road. And very good it was too. The avocado was simply stuffed with julienne strips of white chicken meat and tongue, crabmeat, chopped green peppers and thinly sliced celery which was all masked with Cocktail sauce (page 161) and served on crushed ice.

PIEDE DI MAIALE 'GRIBICHE'
Pigs' trotters with piquant sauce

Cook four split pigs' trotters (wrapped in muslin to hold them together) in salted water with some sliced carrot, onion, celery, a bay leaf and a few peppercorns. Simmer them for not less than three hours. If they are to be eaten hot, then simply drain well and serve them with Gribiche sauce (page 162) or Vinaigrette (page 165) or a mustardy Mayonnaise (page 162). If you wish to serve them cold, then leave them to cool under a weight in their own cooking liquor. Serve slightly chilled with the same sauces.

Cooked pigs' trotters may also be brushed with melted butter and grilled, or breaded and fried and served with any sharp piquant or mustardy sauce.

PINZE DI GRANCHI FRITTE
Cornish deep-fried crab claws

For the restaurants I used to have a regular contract for the supply of the meaty and delicate crab claws from Cornwall. As they are usually difficult to obtain, I am afraid that you will have to hunt them down, but they are worth the trouble. Other sorts can occasionally be bought frozen in domestic packs and these are very good to use for the following recipe. Allow five or six crab claws per portion.

Cook them in boiling water for 15 minutes to 450g (1 lb) and cool. Crack and remove the shells exposing the meaty claw but leaving the pointed shell tip. This will make them suitable for 'finger-eating' and for sauce-dipping. Roll each one in flour, then dip into Parmesan-flavoured, beaten eggs and coat them thickly with a mixture of breadcrumbs, chopped parsley and cayenne pepper. Deep-fry until golden. Serve with a mustardy Tartare sauce.

PIZZA

Pizza is Mediterranean and is typical Arab food. It also has Chinese and Indian overtones. Pizza, like Mandarin pancakes, pitta, chapati and paratha and other flat bread-like preparations, is filled or garnished with savoury fish, meat, cheese or vegetable mixtures. In the absence of plates or forks it should be folded to be comfortably eaten with the fingers.

Pizza is a filling and basic food. It is very satisfying, as is pasta in all forms. Like many Neapolitan dishes, pizza was obviously contrived, as a result of poverty, by ingeniously combining local cheap ingredients. Today, Neapolitans, wherever they are, constantly yearn to be comforted by their adored, savoury pizza. But, I am sorry to say, to be able to relish today's mediocre standard of pizza one has to be quite hungry, poor, or desperate.

I have tried, without success, to track down the perfect old-time pizza and I am now beginning to believe that it no longer exists. I have been dispatched to many recommended places by local pizza connoisseurs. They must have been the possessors of highly inadequate palates for, almost without exception, I have been presented with a rubbery dough topped with haphazardly scattered so-called pizza garnish.

I have eaten my worst pizza in Greenwich Village, New York, my second worst in an establishment in the Naples area, and the ones served to me on the Champs Elysées or the yard-long one in an authentic Sorrentine pizzeria were close contenders.

My personal preference for this type of food, although I must confess that I rarely get the urge to eat pizza, is the French Pissaladière (supposedly derived from Pizza Sant'Andrea, a Ligurian speciality) or the more subtle Armenian pitta.

Pizza, being strictly pizzeria food, has no place on a regular restaurant menu. This is just one reason why I am not giving any recipes for it. It is highly unlikely that any reader will go to the trouble of making a complicated yeast dough which, when twice-risen, has to be rolled, flattened, punched, pulled into regular rounds, blessed, sworn and hissed at, possibly spun into the air, caught, suitably garnished and finally baked, preferably in a baker's wood-fired brick oven. It is that much simpler to go out and buy one.

If you really must have a pizza, then try it topped with slices of fresh Mozzarella, generously sprinkled with grated Parmesan, doused with olive oil and then strewn with shredded, fresh basil. The classic version, however, is liberally scattered with roughly chopped, fresh and very ripe tomatoes, anchovies, sliced, fresh garlic, oregano and lots of olive oil.

POLIPO ALLA LUCIANA
Octopus salad
It is possible, on very rare occasions, to get hold of a real octopus. If you really want one (and I cannot think why you should) then, if you live in London, you may sometimes order it in advance. Myall's, the best wholesale fishmonger in London, may be able to procure one for you. Once purchased, you may have to beat the octopus hard on the kitchen-wall tiles to make it tender. The fishmonger, I hope, will have removed the sack, eyes and beak. Place it in salted water with a little vinegar, a few carrots, onion, bay leaf, some celery and sprigs of parsley. Cover. Cook for three-quarters of an hour or longer, depending on tenderness and size. Drain.

Presented whole on a large dish, the octopus will actually look very pretty, rather like an exotic flower, and you can cut portions off as they are required. Pass a lemon and olive-oil dressing spiked with some hot chilli, chopped parsley and crushed garlic. Or you can cut it into small pieces and dress them with the same condiment.

POMPELMO VAN DER HUM
Grapefruit 'Van de Hum'
Cut the tops off four large, ripe grapefruits. Cut through the segments in the usual way. Pour in a little Van der Hum, that very good South African liqueur. Top with brown sugar. Bake for ten minutes in a hot oven. If necessary, glaze the sugar by passing the grapefruit under a very hot grill. Sprinkle just a little more Van der Hum on top before serving.

PROSCIUTTO
Raw, cured ham
'I'll have the prosciutto with melon to start with, thank you, waiter.' How many times and in how many languages has that phrase been heard? And, almost without exception, certainly in the better hotels, restaurants and trattorie all over the world, prosciutto di Parma has been produced without question, as though it were the most natural thing in the world. Not jambon de Bayonne, de Toulouse, d'Ardennes, not even the fine, smoked Speck ham from the Alto Adige of the Italian Tyrol region but, unhesitatingly, prosciutto from the province of Parma. What a compliment!

Nowadays Parma hams, which incidentally are not smoked but simply air-cured, are produced and matured in most parts of the region of Emilia. In addition to their hams, the Emilians produce the exceptionally delicate and perfect culatello. A speciality of the Salsomaggiore, Bacedasco and Castell'Arquato areas, this is the choicest part of the finest Parma hams. For this reason, culatelli are horrendously expensive and are only rarely seen in Britain. Parma ham, despite its undoubted qualities and international fame, is not the finest of all Italian hams. That title must, unreservedly, go to the exquisite pale and sweet-tasting product of tiny San Daniele, in the Friuli area of the Veneto region.

Prosciutto is normally served plain with butter curls, sliced ripe melon or syrupy 'tear-drop' figs. One thing I can say with pride on the subject is that I first combined, at a desperate time when suitable melons were unavailable, prosciutto with a ripe, peeled comice pear. I also introduced another prosciutto variation at one of my restaurants. I asked the chef to poach some fine, firm, ripe peaches in syrup and pickle them in spiced brandy. When served with tissue-thin slices of moist and succulent cured ham, the two flavours blended and complemented one another.

RATATOUILLE ALLA NIZZARDA
Sautéed, savoury vegetables

It was nearly closing time. The lights had been discreetly dimmed. The Mayfair restaurant was practically empty. Waiters in dark corners waited. Sitting quietly, after a lone dinner, near the softly playing musicians with some bottles of wine, her beautiful face relaxed, Ava Gardner reminisced. Maybe her thoughts were of Spain or some other hot country which produces spicy, piquant dishes like the one she had eaten that evening. This is how the chef played it.

Sauté three crushed garlic cloves in a large frying pan in six tablespoons of olive oil and discard when golden. Then place in the pan one large, sliced onion, four sliced, unpeeled zucchini, four skinned chopped tomatoes, four yellow or red (seeded and cut into wide strips) peppers, a small sprig of fresh tarragon, one sprig of thyme, salt and milled black pepper. Cover. Cook briskly for a few moments and then simmer for half an hour. Turn the mixture over fairly frequently. Meanwhile, in another pan, sauté two medium sized, unskinned, cubed egg-plants in olive oil. Drain them well and add to the other pan. Continue to simmer uncovered, turning the vegetables now and then, for a further 15 minutes. Although this very well-known dish may be eaten either hot or warm, it is in my opinion much better when served cold.

SALMONE AFFUMICATO
Smoked salmon

Smoked salmon is undoubtedly one of the most popular of all hors d'oeuvre served today. I should hate to hazard a guess at how many portions are carved and scoffed in any one year. Where do they all come from? The practice of smoking salmon was already well known in the early eighteenth century in Russia. It is probably from there that Jewish emigrés brought their favourite delicacy to the West.

Smoked salmon must be bought from an experienced supplier. One who will choose the sides well, is jealous of his good name in this very particular trade and whose business enjoys a good turnover. The fish should be large, fresh, tender, moist and pink. It should smell sweetly and be naturally smoked. Scotch smoked salmon is the finest of them all. Salmon must always be carved towards the tail with a long, keen knife; it should be held only very slightly inclined, almost horizontal. This is to achieve the barely slanting, full width slices which should, certainly as the middle part of the salmon is approached, completely cover an hors d'oeuvre plate. The slices must be very, very thin and should bear no visible ridge marks – that is the sign of a poor carver.

Portions that are composed of bitty pieces or seem to be patched up with slices of varying degrees of moisture, hues and thicknesses should be firmly refused. They can go straight back to the chef who should know how to use them up.

It is gastronomically incorrect to garnish portions of smoked salmon with gherkins, radishes, lettuce, cucumber, olives, capers or parsley. Only half a lemon, thinly sliced, fresh, buttered brown bread (never toast), cayenne pepper or freshly milled black pepper should be offered – nothing else!

Smoked salmon served hot on freshly made Blinis (page 160) or unsweetened pancakes, topped with sour cream, sprinkled with lemon juice and black pepper, makes a memorable first course for any lunch or dinner, formal or informal. So will thin slices of rolled smoked salmon filled with real caviar or potted shrimps. Tinned or frozen smoked salmon should never be served, it is absolutely awful and is instantly recognizable.

SALUMI VARI
Salami and pork produce

Italy produces an almost boundless variety of pork products. And without exception they are excellent. While in no way do I claim that they can all compete with the profusion of superb pork specialities so proudly displayed in the *charcuteries* of France, I do insist that most Italian pork produce (except the pâtés and terrines, which are awful) defend themselves very successfully against comparisons.

The space of an entire volume would not suffice to give a complete description of the whole galaxy of Italian salami and pork produce. This huge tray, however, expresses my own personal preferences.

Prosciutto di San Daniele, the best cured ham in the world; culatello, the very heart of Parma ham; finocchiona, a sort of cooked fennel-flavoured sausage; capecuollo, a Campanian rolled 'whole meat' salami; salame gentile, a rare Emilian delicacy; Speck Tyrolese, smoked ham; mortadella di Bologna, a very large, cooked sausage; salam'd la duja, Piedmontese salami preserved under lard; sopressata di Siena, Italian-style brawn; salame di cinghiale, made from boars' meat – but that's enough. I could get carried away! Don't forget the crusty bread and plenty of robust young red wine. That's the way to eat when you're really hungry!

SCAROLA RIPIENA
Stuffed escarole

Discard the outer leaves from four young and tender escaroles – broad-leaved, non curly endives. Wash and blanch them for a few moments in boiling, salted water. Drain well. In a frying pan, sauté three crushed cloves of garlic in six tablespoons of olive oil and remove when golden. Add four heaped tablespoons of soft breadcrumbs, one dessertspoon each of capers and coarsely chopped parsley, four cut-up anchovies, 12 stoned, halved black olives, salt and milled black pepper. Stir well and sauté for a few minutes. Stuff the escaroles with the filling and close them as firmly as you can without pressing or squeezing too much. Arrange them in an oiled oven dish. Sprinkle with soft breadcrumbs and moisten with a little olive oil. Cover with foil. Cook in a moderate to hot oven for 30 minutes, remove the foil for the last ten minutes. Serve hot or cold, as a first course or light main course.

SOFFIETTI DI LUCCIO ALLA SERPENTARIA
Pike quenelles with wine tarragon sauce

One afternoon Quentin Crewe, the well-known British writer, journalist and gourmet, telephoned me. Together we organized the menu for a small dinner party he was giving at his London home that evening. There was to be an important guest and, as I was worried about the restaurant's reputation and concerned as to what unfamiliar cooks might do to the food I was to provide, I offered to send over one of my second chefs. To make doubly sure I made several trips there myself during the evening.

Thinly sliced prosciutto di San Daniele with comice pears were served as antipasto; this was followed by pike quenelles with a tarragon and wine sauce; the main course consisted of tiny roasted quails spiked with just a hint of garlic and rosemary, accompanied by a salad of Romaine lettuce, sliced avocado, pineapple, hearts of palm and orange segments tossed with a mild vinaigrette; marinated fresh strawberries served with a chilled Zabaglione sauce; petits fours and coffee completed the meal. Quentin Crewe supplied his own wines.

The next day he sent me a thank-you note in which he told me that H.R.H. Princess Margaret had complimented him on the dinner which she had enjoyed tremendously. As a result of that evening's work, sometime in the near future I was to have the honour and pleasure of seeing the Princess at my new, luxurious Mayfair restaurant. Here is the recipe for the amazingly light pike quenelles.

Finely mince twice or liquidize 450g (1 lb) of skinned, boned pike. Or you can use any sort of suitable good quality fish or shell fish. Put it into a mixing bowl, season with salt and white pepper and very slowly add the whites of four eggs and work them in fiercely. Pass this through a fine sieve. Place in a refrigerator and chill for an hour. Stir in 570ml (20 fl oz) of heavy cream, and a cup of prepared béchamel sauce, a little at a time, with a wooden spoon. Test the seasoning. Form into small egg-shapes with the aid of a wetted dessertspoon. Range them carefully in a buttered dish and pour gently boiling salted water over them until covered. Poach the quenelles delicately by keeping the water barely shimmering. Do not let it boil. When they begin to firm, they are ready. Drain them well on a cloth. Mask them with Sauce au vin blanc à l'estragon, Lobster or Aurore sauce (pages 165, 162 and 159).

SPUMA DI MERLUZZO AFFUMICATO
Mousseline of smoked haddock

Finely mince 450g (1 lb) of cooked, skinned and boned smoked haddock of the finest quality. Season with salt, a little nutmeg and cayenne pepper. Slowly add three whites of egg and work into the fish fiercely. Rub through a fine sieve. Let it stand in a cool place for two hours. Then, with a wooden spoon, smoothly work in 140ml (5 fl oz) of heavy cream and a cup of prepared béchamel sauce. Turn the mixture into four buttered individual soufflé cases. Poach in a bain-marie on the stove for about 30 minutes. Turn them out and serve with Sauce au vin blanc (page 165) to which you have added a little chopped dill.

STORIONE AFFUMICATO
Smoked sturgeon

Now and then I was able to get hold of a consignment of genuine smoked sturgeon. There is always a tremendous rush for it, and then there is no more for quite a while. Smoked sturgeon is quite deliciously delicate. It has a particularly light and smoky flavour, somewhat reminiscent of the finest Dutch smoked eels. It should be sliced very thinly and served in the same way as smoked salmon. That is to say with lemon halves, cayenne or milled black pepper and thinly sliced, buttered, fresh brown bread. But with the important addition of creamed horseradish.

Try thin slices of smoked sturgeon with hot Blinis (page 160) topped with sour cream or rolled and stuffed with caviar, potted shrimps or a little creamed cods'-roe.

TERRINA D'ANITRA
Terrine of duck

An order had just arrived from the busy kitchen. The dish containing four large, spit-roasted ducks was presented to the guests and placed on the guéridon trolley, which was already alongside the customers' table, awaiting the arrival of the two *trancheurs,* the restaurant's official carvers. But they were both busy in the general rush and occupied with work at other stations. It was, therefore, left to the young Chef de rang to carve the ducks himself. He took his short, black-handled carving knife and gave it a final, flamboyant sharpening.

He turned one of the ducks onto its side in the correct manner and cut through the crispy skin and flesh around the legs. Following normal procedure he then inserted a fork into the joint and firmly pulled the drumstick upwards. The duck resisted. He tugged harder. That evening the duck had no intention of surrendering. He drove the fork deeper into the thigh and strained to wrench the leg up and away from the carcase. It would not budge. So he gave a really fierce jerk. The drumstick abruptly came away and for an instant it was held high in the air, impaled on the fork. At the same time, the force of the movement caused the wheeled trolley to skid away along the shiny terrazzo floor, colliding with tables, chairs, customers and diving waiters. Simultaneously, the four ducks were propelled in a crazy surrealistic flight into a corner of the restaurant. One well-known and pompous lady was acutely surprised to see a plump, spit-roasted duck swooping down from nowhere, making a very fast one-legged, emergency landing towards the runway of her ample lap.

Here is a recipe for a two-legged duck terrine. Strip a small, raw duckling of its meat. Chop it together with 150g (6 oz) each of fat belly of pork and veal, 50g (2 oz) of pork fat and the sautéed duck's liver. Put everything into a bowl together with half a cup of strong stock (made from the duck's carcase and giblets), two chopped garlic cloves, one bay leaf, a little thyme, one teaspoon of canned green peppercorns, a few pistachio nuts, one wine glass of mixed brandy and Marsala. Season with salt and plenty of milled black pepper. Mix well.

Turn the mixture into a larded terrine and dot with lard. Cover with foil. Stand the terrine in a pan of boiling water. Cook it in a moderate oven for at least two hours. Remove the foil for the last ten minutes. Cool and chill slightly. Serve it cut into slices with thick, hot, toasted farmhouse bread, fresh butter and gherkins, and a few glasses of ordinary red wine. Terrine-making is no problem at all – but carving a duck sometimes can be. An especially sharp knife always helps.

TORTA DI PORRI
Leek flan

Line a 25cm (10 in) flan tin with Plain shortcrust pastry (page 164). In a frying pan, gently cook two roughly chopped slices of streaky bacon in oil and butter. Add a chopped small onion and sweat it with the bacon until soft. Add, and quickly sauté, two chopped leeks. Place the mixture in a sieve, strain off all the fat and set it aside. (Use the fat for starting off a soup – the flavour is very good). Whisk one whole egg and three yolks with two tablespoons of grated Parmesan cheese and smoothly blend in 280ml (10 fl oz) of heavy cream. Mix this well with the bacon and leek mixture. Season with salt and milled black pepper and pour into the pastry case. Bake in a moderate oven for 30 minutes or until set. Let the flan cool. Serve barely warm or cold as a first course or a light main dish.

ULIVE NERE AL FINOCCHIO
Black olives with fennel seeds

This is not a recipe at all. Merely a delicious hint. Choose the nice, ripe, soft, fleshy, black, shiny Greek olives and put them in a bowl. Douse with olive oil, sprinkle them lightly with fennel seeds, a roughly chopped chilli and a sliced garlic clove. Leave them a while to absorb the flavours. And then see whether you have ever eaten such marvellous olives.

ZUCCHINE RIPIENE 'TRAGARA'
Zucchini with savoury stuffing
Cut off the ends and hollow through four large zucchini. Blanch them in boiling salted water. Sauté two crushed garlic cloves in olive oil and discard when golden. Add and cook two finely chopped slices of streaky bacon and a tablespoon of chopped onion. Mix in 150g (6 oz) of minced cooked chicken and veal, four tablespoons of fresh soft breadcrumbs soaked in milk, one tablespoon of grated Parmesan cheese, one egg, one teaspoon of fresh (or a pinch of dried) basil, salt and milled black pepper. Stir and cook for a few moments. Stuff the marrows lightly. Lay them in a baking tray and pour in a little stock. Dot with butter. Cover with foil and bake in a hot oven for 40 minutes, uncover for the last ten minutes. Serve hot or cold.

More recipes which are suitable as antipasti can be found in other sections of the book:

Soup
ZUPPA DI COZZE ALL'AMALFITANA Mussel soup, Amalfi style
ZUPPA DI VONGOLE Clam soup

Eggs
FRITTATA ALLA CAMPAGNOLA Country-style omelette
FRITTATA DI CIPOLLE Onion omelette
FRITTATA DI SPAGHETTI Spaghetti omelette
OMELETTE ARNOLD BENNETT Omelette of smoked haddock
This great omelette is often served as a delicious first course.
UOVA ALL BORBONA Baked eggs, southern style
UOVA 'DONNA CARMELA' Croûtes with savoury egg filling
UOVA ALL PAESANA Baked eggs, peasant style
UOVA DEL VESCOVO Poached eggs, the bishop's way
UOVA ALL VIRGILIO Baked eggs on stuffed artichoke hearts

Fish
BRIOCHE 'TORRE NORMANNA' Hot brioche filled with seafood

COZZE AL GRATIN Gratinéed mussels
This is another of those southern Italian dishes which can be served either as a first or main course. It is a famous Neapolitan seafood dish and a lovely way of presenting hot mussels in the shells.
VONGOLE ALLA ALESSANDRIA Sautéed clams, Alexandria style

Vegetables
PORRI ALLA 'VINAIGRETTE' Leeks with vinaigrette
ZUCCHINE ALLA SCAPECE Sweet and sour zucchini
This wonderful but time-consuming way of preparing zucchini can be directly traced back to ancient Capri-Roman cooking. It has an intriguing sweet and sour flavour. Very good as part of a composite hors d'oeuvre, a vegetable accompaniment or side-dish.

Meat
VITELLO TONNATO Cold sliced veal with tuna fish sauce
This subtle veal dish, with its unique creamy tuna fish sauce, is one of Italy's most famous cold specialities. Strangely, for a country with such a hot climate, very few classical cold dishes of this type exist in the Italian cooking repertoire. Vitello tonnato is almost certainly the product of a highly inventive and extremely creative mind. This most refined dish is being served more and more, well-chilled and very thinly sliced, as an hors d'oeuvre on a hot summer's day.

ZUPPE
Soups

I can assure you that at least 90 per cent of Italian restaurants and trattorie in Italy or abroad will restrict the soup choice to a broth garnished with rice, noodles, pastina, ravioli or to a farmhouse minestrone-style, fresh vegetable soup thickened with beans, pasta, rice or variations on the theme. Occasionally menus may offer a Passato di verdura which is simply a sieved fresh vegetable soup served with crispy *crostini* or croûtons and grated Parmesan cheese, and these can be very good indeed.

When in Italy, do steer clear of restaurant soups which include the word *crema*, for example Crema di pomidoro and Crema di asparagi. They aren't! When they are not packaged and factory made, they are invariably very poor copies of the superb French originals and, as a rule, congealed with Besciamella, that good old Italian stand-by white sauce.

In the following soup section I have given the recipes for a few unusual and extremely good soups. The Italian ones deserve to feature more often on local menus. They are easy to prepare and worth trying.

I have included some fish soups which may be served as first courses and are called *zuppe*, but they are more suitable as main dishes. Please do remember that, as with all food, soups (except Minestrone alla Milanese and Cianfotta which may be eaten at room temperature) must be served very hot or, if they are cold, they should be iced. Tepid temperatures just won't do, so don't let your standards drop.

BORTSCH FREDDA
Cold beetroot soup

This is only one of the many versions of this famous soup. Put into a saucepan one teaspoon of tomato purée, six small, raw, grated beetroots, one chopped, medium-sized onion, one large, chopped leek, one crushed garlic clove and 1l 700ml (60 fl oz) of simple beef stock. Bring to the boil and simmer uncovered for 45 minutes. Strain through fine muslin and season with salt and white pepper. Sharpen slightly with a little lemon juice or malt vinegar. Add a small wine glass of dry sherry and sweeten to taste. Serve hot or very cold. Pass sour cream at the table. Curry puffs (page 13) accompany this soup admirably as would a garnish of cooked duck julienne.

BRODO DI MANZO
Beef broth

Put into a large saucepan 900g (2 lb) of shin of beef, one quartered onion, one sliced carrot, two roughly chopped celery stalks and the leaves, and one large, ripe tomato. Cover with 2l (70 fl oz) of salted water. Bring to the boil. Skim off the froth and then simmer gently for at least two hours. Skim again as necessary. Check the seasoning. If the soup appears to be too strong, add a little boiling water. Remove the beef (which may be used in one of the recipes described in the meat section). Let the soup rest. Remove the risen fat carefully and thoroughly and strain. Serve hot either plain, with rice, pasta, pastina, noodles, ravioli, croûtons, Palline di Rita (page 43) or any other suitable garnish. Pass grated Parmesan cheese at the table and black pepper.

BRODO DI POLLO
Chicken broth
The ingredients and the method are the same as those of Brodo di manzo (above), except, of course, that the beef is replaced by a 1kg 350g (3 lb) boiling fowl. Use the cooked chicken in one of the different ways suggested in the meat section. Serve broth hot with the same garnishes as mentioned in the previous recipe; pass grated Parmesan cheese at the table.

BRODO DI POLLO E MANZO
Chicken and beef broth
This combination makes a better, richer broth than either plain chicken or beef. The method is the same as the two previous recipes but you will need a smaller boiling fowl and only 450g (1 lb) of shin of beef. Use up the boiled beef and chicken by following the suggestions in the meat section.

CIANFOTTA
Spicy, vegetable stew-soup
This dish is a little like those various Hungarian soup-stews and I am never quite sure how to describe it. It certainly is more like a stew than a soup but then it is always served at the start of a meal. On the other hand, it could be served hot or cold, as an antipasto or as a vegetable accompaniment, side-dish or as a vegetarian main course.

Put into a large saucepan three seeded, roughly cut-up, red, yellow or green peppers, two large, cubed zucchini, two finely sliced carrots, one finely sliced, medium-sized onion, eight small, new potatoes, four bruised, fresh basil leaves, three crushed garlic cloves, one teaspoon of oregano, 450g (1 lb) of roughly chopped, undrained, canned tomatoes, one cup of olive oil, salt and milled black pepper. Cover and simmer for 30 minutes. Meanwhile, fry one cubed, medium-sized eggplant in olive oil until golden, drain and add to the vegetables. Uncover and simmer for a further ten minutes. This dish should not be too runny but should have enough juice to mop up.

CREMA DI FAGIOLI
Neapolitan cream of haricot beans
Soak 450g (1 lb) of dried, white Italian cannellini beans overnight. Put into a large saucepan and cover them by 10cm (4 in) with cold, unsalted water. Cook them for two hours or until they are soft. Now make sure that the beans are still covered; if not, add more boiling water. Mix in six large, crushed garlic cloves, one heaped tablespoon of coarsely chopped parsley, one dessertspoon of tomato purée, one and a half cups of olive oil, salt and milled black pepper. Stir well. Cook gently, stirring occasionally to prevent sticking (which can easily happen), until the garlic is soft. Remove the garlic, and then pass the soup through a fine sieve.

This is a thickish soup, it should have the consistency of heavy cream. Serve hot with toasted or fried croûtons.

CREMA FREDDA DI PERA AVOCADO
Chilled avocado soup
Mash the pulp of two large, ripe avocado pears and rub through a fine sieve. Blend in 125ml (5 fl oz) of heavy cream. Whisk in 570ml (20 fl oz) of strong chicken stock until creamy. Strain. Season with salt, white pepper and a few drops of Worcester sauce. Bring gently to the boil. Cool and serve well chilled in cups. Garnish with yoghourt, a few cooked shrimps, and some chopped chives, chervil or fresh mint.

CREMA DI PATATE E PORRI
Leek and potato soup
Gently sauté two chopped slices of streaky bacon and a small chopped onion in one

tablespoon of olive oil and a knob of butter. Add four chopped leeks and five medium-sized cubed potatoes. Sauté for a few minutes. Cover with chicken stock. Simmer until the potatoes are soft. If the liquid runs short, add a little more hot water. Pass through a medium sieve or blend for ten to 20 seconds in a liquidizer. Add half a cup of heavy cream. Check the seasoning. Reheat gently and serve hot, sprinkled with chopped chives and fried croûtons.

CREMA DI SEMOLINA
Semolina 'hangover' soup

If you have that 'morning after the night before' feeling or you have a delicate stomach, this soup is just the thing. Likewise, if you're expecting to have to do a lot of 'elbow-bending', then eat a large amount of it before you go out: you'll enjoy an even better, longer evening.

Bring 1 l (35 fl oz) of chicken or beef stock to the boil. Blend in, stirring constantly, 100g (4 oz) of fine semolina in a thin steady stream. Do not allow lumps to form. Simmer for 20 minutes, stirring occasionally. Melt in two tablespoons of butter and two tablespoons of grated Parmesan cheese. Check the seasoning. Serve hot. Pass more grated cheese, if needed, and the black pepper mill.

CREMA SENEGALESE FREDDA
Chilled, curried chicken and cream soup

Bring 1 l (35 fl oz) of good chicken stock to the boil. Add a level dessertspoon of curry powder, one dessertspoon of powdered coconut and a little mango chutney.

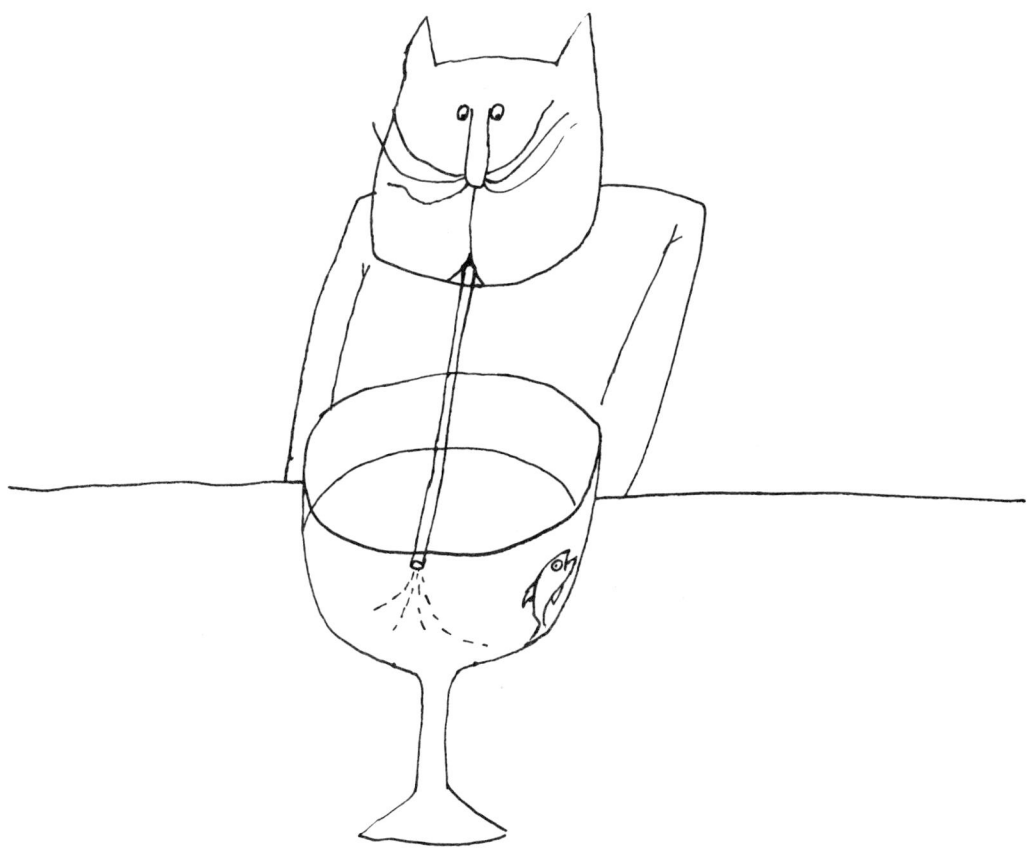

Smoothly blend in 125ml (5 fl oz) of heavy cream and two egg yolks. Stir constantly to avoid curdling. Heat through carefully – do not allow to boil – and season to taste. Allow to cool and chill well. Serve in cups garnished with finely chopped white chicken meat and sprinkled with chopped parsley. A few Curry puffs (page 13) will go well with this delicious cold soup.

GAZPACHO
Iced, piquant tomato soup

In Beverly Hills, California, Le Bistrot restaurant, when it comes to décor, is an eye-opener in every sense of the word. Of course, being right in the centre of the fantasy world that is Hollywood, it naturally follows that this faithful reconstruction of a typical fin de siècle Parisian bistro is a truly noteworthy piece of design.

Of the Bistrot's food I cannot, in all honesty, say very much. It is just not food that anyone would remember for long. In any case this has hardly anything to do with it. The thing is to be seen, seen, seen! – and at the right time, with the right people and at the right tables. What I especially remember about the place is that the very sympathetic, highly expert bartender (as they all are in the United States) mixed me a couple of Bullshots (strong hot beef bouillon well charged with vodka) that not only revived me, but set me up for the next 48 hours. After which I needed a couple more of them. And, as that sort of thing could have gone on for ever, I left town for a while. Here is a soup which, served chilled, can also stand a couple of well-aimed blasts of Russian vodka. Try it.

Mince finely half a cucumber, six peeled, ripe tomatoes, one small onion, one seeded pepper, two large garlic cloves, one large chilli and 150g (6 oz) of crustless bread. Rub through a sieve and discard the left-over pulp. With a wooden spoon blend in 750ml (26 fl oz) of cold chicken or beef stock, two tablespoons of light vinegar, three dessertspoons of olive oil and one heaped teaspoon of tomato purée. Season with salt and milled black pepper. Cover and place in the refrigerator to chill for at least an hour. Mix well and serve cold in cups. Pass tiny cubes of toasted bread, finely chopped cucumber, onion and peppers at the table, to be sprinkled, according to taste, on top of the soup.

MINESTRA DI LILLI
Lilli's spinach soup

Sweat one chopped, medium-sized onion in butter and oil until soft. Add two chopped, medium-sized leeks and cook for a few minutes. Pour in 750ml (26 fl oz) of chicken stock and simmer for 20 minutes. Stir in 100g (4 oz) of Italian rice and 225g (8 oz) of chopped spinach. Cook for a further 20 minutes. Check the seasoning. Serve hot with grated Parmesan cheese.

MINESTRA MARITATA
Neapolitan green vegetable soup

In a saucepan, melt two chopped slices of streaky bacon with one tablespoon of lard and sweat one chopped, medium-sized onion and two crushed garlic cloves; then discard the garlic. Add one large, cubed potato, a chopped, tender celery stalk and 1l 500ml (52 fl oz) of mixed chicken and beef stock. Boil for 15 minutes. Then add four heads of curly endives or escaroles (broad-leaved and non-curly endives) which have been previously cooked in salted water – reserving the tender hearts for salads, 450g (1 lb) of cooked spring greens and 225g (8 oz) of cooked leaf-spinach. Boil for a further five minutes. Add two tablespoons of diced, boiled bacon, two tablespoons of grated Parmesan cheese and one heaped teaspoon of fennel seeds. Check the seasoning. Remove from the stove and let cool for two hours. Then reheat and serve hot. This absolutely marvellous soup is even better when eaten, as the shrewd Neapolitans do, the next day. I recommend pouring in some red wine.

MINESTRINA DI SARA 'FRETTOLOSA'
Sara's quick vegetable soup

Using a chicken or beef stock-cube this soup can be made relatively quickly. It may even be served with impunity to guests. It is very good and no one will ever guess that you have cheated on them. They will enjoy it, I promise you!

Sweat a small, finely chopped onion in two tablespoons of lard until soft, but do not let it turn colour. Add one diced potato, one diced carrot, a cut-up tender celery stalk and the leaves, two ripe, skinned tomatoes, one sliced zucchini and one beef or chicken stock cube. Stir and cook gently for a few moments. Pour in 1 l (35 fl oz) of water and simmer for 30 minutes. Check the seasoning. Add 75g (3 oz) of small pasta and cook for a further ten minutes. Serve hot. Pass grated Parmesan cheese at the table. Croûtons could be served instead of pasta, but it isn't really that kind of a soup.

MINESTRONE ALLA 'LUISA'
Vegetable soup the way my Mother made it

Soak 225g (8 oz) of dried, white Italian cannellini beans overnight. Cover well with unsalted water. Cook, adding more boiling water if necessary, until tender. Add one tablespoon of lard, three tablespoons of olive oil, half a sliced leek, one sliced zucchini, two crushed garlic cloves, one chopped, medium-sized onion, one cubed, medium-sized potato, two chopped, tender celery stalks and leaves, two diced carrots, two heaped teaspoons of tomato purée, a small, shredded cabbage, salt and milled black pepper. Cover with cold water and bring to the boil. Simmer for 45 minutes or until the vegetables are tender. Add 225g (8 oz) of cooked, drained leaf-spinach and 50g (2 oz) of Italian rice. Cook slowly for a further 20 minutes. Check the seasoning and serve slightly cooled in soup plates. Pass grated Parmesan cheese at the table.

In summer or on hot days this classic vegetable soup can be eaten quite cold. Remember that a Milanese will not eat minestrone unless it is so thick that a spoon will stand up in it. So, if you should be entertaining guests from Milan, make sure that you follow the above directions carefully or else have a trick spoon handy.

MINESTRONE CON LA ZUCCA
Vegetable soup with pumpkin

In a saucepan, sauté two crushed garlic cloves and one chopped, medium-sized onion in a cup of olive oil until golden. Add (all chopped) 450g (1 lb) of ripe pumpkin flesh, two celery stalks and leaves, two carrots, one large potato, one leek, two zucchini, a small cabbage, two ripe tomatoes, one dessertspoon of parsley, salt and milled black pepper. Toss the ingredients until they are well coated with the fat. Barely cover with cold water. Bring to the boil and simmer for 45 minutes or until the vegetables are tender. Add 50g (2 oz) of Italian rice. Cook for a further 20 minutes. Check the seasoning. Serve in soup plates letting this soup cool a little before eating (you can't drink this one). Grated Parmesan cheese can be passed, but it should not be needed because of the slight sweetness of the pumpkin. Pass the black pepper mill instead.

PALLINE DI RITA
Delicate soup dumplings

Melt 25g (1 oz) of butter in a saucepan and, away from the heat, carefully blend in the yolk of an egg. Add three tablespoons of fresh, dried breadcrumbs, three tablespoons of grated Parmesan cheese and one tablespoon of very finely chopped, cooked ham. Season and fold in smoothly one stiffly beaten egg white. Chill for 30 minutes. Roll into small marble-sized balls. Poach them for five minutes in the chosen broth. Pass grated Parmesan at the table and black pepper if desired.

RISO E FAGIOLI
Rice and bean soup
Soak 100g (4 oz) of white Italian cannellini beans overnight. Cook them in unsalted water, adding more boiling water if necessary, until tender. Do not drain. Add 850ml (30 fl oz) of beef or chicken stock, one crushed garlic clove, one thinly sliced onion, two sliced celery stalks and leaves, one teaspoon of tomato purée, four tablespoons of olive oil, salt and milled black pepper. Simmer for 20 minutes. Add 50g (2 oz) of Italian rice. Cook for a further 20 minutes. Serve hot. Grated Parmesan cheese may be offered although it is not necessary, but freshly milled black pepper should be.

RISTRETTO ALLA MADRILENA IN GELATINA
Jellied tomato consommé
Bring to the boil 750ml (26 fl oz) of strained, clarified, well-flavoured chicken stock with six large, coarsely chopped, skinned and seeded tomatoes and one dessertspoon of tomato purée. Simmer for 20 minutes. Season with salt and white pepper. Add a little sugar to counter the acidity of the tomatoes. Allow to cool. Strain through fine muslin. Stir in one dessertspoon of powdered gelatine which has been dissolved in water over a gentle heat. Let the soup set in the refrigerator. Serve well chilled in individual bowls. Garnish with chopped, seeded and skinned tomatoes and chopped parsley. Serve with lemon wedges.

STRACCIATELLA ALLA CASALINGA
Chicken broth with whisked eggs
Bring 850ml (30 fl oz) of strong, well-flavoured chicken stock to the boil. Quickly stir into the hot soup two whole, seasoned eggs whisked up with two heaped tablespoons of grated Parmesan cheese and a dessertspoon of chopped parsley. Do not blend too smoothly, the eggs should more or less only scramble. Serve very quickly before the eggs harden and overcook with the heat of the broth. Pass more grated Parmesan cheese if required.

ZUPPA DI CAVOLFIORE 'PETRIT'
Cauliflower soup
In a saucepan, sauté four crushed garlic cloves in two tablespoons of olive oil and one of lard and discard when golden. Add the parboiled florets of two medium-sized cauliflowers. Sauté for a few minutes and let them take on a little colour. Add one heaped tablespoon of chopped parsley, two roughly chopped chillis and one heaped dessertspoon of tomato purée. Cover with salted water. Simmer for 20 minutes or until the cauliflower is tender. Check the seasoning. Do not pass cheese, just a lot of crusty French bread, and mind those chillis.

ZUPPA DI COZZE ALL'AMALFITANA
Mussel soup, Amalfi style
In a large saucepan, sauté four crushed garlic cloves in one and a half cups of olive oil and discard when golden. Add 450g (1 lb) of roughly chopped, drained, canned tomatoes, one heaped tablespoon of coarsely chopped parsley and milled black pepper. Cook for a few minutes. Add 1kg 800g (4 lb) of well-scrubbed mussels to the saucepan. Cover. Shake the pan over a high flame until the mussels open and discard those that don't. Check the seasoning. Serve in soup plates and pass thick rounds of toasted French bread. Do try to reserve some of the mussel-tomato sauce – it goes admirably with cooked pasta such as rigatoni or linguine.

ZUPPA DI COZZE 'CHOWDER'
Mussel chowder 'King Bomba'
I first tasted a real American chowder at a lunch in the extremely attractive and well-run Cape Cod Room at the Drake Hotel, Chicago. I liked it so much that the helpful

Restaurant Manager gave me the recipe, which I promptly lost, I am sorry to say. I never forgot the subtle, creamy taste of that soup. This is how I had it prepared for my restaurants.

In a saucepan, melt four chopped slices of streaky bacon in olive oil and butter. Sweat one chopped, medium-sized onion. Add one diced, medium-sized potato and one chopped, tender celery stalk and leaves. Cook for a few moments and set aside. In a separate saucepan put 1kg 800g (4 lb) of scrubbed live mussels together with a wine glass of dry white wine. Cover. Shake the pan over a high flame until the mussels open – discard those that don't. Shell and set them aside. Strain the mussel and wine liquor into the vegetables. Add a dessertspoon of chopped parsley and 570ml (20 fl oz) of light fish stock, and simmer for 20 minutes. Blend in two cups of heavy cream. Gently heat through. Season to taste and serve this creamy soup with its wonderful flavour in large soup bowls garnished with some of the mussels and a generous sprinkling of finely chopped, crispy bacon. Pass dry, crunchy water biscuits.

ZUPPA DI FAGIOLI ALLA MINORESE
Bean soup, Minori style
Soak 450g (1 lb) of white Italian cannellini beans overnight. Cook them in unsalted water until tender leaving 5cm (2 in) of cooking liquid above the cooked beans, or correct the level with boiling water. Set aside.

In a saucepan, lightly brown six large, crushed garlic cloves in one and a half cups of olive oil. Add the cooked beans with the liquor, one heaped tablespoon of tomato purée, eight bruised, fresh basil leaves (or a pinch of dried), salt and milled black pepper. Simmer for 20 minutes or until the garlic is soft. Be very careful that the beans do not stick or burn, this can be surprisingly easy! Remove the garlic. Adjust any sharpness that might occur with sugar.

The finished consistency should be similar to that of a thin minestrone. If at any time during the cooking the liquid runs dry, add enough boiling water to correct the situation. Pass thick rounds of toasted French bread. No cheese, but plenty of black milled pepper.

ZUPPA DI FAGIOLI CON SCAROLA
Bean soup with escarole
In a large saucepan, sauté four crushed garlic cloves in one cup of olive oil until golden. Add one teaspoon of tomato purée, 225g (8 oz) of white Italian cannellini (soaked and cooked as in the previous recipe) together with abundant cooking liquor, four whole (previously cooked) escaroles, two sliced, tender celery stalks and leaves, salt and milled black pepper. Simmer until the celery is cooked. If this seems to be too thick add some lightly-flavoured boiling stock. Remove the garlic (if you can find it!). Serve very hot with thick rounds of toasted French bread.

ZUPPA DI FAGIOLINI
French-bean soup
In a saucepan, sauté until golden four crushed garlic cloves in four tablespoons of olive oil. Add 450g (1 lb) of thin, tender French beans, 450g (1 lb) of roughly chopped, undrained, canned tomatoes, eight bruised, fresh basil leaves, salt and milled black pepper. Barely cover with water. Cover and cook for 40 minutes or until the beans are tender. Remove the garlic. Pour the beans and soup over large rounds of toasted, country-style bread in deep soup plates. Do not attempt this dish with old, tough or stringy beans.

ZUPPA FORTE O SOFFRITTO
Chilli-hot sauté-soup
For many years one of the traditional Neapolitan specialities at one of my

London restaurants was Zuppa forte which, because of its unusual features, became a favourite 'starter' among the customers. The press and food critics acclaimed it. The English menu-description was deliberately ambiguous, casually referring to it as 'a rich and piquant sauté-soup' and left it at that. The manager, head waiters and waiters were instructed (and closely watched to see that they complied) never to divulge the secret of the main ingredients. Should an unsure or inquisitive customer be too insistent, they were to become suddenly vague and incoherent.

Zuppa forte is a winter dish. It is red, succulent and tasty. It has varying textures, a strong flavour with delicate undertones and it is very chilli-hot – and gorgeous! It burns your mouth and then gently warms you and makes you glow.

Cube (just under 25mm (1 in) square) 900g (2 lb) of pigs' lights (including the lungs, heart and spleen). Soak them overnight in slowly running water until the water runs clear. Drain well and pat dry. In a large saucepan, heat two tablespoons of olive oil and 50g (2 oz) of lard. Add the lights and toss them around over a brisk flame until they are well coloured and their liquid has evaporated. Pour in a wine glass of dry red wine and let it reduce. Add 225g (8 oz) of tomato purée, one bay leaf, a sprig of rosemary, four crushed hot chillies, three cups of plain water and salt to taste. Cover and simmer gently for at least two hours. The consistency should be more sauce-like than soupy. Serve very hot. Pour this marvellous taste-experience over thick, oven-toasted slices of farmhouse bread. But, to be on the safe side, keep the ingredients to yourself and a couple of eggs for quick frying handy.

ZUPPA DI LENTICCHIE
Thick lentil soup

For many years one of the last jobs to be done at night at some of my restaurants was to put an enormous quantity of lentils to soak, ready for the next day's soup. And it was a relatively simple one to prepare. This is how.

Soak 450g (1 lb) of brown Italian lentils overnight. Rinse well. Cook them in unsalted water until tender. A couple of centimetres of cooking liquor should remain above the level of the cooked lentils – if not, add some boiling water. Add to the saucepan six crushed garlic cloves, one and a half cups of olive oil, one heaped tablespoon of coarsely chopped parsley, one dessertspoon of tomato purée, salt and milled black pepper. Cover and simmer for 20 minutes or until the garlic is soft. Remove the garlic and the soup is ready. Serve it hot, and, if you should have a few slices of cooked, savoury continental sausage such as cotechino or Polish, these may be successfully added. No cheese with this one but toasted rounds of French bread and lots of black pepper.

ZUPPA DEI RONCHI
Chicken, onion and egg soup

Onion soup usually reminds the older generation of exciting Parisian dawns at Les Halles. But it always reminds me of general elections! At the time of the first post-war election I worked in a West End nightclub. During the wee hours, we served gallons and gallons of thick, hot, savoury onion soup to the hundreds of customers.

There was still no television service, so the radio and the phoned-in results were written on glass slides and projected onto a large screen above the bandstand to triumphant fanfares or slow dirges played by the partisan musicians.

My boss, who usually infinitely preferred cocktail parties to political parties, was depressed by the limp, stunned atmosphere as well as by the sadly flagging champagne sales. But, ever wily, he thought matters over and stopped all further projection. He allowed the incoming results to accumulate and rearranged their order more to his, and to his customers', liking. When a sufficient quantity had been built up he gave the command to release them. They were flashed in happy, victorious bursts. The reaction was immediate. The waiters, barmen and cellarmen were instantly overwhelmed with joyous orders. Krug! Louis Roederer! Lanson! Mumm! Bottles! Magnums! Jeroboams! My boss walked through the packed and jumping room puffing busily at his Havana cigar, beaming at his suddenly celebrating customers. The popping corks drowned the triumphant fanfares played by the now unhappy band. And so great was the confusion that no one noticed that many results were projected twice and even three times. It would not have mattered anyway.

Very much later, after their onion soup, kippers, and bacon and eggs, the election revellers staggered out into the bright daylight, inebriated with the mistaken idea that the voting had gone well for them. But Labour had romped in. They were blissfully oblivious of the strange looks they were getting from the better informed workers already arriving at work. Their subsequent hangovers must have matched the sorry state of their badly depleted pocket-books.

Here is a recipe for an onion soup which, election or no election, will unquestionably make you feel much better the morning after the night before. In a saucepan, gently sweat two thinly sliced, large onions in one tablespoon each of butter and olive oil until they are soft and golden. Pour in 1l (35 fl oz) of chicken stock. Simmer for five minutes. Check the seasoning and pour, while still boiling, into four earthenware crocks. Break an egg into each one. Top with rounds of lightly toasted French bread; dust with a mixture of grated Parmesan and Gruyère cheeses. Brown under a hot grill and season with black pepper if desired.

ZUPPA RUSTICA
Chicken, egg and spinach soup

This is a very simple soup to make and was tremendously popular in my restaurants. In a saucepan sauté two crushed garlic cloves in two tablespoons of olive oil until golden. Add 450g (1 lb) of cooked leaf-spinach and toss it around in the hot oil. Remove the garlic. Pour in 750ml (26 fl oz) of chicken stock. Simmer for five minutes. Stir quickly into the soup two whole, seasoned eggs beaten up with two tablespoons of grated Parmesan cheese, and let them scramble. Check the seasoning. Pass more grated Parmesan cheese at the table.

ZUPPA DI SCIURILLI 'AGNESE'
Zucchini-flower soup

Although marrows and zucchini (courgettes) are cultivated in profusion, their pretty yellow flowers are sadly always left to die on the plants. It would be worth marketing them as there is a ready demand for them among the more knowledgeable Italian and French restaurateurs and, certainly, in the markets and stores supplying the Italian communities.

These zucchini-flowers are very good when crisply fried in Batter (page 160), and in the following soup. In a large saucepan, sweat one medium-sized, chopped onion and two crushed garlic cloves in two tablespoons of olive oil and one tablespoon of pure lard. Remove the garlic when golden. Add to the pan two large, cubed potatoes, one chopped leek, one chopped, tender celery stalk with leaves, two chopped, canned tomatoes and four cubed zucchini. Sauté for a few minutes. Pour in 1l (35 fl oz) of chicken stock and bring to the boil. Add six slices of chorizo sausage and simmer for half an hour. Plunge in 450g (1 lb) of small zucchini-flowers (pistils and stalks removed) together with 225g (8 oz) of lightly cooked spring greens or spinach. Simmer for a further 15 minutes. Mix in one tablespoon of grated Parmesan cheese and check the seasoning. No more cheese at the table, just hunks of crusty French bread, and glasses and glasses of cheerful red wine!

ZUPPA DI SPINACI
Quick spinach soup

In a saucepan, sauté four crushed garlic cloves in one cup of olive oil until golden. Add 450g (1 lb) of cooked, roughly chopped spinach. Toss this around in the heated oil a few minutes. Pour in 750ml (26 fl oz) of chicken stock. Simmer for ten minutes. Remove the garlic and add two tablespoons of grated Parmesan cheese. Check the seasoning. Stir and allow to settle before serving – although it should be hot. No more cheese at the table.

ZUPPA DI VONGOLE
Clam soup

I have visited all those Italian restaurants in Los Angeles recognized by the *conoscenti* as being, for one reason or another, the best. And I won't argue for, generally speaking, they are very good. They have to be, considering the prices most of them charge. But the restaurant which received my own personal award and to which I returned time and again, was the one that served the best Zuppa di vongole in the whole sprawling delightful city – the Dolce Vita Restaurant on Santa Monica Boulevard at Wilshire.

In a large saucepan, sauté four crushed garlic cloves in one and a half cups of olive oil and discard when golden. Add 450g (1 lb) of roughly chopped, drained, canned tomatoes, two crushed chillies, one level teaspoon of oregano, one heaped tablespoon of coarsely chopped parsley and milled black pepper. Cook for a few minutes. Plunge 2kg (4½ lb) of scrubbed, live clams or the small French clams known as *praires* into the saucepan. Cover. Shake the pan over a high flame until they open and discard those that don't. That's all, its done! Check the seasoning. Pass thick rounds of toasted French bread at the table.

More recipes for soups are to be found in the **Fish** section:

ZUPPA DI BACCALÀ CON LE PATATE Salt-cod and potato soup
If you wish to serve this unusual dish as a soup, then remember to double the quantity of water stipulated. (See Baccala con le patate on page 80).
ZUPPA DI PESCE Fish soup

UOVA
Egg Dishes

The menu I compiled for my luxurious Mayfair restaurant covered a vast range of dishes. With my constant personal supervision in the kitchen it was possible to ensure that the food emerged properly cooked and beautifully presented. Unfortunately, standards in the trade in general have slipped and such a lavish menu could not be properly produced today.

It used to give me such a thrill to see the commis waiters come out of the buzzing kitchens carrying such dishes as lobster cocktails in silver coupes set in shimmering ice; tissue-thin slices of sweet prosciotto di San Daniele served with a glistening brandied peach; hot, baked Whitstable oysters alla Sergius Orata; pink slices of Scotch smoked salmon accompanied by hot, buttery blinis; crisply gratinéed mussels; stuffed artichokes; delicate pike quenelles in wine and tarragon sauce; homemade tagliolini with saffron-flavoured seafood; feather-light brioches with creamed lobster; glazed soufflé omelettes stuffed with chicken and crabmeat; young lobsters served *à la nage;* dishes of crisply fried seafood that even the Bay of Naples would have trouble in providing; braised chicken with truffle sauce; roasted, honey-spiced ducklings; ribs of tender lamb roasted with Ligurian herbs; bowls of tiny, wild strawberries with fresh orange-juice; marinated, fresh raspberries soon to be covered with a sauce of port, Curaçao and thick cream whipped to a magenta colour; silver sweetmeat trays filled with *friandises* to accompany the espresso coffee.

And that was only a tiny part of that great selection. I was terribly proud as the Head Waiter handed a menu to Elizabeth Taylor. It was her first visit to the restaurant. What would she order, I wondered. She gave it a brief scanning, handed it back and promptly punctured my swelling ego by asking for 'A plain omelette, please. Well cooked.'

Her unintentional rebuff not only wilted my ego but was made all the worse because, while her modest order was being prepared by a similarly deflated cook, she found time to have an almighty row with Richard Burton, leave him and the rest of the party, call loudly for her Rolls and storm upstairs to the street.

FRITTATA ALLA CAMPAGNOLA
Country-style omelette
Sauté together in butter and oil diced, cooked potatoes, sliced onions, diced, chorizo sausage, chopped bacon, sliced peppers, tomatoes, peas or anything that may take your fancy. Beat and season six eggs and mix into the filling. Fry in a heavy pan with butter and oil in pancake fashion until golden. Turn it over with the aid of a large plate, slide it back into the pan and cook the other side. Do not overcook or you will ruin it.

FRITTATA DI CIPOLLE
Onion omelette
In a heavy frying pan, gently sweat two large sliced onions in a mixture of lard and oil until soft and golden. Remove and

drain the onions well. Beat six eggs together with a tablespoon of grated Parmesan cheese, salt and milled black pepper and mix in the cooked onions. Heat the pan and the original fat and pour in the mixture. Cook the omelette on both sides in pancake-style until nicely coloured, set, yet still moist inside.

FRITTATA DI SPAGHETTI
Spaghetti omelette
Beat four eggs together with two tablespoons of grated Parmesan cheese, season with salt and milled black pepper. Mix well with some roughly cut-up, cold, leftover, unsauced spaghetti (or cook some especially, but somehow it just won't be the same). Cook in pancake style in hot olive oil until golden and crisp on both sides.

OMELETTE ARNOLD BENNETT
Omelette of smoked haddock
Because the Pizzala restaurant, once the famous Mitre Public House, was just around the corner from London's Fleet Street where journalists, writers and critics work or gravitate to at drinking time, the Pizzala brothers thought that they would try out the favourite omelette of Arnold Bennett, the London *Evening Standard*'s most famous theatre critic. Until they sold their restaurant they weren't able to take it off the menu once!

Beat six eggs and season them with salt and cayenne pepper. Pour the mixture into a hot, buttered and oiled frying pan. Shake and move the eggs with a fork over a medium flame so that the uncooked parts run continually under those setting. When nearly set, but still moist, quickly spread with a hot mélange of flaked (skinned and boned), smoked haddock and grated Gruyère and Parmesan cheeses. Pour a cup of heavy cream over the top. Pass the omelette under a hot grill and let the top glaze and brown nicely. Do not fold this omelette. Do not overcook it. Serve it hot.

OMELETTE SOUFFLE 'TRIANON'
Omelette stuffed with chicken and crabmeat
Beat and season five egg yolks and two whites with two tablespoons of heavy cream. Whip three egg whites very stiffly. Fold them gently into the beaten egg mixture. Pour into a hot, buttered and oiled pan and cook in flat omelette style. It will rise and become quite fluffy. Place a hot mixture of sautéed, finely chopped, white chicken meat, crabmeat and mushrooms covered with a little Lobster or Aurore sauce (pages 162 and 159) in the centre. Fold the omelette over. Press it lightly down. Mask with more of the sauce. Cover with heavy cream and glaze under a hot grill. Serve it very hot immediately.

UOVA ALLA BORBONA
Baked eggs, southern style
Put all together into a frying pan 225g (8 oz) of drained, chopped, canned tomatoes, one crushed garlic clove, two tablespoons of olive oil, four bruised basil leaves (or a quarter-teaspoon of oregano), salt and freshly milled black pepper. Stir now and again over a medium flame and let everything amalgamate well. Remove the garlic. Spoon this sauce onto the bottom of four individual egg dishes. Break one egg into each. Cover them with a very thin slice of Fontina cheese. Bake in a hot oven until the eggs are set and the cheese is melted.

UOVA 'DONNA CARMELA'
Croûtes with savoury egg filling
To serve someone a meal of two plainly fried eggs (other than at breakfast-time) could be regarded as very ordinary. To go to the trouble of serving the same two eggs in an omelette is a much more complimentary thing. But to serve those eggs in the following fashion is pure, unadulterated flattery.

Mind you, my wife's grandmother, annoyed with her husband but not wishing to be overtly rude to him, once left a note (which her husband later found) for the cook, instructing her to prepare and serve '. . . an omelette for the Count, using only one egg, but don't tell him!'

Cut four 37mm (1½ in) thick, round slices of stale sandwich bread and trim off the crusts. Carefully hollow out the centres with a sharp knife leaving the sides and base about 6mm (¼ in) thick. They should look rather like round, open boxes. Drench them with melted butter and bake them in a hot oven until they are golden and crispy. Or you can deep-fry them. Set aside.

In a frying pan, sauté two crushed garlic cloves in olive oil and discard when golden. Add six skinned, seeded, chopped tomatoes, four chopped anchovy fillets and a pinch of oregano. Season with salt and black pepper. Sauté for a few moments over a brisk flame and set aside. Medium-poach four eggs and drain them well. Put a little of the sauce at the bottom of each bread-case. Place a poached egg in each. Cover with the rest of the sauce and sprinkle with fresh soft breadcrumbs. Moisten with a little melted butter and brown quickly under a hot grill.

UOVA ALLA PAESANA
Baked eggs, peasant style

Sauté two chopped slices of bacon with two tablespoons of finely chopped onion in butter and oil until soft and golden. Add four thinly sliced mushrooms, a sprinkling of chopped fresh tarragon, salt and milled black pepper. Cook for a few minutes. Divide this into four buttered individual egg *plat* dishes. Break one or two eggs into each. Mask with a little heavy cream and bake in a hot oven until the eggs are set. Sprinkle with chopped parsley.

UOVA ALLA TRIPPA
Eggs cooked as tripe

This is a very easy, light dish to prepare. It is suitable for an hors d'oeuvre and as a main luncheon course. Years ago I used to serve it a lot to the smart ladies lunching at the Mirabelle restaurant. Poor dears, they were so tired after a hard morning's shopping in Bond Street. Then, when I opened the Mayfair restaurant, I introduced it to the ladies there. They were just as tired, but always so pretty and charming—flowers weren't really needed around the place.

Generously mask the bottom of a flat oven cocotte dish with béchamel sauce (enriched with an egg yolk). Gently sweat a finely sliced onion in butter until soft. Spread half on top of the béchamel sauce. Cover this with four sliced, hard-boiled eggs in an overlapping arrangement. Season with salt and milled black pepper. Spread the remaining sautéed onions over the eggs. Lay a row of thinly sliced tomatoes down the centre. Mask with the rest of the béchamel sauce. Sprinkle with grated Parmesan and heat through in a moderate to hot oven. Give a finishing glaze under a hot grill. Sprinkle with chopped parsley.

UOVA DEL VESCOVO
Poached eggs, the bishop's way
Toast four English muffins and butter them well (or fry four round bread croûtes). Top with thick slices of warmed tongue and set a poached egg on each. Cover them generously with Béarnaise sauce (page 159). Decorate with a thin slice of black Umbrian truffle. Serve hot and season with black pepper if desired.

UOVA ALLA VIRGILIO
Baked eggs on stuffed artichoke hearts
Make a fairly thick filling by cooking together some shallots, white chicken meat, mushrooms (all finely chopped), parsley, salt, milled black pepper, and bind with heavy cream. Sauté four cooked (fresh or canned) artichoke hearts in butter. Set them in four individual egg *plat* dishes. Pile the filling on each artichoke heart. Set a poached egg in the centre. Mask generously with Mornay sauce (page 163). Sprinkle with grated Parmesan cheese and glaze under a hot grill.

FARINACEI
Pasta & Rice

PASTA

Pasta, even when eaten as a main course, is very nourishing and, according to the quantity of the condiment or sauce, need not be fattening. Pasta can be either homemade or factory produced. At the turn of the century there was a Ligurian pasta factory which advertised over 140 kinds. I understand that today in Naples well over 300 different shapes are available.

Pasta is made for boiling, for soups, for baking and for stuffing. It can be long, short, thin, wide, flat, wavy, straight, spiralled, slim, fat, solid, hollow, ribbed, smooth, square, round, bunched, coiled or rolled. It can be in the shape of a shell, butterfly, elbow, thimble, hat, wheel, tube or radiator. Whatever its shape, it is always made with the same basic ingredients. It is quite strange, therefore, how the different forms have such a definite and different taste of their own. It is true to say that some sauces only marry well with particular shapes of pasta. It would be unthinkable to prepare, for example, pasta shells with a clam sauce, just as it would be to serve tagliatelle with egg-plants, or baked lasagne with a fish stuffing.

Pasta names vary from region to region and some are quite unrecognizable. Spaghetti becomes vermicelli, tagliatelle becomes fettuccine, agnolotti becomes casoncei and so on. So fiercely proud are Italians of their national food that it is even possible to purchase pasta in shades of red, white and green – the colours of the flag. Another anomaly which exists inside and outside Italy is that ravioli are made with pasta! They're not! Ravioli have no pasta covering at all. They are simply small amounts of savoury mixture rolled or shaped and served in soup or with sauce or butter condiment.

Pasta has come a long way since the times of the ancient Romans who already knew of a similar food. But it has never been more popular than at present. Even in my comparatively short career the pasta industry has made vast progress. I can still remember the hot sun-baked beaches of Minori, Maiori and Amalfi, now so tightly packed with holidaymakers, lined only with long poles over which freshly made macaroni and spaghetti were hung to dry in the gentle, hot breeze. A naive foreign tourist of those days might have been forgiven had he gained the impression that spaghetti was actually growing from those branch-like poles. I wonder if that is not where the B.B.C. found the idea for their fabulous April Fool's Day Spaghetti Tree sketch?

Pasta, on the other hand, must not be cooked as recommended by Eliza Acton, Victorian cookery expert, who, whilst deploring the then current habit of 'soaking macaroni in either water or milk till well swollen', advised her readers that '. . . in about three-quarters of an hour the Naples macaroni will be sufficiently tender'.

Pasta is consumed in such great quantities by Italians that, after a day or two away from home, they may be seen in most European tourist capitals looking as though they were in desperate need of physical reassurance: their nostrils twitching for the subtle scent of any pasta sauce which may waft from around some foreign corner. Once located, there is no more stirring a sight than watching an entire Italian family rushing and pushing each other out of the way in order to reach the glorious, red-sauced, Parmesan-strewn, steaming coils.

Pasta is something that I can usually take or leave. And yet even I have to plead guilty, whenever away from home, to becoming edgy and nervous from a sudden raging desire for pasta. And this only a few hours out of London!

Pasta-eating, particularly over-sauced spaghetti, can sometimes be quite tricky, especially if you are in the middle of a heated conversation *all'Italiana*. Pasta stains are best avoided by adopting the socially approved Italian practice of covering the whole of your front with the aid of a well-spread napkin. Once, my excitable father-in-law, satisfied that he was adequately shielded, thoroughly enjoyed an animated political discussion while busily scoffing a plate of spaghetti. Having saved Italy's future for the third time that day, he removed his napkin, rose from the table and walked in a debonair manner through the restaurant with a large, inexplicable stain on his shirt-front plus the new and interesting addition of two long strands of spaghetti hanging over his left shoulder.

Hints for successful pasta

There is no mystery involved in the proper cooking of pasta. No special flair is required. And you don't have to be Italian; but remember, pasta should be eaten al dente, that is just slightly firm to the bite.

Commercially made pasta can, and does, vary considerably in manufacture and quality. So there can be no hard and fast rule as to the various cooking times. Some of the larger shapes such as rigatoni, mezzani, penne and ditali can take up to 20 minutes to cook, while good quality, hard-grained spaghettini can take between eight and ten minutes. Just follow these few guidelines.

Only buy the finest quality pastas. Allow 75 to 100g (3 to 4 oz) for an ample portion and cook in abundant, salted, fast-boiling water. Spaghetti and other long pasta will bend of their own accord in the water, so don't break! Plunge all the pasta in at the same time and stir it immediately. The water temperature will drop, so cover the pan and uncover when the water returns to the boil. Stir the pasta occasionally and when it is al dente it is ready. Spaghettini and other finer pasta must be removed a little sooner, their own heat will complete the cooking process. Always drain the pasta well in a large colander. Then mix in the chosen sauce. Pass the grated Parmesan cheese and/or the black pepper mill.

If you do not want to ruin your pasta and sauces and waste your precious time, then do make sure that you buy only the best, sweetest, well-aged Parmesan cheese. Grate sufficient quantities freshly as they are required. Never, never buy pre-grated, pre-packed Parmesan. Buy the finest black pepper – it should be of young crop, spicy, hot and very black. Try to buy fresh basil. If you can't get any then use dried basil leaves. Never use the powdered sort. Buy your oregano from a reputable Italian store; never use the commercial kind, it will almost certainly ruin your food. Buy your garlic when it is moist and, if possible, of a new crop; never when it is dry-looking, old and brittle for then it is acrid and sour. Buy only well-known Italian brands of canned tomatoes. This is not just national pride, the others are just not up to it! Never use butter in a fish sauce to be eaten with pasta. Never pass grated Parmesan (or any other) cheese with pasta dressed with fish sauce. Freshly milled black pepper, yes, always!

Fresh home-made pasta

If you can make pastry you can make fresh pasta. You may well make a few mistakes, but then so do most Italians at first. All the quantities given here are sufficient for four portions, so adjust them to suit your particular requirements. This is how it is made.

Mound 400g (14 oz) of finely sieved flour onto a firm, smooth working-surface and make a well in the centre. Break in four large eggs. Mix thoroughly and then knead well. At first the mixture will be a little stiff but later it will become smooth and pliable. Roll into a ball and cover with a cloth. Allow to rest for 20 minutes. Sprinkle flour onto the working surface to prevent sticking and roll the dough out evenly, without any bumps at all, to the thinnest possible 'paper' thickness. If you have one, use a pasta machine-roller.

For lasagne, tortelloni, casoncei, cannelloni, rotolo di Fiorella or any other stuffed pasta, roll it out just a little thicker and cut into the required shapes immediately. For tagliatelle, fettuccine, tagliolini etc., roll the pasta out and let it rest for half an hour. Then roll it up in 'Swiss roll' fashion and cut through into strips with a very sharp knife. Tagliatelle and fettuccine should be 8mm ($\frac{1}{3}$ in) wide, and tagliolini half that width. Pappardelle are cut into long, irregular 37 to 50mm ($1\frac{1}{2}$ in

to 2 in) widths – they are usually made from the left-over trimmings. Shake out the rolled pasta coils and allow them to dry for a few minutes. Cook in abundant, fast-boiling, salted water. Stir occasionally. Remember that fresh pasta takes very little cooking time.

BUCATINI ALL'AMATRICIANA
Spaghetti with piquant sauce, Roman style

Peter Sellers had just married Britt Ekland. Only Peter's family and most intimate friends were invited to a celebration dinner at my Mayfair restaurant. They sat at a long table in a faraway corner. Britt's eyes shone. Peter beamed happiness. The long happy party went on until the wee hours. Slowly seats were unobtrusively changed until, almost without realizing it, the ladies found themselves bunched together. The boys were reunited.

From the queer 'goonish' sounds, chokes, laughs and giggles, it was clear that they were running through some of their old comedy routines. They were enjoying themselves. It was getting late. Britt's eyes shone a little less now. Someone asked the time. Peter Sellers pulled out and consulted a small piece of paper. 'It's three thirty in the morning,' he said. Harry Secombe stopped shaving himself with an oblong ashtray. 'How do you know?' he asked. Peter waved the piece of paper, 'Because it's written down here.' Harry picked up and studied a silver wrapped chocolate from the tray of petits fours 'It's later than that!' he objected. 'You should buy yourself a new piece of paper, Peter,' admonished Spike Milligan, looking at them through two wine glasses held to his eyes binocular-fashion.

A drunken customer, thinking that he recognized Spike Milligan as a long lost friend, rushed over with outstretched arms and promptly knocked a bottle of wine over him. Now embarrassed and aware of his mistake, the horrified drunk offered to buy another bottle. 'Why? Do you want to do it again?' asked Spike with good humour as he busily squeezed out his sodden peaked cap into the wine glass. Here is a pasta dish that Britt Ekland particularly enjoyed.

In a saucepan, sauté 75g (3 oz) of Roman salt lard, or thick slices of streaky bacon cut into short strips, with two crushed garlic cloves in two tablespoons of olive oil. Add 450g (1 lb) of drained, roughly chopped, canned tomatoes, one large crushed chilli, salt and milled black pepper. Cook over a high flame for eight minutes. Remove the garlic. This sauce must be cooked fast. Meanwhile, cook 325g (12 oz) of bucatini. Drain and mix them with the sauce. Grated Roman Pecorino cheese should be passed, although I personally find its flavour overpowering and prefer this dish with grated Parmesan cheese instead. You choose! But don't forget the milled black pepper.

CANNELLONI AL FORNO
Rolled pasta with savoury stuffing

I doubt whether anybody knows the true origin of this very popular restaurant dish. I suspect that an economically-minded restaurateur invented it, for it is undoubtedly a very good way to use up leftovers.

Cannelloni should be made with thin squares of fresh pasta – but very often easy-going cooks prefer to pinch the beloved crêpes from the French and so escape a little hard work. We shall make them the proper way. In a deep frying pan sauté two crushed garlic cloves and one finely chopped small onion in one tablespoon each of butter and oil until soft. Discard the garlic. Add and quickly cook two halved chicken livers. Now mix in 75g (3 oz) each of chopped, cooked veal and white chicken meat, three slices of chopped mortadella sausage and one sliced carrot. Cook these for a few minutes. Mince finely and place in a bowl with two egg yolks, four tablespoons of grated Parmesan cheese, one cup of milk-soaked fresh breadcrumbs, one dessertspoon of chopped parsley, salt and black pepper. Mix well. Bind moistly with a little heavy cream.

Cut eight 12cm (5 in) squares of thinly rolled fresh pasta. Cook al dente, drain on a towel and allow to cool. Divide the filling and place on the pasta squares slightly off-centre. Roll the squares up fairly loosely and range side by side in a buttered baking dish. Mask with Béchamel sauce (page 159) and spoon over some Simple tomato sauce (page 164). Sprinkle with grated Parmesan cheese and heat through in a moderate to hot oven for about 25 minutes

CANNELLONI ALLA SORRENTINA
Rolled pasta with cheese filling, southern style

Mash 225g (8 oz) of Ricotta or fresh curd cheese and roughly blend with one diced fresh Mozzarella cheese, two tablespoons of chopped cooked ham, one tablespoon of chopped mortadella sausage, two whole eggs, four tablespoons of grated Parmesan cheese, 225g (8 oz) of well-squeezed, chopped, cooked spinach, salt and black pepper.

Cut eight 12cm (5 in) squares of fresh pasta. Cook al dente, drain them on a towel and cool. Roll the mixture inside each piece. Range them side by side in a buttered oven dish and sprinkle with chopped fresh basil. Mask with béchamel sauce, strew with grated Parmesan cheese and drizzle with melted butter. Bake in a moderate to hot oven for 25 minutes.

CASONCEI ALLA BOTTICINO
Pasta with savoury stuffing in butter sauce

In a bowl, mix 150g (6 oz) of two-day-old soft, white breadcrumbs and the same quantity of grated Parmesan cheese with a quarter of a teaspoon of allspice. In a frying pan gently melt two tablespoons of butter, two tablespoons of chopped chicken fat and four chopped slices of bacon. Pour this into the mixture. Now mix in 225g (8 oz) of chopped, cooked spinach, two eggs, a little chicken stock, salt and milled black pepper. This filling must be just moist.

Roll out a thin sheet of fresh pasta. Cut out 40 6cm ($2\frac{1}{2}$ in) squares. Put a teaspoon of the filling slightly off-centre on each square. Fold them into triangles. Seal and press the open sides gently but firmly. Cook them in abundant boiling, salted water for five minutes or until tender.

Remove the pasta gently from the water with a draining spoon and place them in a serving dish. In a frying pan, heat three tablespoons of butter with ten fresh sage leaves, let it take a golden colour and pour it hot and foaming, over the casoncei. Strew with grated Parmesan cheese. Serve hot and pass black milled pepper.

CRÊPES ALL FORMAGGIO
Pancakes with cheese stuffing

Prepare and cook eight very thin crêpes (page 163). Set them aside. Make two cups of thick béchamel sauce. Over a gentle heat melt and blend in, stirring constantly with a wooden spoon, 75g (3 oz) each of grated Parmesan, Cheddar, Gruyère cheeses, a few dashes of Worcester sauce, salt and milled black pepper. Allow to cool. Mix in two egg-yolks and 100g (4 oz) of finely diced Mozzarella cheese. Allow to cool. Then place two tablespoons of the mixture, slightly off-centre, on each pancake. Roll them fairly loosely. Trim off the ends and cut them across diagonally into 'lozenges' about 5cm (2 in) long. Place them in a well-buttered oven dish. Douse with melted butter and sprinkle abundantly with grated Parmesan cheese. Bake in a hot oven for 25 minutes or until crisp.

FETTUCCINE ALLA PANNA
Noodles in cream sauce

Cook four portions of dried or fresh fettuccine in the normal way. Meanwhile, prepare this very simple but delicious sauce. In a pan, over a low heat, swirl two cups of heavy cream, two tablespoons of grated Parmesan cheese and two dessertspoons of butter until smooth and thick. Drain the noodles well and return them to their cooking pot. Mix in the cream sauce until the noodles are well coated. Serve very quickly, do not let the heat of the pasta thicken the cream too much. Pass more grated Parmesan cheese and milled black pepper at the table.

FETTUCCINE CON PISELLI E PROSCIUTTO
Noodles with peas and ham
In two tablespoons of butter gently sauté until golden four tablespoons of Parma ham cut into strips. Remove and set aside. Add a dessertspoon of oil and a tablespoon of water to the same pan and gently sweat half of a very small onion. Now mix in 450g (1 lb) of cooked (fresh, canned or frozen), drained petits pois and return the ham to the pan. Season with salt and milled black pepper.

Cook four portions of dried or fresh fettuccine. Drain well. Mix in the sauce together with all the tasty fat. Now add small pieces of butter and a tablespoon of grated Parmesan cheese and, stirring, melt this into the hot pasta. Repeat once more. This will have the effect of thickening the sauce. Pass more grated Parmesan cheese and black pepper at the table.

FUSILLI ALLA PALUMBO
Spiral-shaped pasta with Ricotta cheese
Cook 325g (12 oz) of fusilli pasta in the normal way. Drain well. Mix in one recipe quantity of hot Simple tomato sauce (page 164). Roughly blend in a cup of warm, thick cream, then gently fold in, but do not melt, 100g (4 oz) of slightly mashed Ricotta or fresh curd cheese. Pass more tomato sauce, grated Parmesan cheese and milled black pepper at the table.

GNOCCHI DI PATATE AL POMODORO
Potato dumplings with tomato sauce
Cook 900g (2 lb) of floury potatoes in their skins. Peel and mash them while still hot and place on a floured working surface. Add 225g (8 oz) of flour. Mix together well and knead lightly into a smooth dough. (You may need more or less flour, it all depends on the absorbent quality of the potatoes.) Roll out the dough into long finger-thick rolls. Cut into pieces 25mm (1 in) long. Give each one a gentle, but positive, curling flick with your thumb to give the correct, long, slightly concave shape. This will undoubtedly result at first in quite a few distorted and ruined potato gnocchi – but persevere. Place the gnocchi in abundant boiling, salted water (a few at a time to prevent sticking). Keep the water boiling. When the gnocchi rise to the surface they are ready. Remove and drain them well with a straining spoon. Place in a serving dish and ladle generously with Simple tomato sauce (page 164). Sprinkle with grated Parmesan cheese but pass more cheese if required and plenty of freshly milled black pepper.

LASAGNE PASTICCIATE ALLA MINORESE
Savoury lasagne
This is different from the classical and well-known Lasagne alla Bolognese. It is unusual as it has the sweet undertones reminiscent of ancient Roman cooking. If you have the time and the patience, do try it as it makes a change.

Prepare two recipe quantities of Simple tomato sauce (page 164) and keep them handy or time their preparation to coincide with the frying of the meatballs. Gently sweat one finely chopped, medium-sized onion and two crushed garlic cloves in two tablespoons of lard. Discard the garlic. Drain the onions and put them into a mixing bowl. Reserve the cooking lard. To the bowl add 325g (12 oz) of minced lean pork and beef, one heaped tablespoon of chopped parsley, two whole eggs, two squeezed, crustless slices of milk-soaked bread, two tablespoons of grated Parmesan cheese, one dessertspoon of pine nuts or pine kernels, a few sultanas, one teaspoon of finely chopped candied peel, a little finely chopped lemon peel, a pinch of allspice, salt and milled black pepper. Mix well and form into walnut-sized balls. Roll these in flour and brown quickly in the reserved lard (adding more if necessary). Put them, together with a little of their frying fat, into the tomato sauce and simmer for about 20 minutes.

Roll out thinly three-quarters of the recipe quantity of Fresh home-made pasta (page 55). Cut it out into 10cm (4 in) squares. Cook them al dente. Drain well on a towel. Mask the bottom of an oven pie-dish with a little of the tomato sauce. Cover this with a single layer of pasta and mask with a little more sauce. Strew with some of the meatballs, some chopped Mozzarella, sliced hard-boiled eggs and grated Parmesan cheese. Continue in this way until five layers have been built up. Finish with a generous masking of tomato sauce and a sprinkling of grated Parmesan cheese. Bake in a moderate to hot oven for 30 minutes or until the lasagne are well heated through and crispy on top.

This dish may be prepared by omitting all the sweet ingredients in the meatballs, but it is not as good and certainly less interesting.

LASAGNE ALLA VINCIGRAS
Lasagne with a special stuffing

This is another unusual lasagne recipe. It was very successful for many years at my Mayfair restaurant. It has always been my own favourite. I don't have the written recipe any more, it was lost somewhere along the years. But it went something like this.

Mask the bottom of an oven pie-dish with a creamy béchamel sauce which has been flavoured with Marsala wine. Cover this with a single layer of cooked lasagne squares as in the above recipe. Strew this liberally with a mixture of chopped cooked ham, sweetbreads, white chicken meat, diced white mushrooms, veal meatballs, tiny cubes of Fontina cheese and sprinkle with chopped, black, Umbrian truffles. Mask with more of the flavoured béchamel and sprinkle with grated Parmesan. Carry on in this way until five layers are completed. Top with béchamel sauce and Parmesan cheese. Bake in a moderate to hot oven for 30 minutes.

LINGUINE AL SUGO DI PESCE
Flat pasta with fish soup sauce

This dish is traditionally served on Christmas Eve in the Neapolitan area. However, as Christmas comes but once a year, do prepare this whenever you like. The recipe is in the fish section entitled Zuppa di pesce. Remember to make the sauce a little thicker by allowing it to reduce somewhat. The fish, of course, is to be eaten separately as a main dish. Mix the sauce with 325g (12 oz) of cooked and drained linguine. Serve very hot. No cheese! Black milled pepper, yes!

LINGUINE E CECI
Flat pasta with chick-peas

Gino's, on Madison Avenue, is unpretentious, but it is undoubtedly one of New York's best southern-Italian restaurants. It hardly needs any more favourable comments as there is a constant crowd of customers waiting for tables. They could barely cope with any more clients. Despite this continuity of business and success, neither Gino, his partner Gaetano (Guy) nor their staff have ever lost sight of their obligations to faithful customers. They fully understand that the whole game is about friendly service, quality, reliability and good cooking – the mainstays of any dedicated and professional restaurant. And believe me, Gino's is just that.

Their house pasta speciality is Linguine alla segreta, but don't bother to ask them for the recipe for they won't part with it. I know, I've already tried. So here let me present to you a linguine recipe that is nothing at all like Gino's, and it's one that I hope Gino and Guy will like too. But they will have to go out and buy themselves a copy of this book, for I'll not tell them a thing either!

Soak overnight 225g (8 oz) of *ceci* (dried chick-peas) with one teaspoon of flour. Rinse well in lukewarm water. Cook in unsalted water for four hours or until the peas are soft and nearly mushy. Stir occasionally, do not allow them to burn. When cooked, see that they are covered with their cooking liquor by 25mm (1 in), and, if not, correct level with boiling water.

In another saucepan, sauté five crushed garlic cloves in one and a half cups of olive oil until golden. Add one tablespoon of coarsely chopped parsley and one chilli and stir well. Pour this into the chick-peas and season with salt and milled black pepper. Simmer for 15 minutes. Remove garlic and the chilli.

Cook 325g (12 oz) of broken-up linguine. Drain well. Mix with the chick-peas. Let this rest for a few minutes before serving. No cheese here at all, but load that black pepper mill instead.

LINGUINE 'JONI JAMES'
Flat pasta with squid

Place in a medium-sized saucepan 450g (1 lb) of squid cut into rings together with tentacles, 450g (1 lb) of undrained, canned tomatoes, one heaped tablespoon of

chopped parsley, four crushed garlic cloves, four tablespoons of olive oil, salt and milled black pepper. Cover and cook gently for 30 minutes or until the squid is tender. Stir occasionally to prevent sticking or burning. Remove the garlic. Cook 325g (12 oz) of linguine in the normal way. Drain well. Mix in the sauce and serve hot. Never serve cheese with this dish, just plenty of milled black pepper.

LINGUINE AL LARDO E BASILICO
Flat pasta with lard and basil

This was a 'poor man's' dish in the deep south of Italy, and as such is a very tasty and simple one. The poor in those days were rich in taste, in flavours and in ideas, but unfortunately, that's about all. But they certainly enjoyed dishes like this one.

On a heavy chopping board and with a 'half-moon' cutter or a heavy knife, coarsely chop 100g (4 oz) of Italian salted lard (do not use commercial soft lard) together with five crushed garlic cloves. Sauté gently in a heavy frying pan until the lard has dissolved and the garlic has turned nearly golden. Take care not to burn either of them. Throw in, at the last minute, ten julienned fresh basil leaves and remove the garlic. Meanwhile, cook four portions of linguine. Drain well, mix in the sauce and pass grated Parmesan cheese and plenty of freshly milled black pepper.

LINGUINE ALLE VONGOLE
Flat pasta with red clam sauce

It may sound unbelievable to American readers that, whereas in the United States Spaghetti with clam sauce has been a well-known dish for donkey's years, it took my restaurants to introduce it a comparatively short while ago to Britain!

Of all the new dishes and ideas that I presented to my clientele, none became as well loved as Linguine alle vongole. It was featured on all the menus. Over the years its fame spread so far that hardly any Italian restaurant or trattoria in the United Kingdom did not include this speciality in their menus.

Apart from my own restaurants, modestly speaking, the best linguine with clam sauce I have enjoyed were those served at that extremely good Italian restaurant in Paris, the San Francisco, and those quite fantastic ones that I had at the modest, but superbly traditional Blue Grotto on Mulberry Street in New York's Little Italy.

In a sauteuse or similar pan, cook six crushed garlic cloves in a cup of olive oil until golden. Now, a secret: add one chopped, unsalty (and that's important) anchovy fillet; it will frizzle and disappear and no one will ever know. Add 450g (1 lb) of roughly chopped, drained, canned tomatoes, one heaped tablespoon of coarsely chopped parsley, salt and milled black pepper. Cook over a brisk flame for five minutes. Add 900g (2 lb) of washed and scrubbed live clams (or equivalent canned or frozen) and toss them around until they open. Discard any that do not. Mix with 325g (12 oz) of cooked and drained linguine or spaghettini. Serve hot. Plenty of freshly milled black pepper but no cheese at all.

LINGUINE ALLE VONGOLE IN BIANCO
Flat pasta with white clam sauce

This pasta and clam dish is particularly well liked in the United States. Follow the same procedure as in the previous recipe, but omit the tomatoes. Add a crushed chilli at the start. Again, never serve any cheese with this, but black pepper, plenty!

MACCHERONI ALLA GENOVESE
Macaroni with onion sauce

See Manzo brasato alla genovese in the meat section on page 98. The absolutely delicious sauce, when mixed with cooked macaroni or rigatoni, produces one of the best Italian pasta dishes known.

MACCHERONI AI QUATTRO FORMAGGI
Macaroni with four cheeses

Cook 325g (12 oz) of penne or similar macaroni in the usual way. When they are al dente drain, set them aside and keep warm. Leave one and a half cups of the cooking water in the saucepan and add 50g (2oz) of chopped fatty ham, 75g (3 oz) of butter and 75g (3 oz) each of grated Parmesan, Mozzarella, Gruyère and mild Cheddar. Stir over a medium flame until the cheeses have melted. Now mix in the cooked pasta. This should be done quickly. Do not allow the macaroni to become overcooked. Pass more grated Parmesan at the table if required (unlikely) and lots of freshly milled black pepper (most likely).

MANICOTTI AL FORNO
Macaroni stuffed and baked

Cook 16 large manicotti (giant-sized hollow pasta) in the normal way. Drain and let them cool. Fill a wide-nozzled piping bag with a roughly blended mixture of 325g (12 oz) of Ricotta or fresh curd cheese, four heaped tablespoons of grated Parmesan cheese, two egg yolks, four tablespoons of cooked fatty ham, two tablespoons of heavy cream, salt and milled black pepper. Fill the manicotti while still warm. Arrange them in individual buttered oven-proof dishes. Mask them with a little Simple tomato sauce (page 164) and sprinkle with grated Parmesan cheese. Bake in a moderate to hot oven for 20 minutes or until the manicotti are heated through.

MEZZANI AL RAGÙ NAPOLETANO
Macaroni with Neapolitan meat sauce

In the Naples area, before the war, meat was expensive and money was really tight. However, even the poorest families somehow managed to buy, usually on the slate, a thin slice or two of tough old beef to be stuffed and rolled into the savoury *braciola* with which to make the marvellous pasta sauce for Sunday's mezzani al ragù. No one needed to ask his neighbour what he was having for lunch. It was obvious, judging from the delicious aromas which came from the heavy iron pots bubbling and simmering over the tiled charcoal ranges and wafted around the closely packed houses. As the great moment drew near impatient children would dart from behind their mothers' skirts to dip a piece of bread into the magic sauce. Their subsequent look of rapture announced very plainly 'It's Sunday!'

After the macaroni had been eaten there came the second ritual of the meal: the careful unwinding of the cotton which had held the rolled beef together and the cautious slicing of the meat into portions. A little more of the dark rich sauce coated onto each slice and then it would be eaten slowly, as though it were ambrosia, with a large piece of crusty bread so as to give more substance to the flavour and to make the exquisite sensation last for as long as possible. Oh! It was Sunday all right!

And now back to earth! Make a mixture of two tablespoons of coarsely chopped parsley, four crushed garlic cloves, one dessertspoon of pine nuts or four teaspoons of grated Parmesan cheese, two teaspoons of sultanas, eight bruised, fresh basil leaves, salt and freshly milled black pepper. Divide into four parts and place in the middle of four, well-flattened slices of raw beef silverside, about 450g (1 lb) in total. Roll them up and secure with cotton.

In a large saucepan, put two heaped tablespoons of pure lard, one finely chopped, medium-sized onion and the rolls of beef. Over a moderate heat sauté the onions and the beef to a golden colour stirring continuously. Do not allow it to burn. Now add a wine glass of red wine and let it reduce. Stir in one heaped tablespoon of tomato purée. Add 900g (2 lb) of roughly chopped, undrained, canned tomatoes, salt and milled black pepper. Cover. Simmer very gently for at least two and a half hours. Add a little sugar if the sauce seems too sharp. Cook and drain 325g (12 oz) of mezzani or similar tube-shaped macaroni. Mix in the sauce. Serve with Parmesan cheese and pass the milled black pepper. If you wish, you may garnish each portion with a slice of the beef olives.

Despite the hundreds of ways that pasta can be prepared, once you have tasted a lovingly and carefully cooked Ragù alla Napoletana, you are hooked for life. No other pasta will ever taste quite as good. Unfortunately this delicious sauce is never offered in its original and proper form by any restaurant, not even mine. It is a lot of trouble for the cooks, even the Neapolitan ones, I am sad to say.

MEZZANI CON LA SALSICCIA
Macaroni with Italian sausage

In a saucepan gently sweat two crushed garlic cloves with a small, finely chopped onion in one tablespoon of lard. Remove the garlic when it turns golden. Add 450g (1 lb) of undrained, roughly chopped, canned tomatoes and one tablespoon of tomato purée. Bring to the boil. Add three parboiled (eight if they are going to be eaten later as a main course) pure pork, Italian-style sausages and six bruised, fresh basil leaves. Season with salt and milled black pepper. Cover. Simmer for at least 45 minutes. Check the seasoning. If it is too sharp, correct by adding a little sugar. Cook 325g (12 oz) of mezzani or similar tube-shaped macaroni. Drain well. Mix with the sauce and garnish with some slices of the sausage. Pass grated Parmesan cheese and freshly milled black pepper.

PAPPARDELLE ALLA PAPALINA
Pasta ribbons with cream and tomato

Before I am accused of being biased or partisan, let me beat you to it by readily admitting that I am. But, in this instance, most justifiably so. During the exploratory market-research trips to the provinces before I opened my first out-of-town restaurant, I was regularly served the weirdest collection of gooey, overcooked and gummy pasta dishes. On good days I was served the canned variety! That was one reason why the decision was taken to expand out of London.

This is one of the fresh, home-made pastas that the northern customers came to like so much in the old days. As far as I know you can enjoy a similarly good plateful at Walter's and Enzo's La Meridiana restaurant in London.

Make four portions of pappardelle (page 55). Cook and drain them. Mix with two cups of hot Simple tomato sauce (page 164), then fold in, but do not stir, half a cup of warm, heavy cream. The cream should form separate 'harlequin' streaks across the tomato sauce. Serve very hot. Pass lots of grated Parmesan cheese and freshly milled black pepper. That's all!

PASTA E CAVOLFIORE
Pasta with cauliflower

This is one of the many very good Campanian pasta recipes which makes good use of local vegetable produce. It is rarely seen on restaurant menus. I used to have it prepared only by special request. Put in a saucepan the florets from a medium-sized cauliflower, three garlic cloves, one tablespoon of coarsely chopped parsley, two tablespoons of olive oil, one cup of cold water, one roughly chopped chilli, salt and milled black pepper. Cover and cook gently for between 20 to 30 minutes or until the florets are tender and soft. Cook 325g (12 oz) of penne or rigatoni. Drain well. Mix with the sauce and leave to stand on a warm part of the stove for five minutes before serving.

PASTA E CAVOLFIORE 'SARA'
Sara's pasta with cauliflower

Cook the florets from a medium-sized cauliflower until barely tender and drain.

In a saucepan, sauté two julienned slices of streaky bacon in oil and butter. Add, and sweat, one small, finely sliced onion. Mix in the florets and cook, turning occasionally, until they are soft and golden. Season with salt and milled black pepper. Add one dessertspoon of finely chopped parsley. Cook 325g (12 oz) of penne or rigatoni pasta and drain well. Put them into a large serving bowl together with a tablespoon of butter. Mix in the cauliflower mixture. Serve hot. Pass grated Parmesan cheese and freshly milled black pepper.

PASTA E FAGIOLI
Pasta with beans

This recipe is another of my restaurant's English firsts. It had never been served in any Italian restaurant in England before. It was one of the traditional Neapolitan dishes that I wanted to introduce from the start. Sophia Loren regularly enjoys a plate of Pasta e fagioli. Roger Moore and his lovely wife Luisa adore it and get their friends to join in and order some. As soon as Mary Rand returned from Tokyo with her Olympic Gold Medal, she made a long-jump for a plate of Pasta e fagioli. But even I would acknowledge that there is a time and a place for the consumption of Pasta e fagioli. One evening my cousin, Adolfo Arpino, dined at my elegant Mayfair restaurant with Anna, his bride of only a few hours. They were due to fly away later that evening to their honeymoon destination. Adolfo could have ordered anything his heart desired as an hors d'oeuvre: the finest caviar, the most succulent smoked salmon, a little truffled foie gras from Strasbourg or some plump oysters. Adolfo shook his head, quite firmly, ordering a plate of sustaining Pasta e fagioli, please! I always knew that he was a man of impeccable taste. Or perhaps he had other things on his mind? In any case, Anna immediately understood that married life with Adolfo was going to be definitely 'Heinz-like' and mean 'beanz'.

You make it this way. Soak 225g (8 oz) of white Italian cannellini beans overnight. Rinse and change the water. Put them in a large saucepan and cover, by 10cm (4 in), with cold unsalted water. Cook them until soft. This will take about two hours. Do not allow them to stick or burn, make sure that there is 3cm ($1\frac{1}{2}$ in) of cooking liquor left over the cooking beans, and if not, correct the level with hot water. Now add one and a half cups of olive oil, one dessertspoon of tomato purée, one heaped tablespoon of coarsely chopped parsley, six large, crushed garlic cloves, salt and freshly milled black pepper. Stir well and cover pan. Cook gently until the garlic is soft, then fish around and remove it.

Cook 325g (12 oz) of ditali pasta. Drain and mix well with the beans. It should be thick enough to eat with a fork and should never be runny. Do not pass any cheese but do pass the black pepper mill – and red wine.

Pasta e fagioli may be served hot, warm or even cold. Invited to a picnic, my wife and I once carried a huge saucepan of this pasta halfway across London's Hampstead Heath. It contrasted admirably with the daintier sandwiches the others had brought along – and it certainly caused a sensation.

PASTA E FAVE
Pasta with broad beans

Soak 225g (8 oz) of dried broad beans overnight in water. Drain them. Remove the outer husks. Now follow the recipe for Pasta e fagioli (above).

PASTA E PATATE
Pasta with potatoes

After a lot of soul-searching, I would have to admit that this is my favourite pasta of them all. Pasta and potatoes do go perfectly well together.

In a saucepan sweat a chopped, medium-sized onion in two tablespoons of lard and one tablespoon of oil until soft and golden.

Add five floury, medium-sized potatoes cut into 18mm (¾ in) cubes, and two roughly chopped, tender celery stalks with leaves. Stir these around until they are well coated. Now add one heaped dessertspoon of tomato purée and enough cold water barely to cover the potatoes. Season with salt and milled black pepper. Cover and simmer for 30 minutes or until the potatoes are cooked and start to break up. Cook 325g (12 oz) of ditali or penne, drain well and mix with the sauce. Serve hot with plenty of grated Parmesan cheese and freshly milled black pepper.

PASTA E PISELLI
Pasta with peas
In a saucepan, sweat one finely sliced, medium-sized onion in one and a half tablespoons of lard with three chopped slices of streaky bacon until they are lightly coloured. Add four tablespoons of water and cook for a few more minutes. Mix in 450g (1 lb) of drained, canned or cooked, fresh petits pois. Do not use frozen peas. Cook the peas for a few minutes. Cook 325g (12 oz) of ditalini and drain well. Mix with the peas and bacon. Add a knob of butter. Serve hot with plenty of grated Parmesan cheese and milled black pepper.

PASTA CON LA ZUCCA
Pasta with pumpkin
In a saucepan, sauté four crushed garlic cloves in four tablespoons of olive oil and discard when golden. Mix in 450g (1 lb) of peeled, seeded and cubed pumpkin and toss it around until it is well coated with the fat. Add enough water to reach halfway up the pumpkin, two heaped tablespoons of chopped parsley, one roughly chopped, large chilli, salt and milled black pepper. Cover and cook gently for half an hour or until the pumpkin is soft and tender but not pulpy. Cook four portions of tagliatelle, drain well and mix with the sauce. Remove the chilli if you can find it. No cheese, but black pepper definitely.

PENNE ALLA CARBONARA
Macaroni with bacon and eggs
The Romans (not the ancient, but today's elegant ones) have always been credited with this very good way of preparing macaroni. In reality it is an Umbrian method. It was brought to Rome by Umbrian charcoal burners, hence the name *carbonara* or coalmen. It used to be an extremely popular dish at all of my restaurants. I recall, too, that I devoured a fantastic amount of the most marvellous Spaghetti alla carbonara at the smoothly run San Marco which is, in my opinion, New York's best Italian restaurant, and that's saying something, for they are all, generally speaking, exceptionally good.

Cut 100g (4 oz) of Roman pancetta or green streaky bacon into strips and sauté until crisp in one tablespoon of lard and a little oil. Set aside. Cook 325g (12 oz) of penne or spaghetti and drain well. Mix with the crisp bacon or pancetta and the hot, melted fat. Quickly stir in two seasoned eggs (lightly whisked with two tablespoons of grated Parmesan cheese) well away from the heat. Pass more grated Parmesan cheese at the table and don't forget that freshly milled black pepper!

Do not allow the eggs to overcook or scramble as 99 per cent of all restaurants do – that is very very wrong!

PENNE PASTICCIATE AL FORNO
Baked savoury macaroni
You will need to prepare in advance two quantities of Simple tomato sauce (page 164), two fried and crumbled Italian pork sausages and 325g (12 oz) of cooked and drained penne or similar pasta. Mix the macaroni with two thirds of the tomato sauce. Rub an oven pie-dish with lard and spread the bottom with a little tomato sauce. Lay one third of the pasta on top. Strew abundantly with roughly chopped hard-boiled eggs, some of the sausage-meat and grated Parmesan cheese. Cover

this with very thin slices of Fontina cheese and mask with more of the tomato sauce. Repeat these layers until the ingredients are used up. Finish with spreading of tomato sauce and grated Parmesan. Bake in a medium to hot oven for half an hour or until the macaroni are well heated and crusty on top.

PENNE CON LE ZUCCHINE
Macaroni with zucchini
I have tried lots of different versions of this pasta-zucchini combination, but this one is the very best there is. So, in my opinion, you need look no further.

In a saucepan, sweat a finely sliced, medium-sized onion together with two crushed garlic cloves in two tablespoons of butter and one tablespoon of olive oil. Add 450g (1 lb) of cubed (unseeded and unskinned) zucchini, season and cook covered until tender. This will take from 30 to 40 minutes. Add six bruised, torn-up basil leaves. Cook 325g (12 oz) of penne or similar macaroni, drain well and mix in the zucchini with all the pan juices. Melt in a large knob of butter and serve very hot. Pass plenty of grated Parmesan and milled black pepper.

RAVIOLI ALLA FIORENTINA
Spinach dumplings with butter sauce
True ravioli do not have a pasta covering of any sort. This is a recipe for true ravioli. Cook 900g (2 lb) of young spinach in a covered saucepan without water until they are barely tender. Cool, drain well and chop very, very finely. Mix with 400g (14 oz) of Ricotta or fresh curd cheese, two whole eggs, three tablespoons of grated Parmesan and salt to taste. Work the mixture into walnut-sized balls. Roll them in flour and poach in boiling, salted water until they feel slightly firm. Remove them with a straining spoon and place in a serving dish. Melt three tablespoons of butter with ten fresh sage leaves, let it colour and pour it hot and foaming over the ravioli.

Sprinkle with Parmesan and pass more at the table. No black pepper here, not even if it does have all the correct hot spicy properties and is freshly milled! I assure you, I know!

RIGATONI ALLE COZZE
Ribbed pasta with mussels
Of all the glamorous tables I have ever seen in my years in the restaurant business I will never forget that splendid table to which the movie producer and writer Jerry Epstein was host. He was discussing his new picture *The Countess of Hong Kong*. His guests included Sophia Loren, Oona O'Neil, Geraldine Chaplin, Charles Chaplin, Marlon Brando, Carlo Ponti and Sidney Chaplin. The rest of the dining-room just could not seem to concentrate on their food.

Sophia Loren was impressed with the restaurant's food. It reminded her of home. So, each evening during the shooting of that amusing movie, she would phone over orders for large portions of Pasta e fagioli, Maccheroni all'Amatriciana, Spaghetti alle vongole, Lasagne al forno, Rigatoni alle cozze, and sometimes even freshly whipped Zabaglione al Marsala. Here is one of Sophia Loren's favourite pasta dishes.

In a large saucepan, sauté six crushed garlic cloves in four tablespoons of olive oil until golden. Add 1kg 350g (3 lb) of scrubbed mussels, one heaped tablespoon of coarsely chopped parsley, 450g (1 lb) of roughly chopped, drained, canned tomatoes and milled black pepper to taste. Cover the pan and shake it over a brisk flame until the mussels open. Discard any that don't. Shell all but 16 of the mussels and return them to the sauce. Cook 325g (12 oz) of rigatoni, drain, mix in the sauce and turn them into a large dish. Garnish with the unshelled mussels. Serve very hot. Do not offer grated Parmesan with this one but pass the pepper mill.

RIGATONI CON LE MELANZANE
Ribbed pasta with egg-plants

You will need to prepare in advance one quantity of Simple tomato sauce (page 164). Cut two medium-sized, ripe egg-plants (unseeded and unpeeled) into 6mm ($\frac{1}{4}$ in) thick slices. Fry them in a cup of olive oil until golden and drain well on absorbent paper. Mix them into the heated tomato sauce. Cook 325g (12 oz) of rigatoni, drain well and mix into the sauce. Stir in three tablespoons of grated Parmesan Serve hot. Pass more grated cheese at the table as well as the black pepper.

RIGATONI AL TONNO
Ribbed pasta with tuna fish

For this recipe you will need a quantity of Simple tomato sauce (page 164). Simply add to the sauce 150g (6 oz) of firm, best quality pieces of canned tuna fish, twelve stoned black olives and a pinch of good oregano. Heat well. Mix with 325g (12 oz) of cooked and drained rigatoni and serve hot. No cheese here.

ROTOLO DI FIORELLA
Spinach and pasta roll

Cook 1kg 350g (3 lb) of young spinach in a covered saucepan without water until barely tender. Drain well and gently squeeze the spinach moistly dry. Chop it very finely. In butter and oil, sauté one finely chopped white of a large leek until soft but not coloured. Add the spinach with two tablespoons of grated Parmesan, salt, milled black pepper and mix well.

Roll out three-quarters of a recipe quantity of Fresh home-made pasta (page 55) into one thin sheet. Spread it fairly thickly and evenly with the spinach mixture leaving a 5cm (2 in) margin all round.

Roll it three times only in 'Swiss roll' fashion. Trim the ends and wrap the roll tightly in muslin and secure well. Cook it in boiling, salted water for 20 minutes. Drain. Cut the roll into slices 18mm ($\frac{3}{4}$ in) thick. Serve with butter flavoured with fresh sage, tomato sauce or a good meat sauce. Pass grated Parmesan cheese at the table.

A very important note–unless your family or guests have steel-like teeth or highly effective digestive systems, it might be as well to remove the muslin cloth before slicing and most certainly before serving.

SOUFFLE DI TAGLIOLINI
Pasta and cheese souffle

In a saucepan, mix two tablespoons of flour in two tablespoons of melted butter and, stirring all the while, cook for a few moments. Do not let it colour. Blend in 430ml (15 fl oz) of lukewarm milk and cook gently for ten minutes. The mixture should be quite thick. Season with salt and pepper. Smoothly stir in a mixture of four beaten egg yolks and 75g (3 oz) of mixed grated Parmesan and Gruyère cheeses. Now mix in two portions of cooked, roughly cut-up, fresh tagliolini. Fold in four stiffly beaten egg whites. Pour into four individual, buttered souffle dishes. Bake for 25 minutes in the middle of a hot oven. Do not wait when they are ready! Run to the table and serve them quickly–but look out for hidden obstacles. Once, in a busy restaurant, I saw the consequences of not doing so: believe me, it wasn't a pretty sight!

SPAGHETTINI CON LE ACCIUGHE
Thin spaghetti with anchovies

This is one of the fastest spaghetti sauces. It can be prepared while the pasta is boiling. Put on 325g (12 oz) of spaghettini to cook in the normal way. Meanwhile, in a frying pan, sauté six crushed garlic cloves, six plump anchovy fillets and two roughly chopped chillies in four tablespoons of olive oil. When the garlic is golden, add one heaped tablespoon of coarsely chopped parsley and a tablespoon of boiling pasta water, mind the spitting and the spluttering, and stir well. Discard the garlic and mix the oily, flavoursome sauce into the drained al dente spaghettini. No cheese under any circumstances but a lot of milled black pepper. Don't forget some crusty French bread to mop up the sauce.

SPAGHETTI ALLA CARRETTIERA
Cart-drivers' spaghetti

In a frying pan sauté four crushed garlic cloves in four tablespoons of olive oil until golden. Give the garlic one last crush and then discard. Now add 50g (2 oz) of chopped mushrooms and a crushed chilli pepper. Cook for a few minutes. Add 75g (3 oz) of broken-up tuna, three plump anchovies, four roughly chopped, drained, canned tomatoes, one dessertspoon of coarsely chopped parsley, a pinch of oregano, salt and milled black pepper. Cook over a fairly high flame for five minutes. Cook and drain 325g (12 oz) of spaghetti and mix with the sauce. This dish needs no cheese but does need milled black pepper.

SPAGHETTI ALL'INSALATA
Spaghetti salad

This is a little known and very unusual way of presenting spaghetti. It is a summertime dish and is served mostly around the chic Roman beach areas.

Put into a very large salad bowl 450g (1 lb) of quartered and seeded, ripe tomatoes, two crushed cloves of garlic, three tablespoons of olive oil, six bruised torn-up basil leaves (or a pinch of oregano), twenty stoned ripe black olives, two tablespoons of chopped Mozzarella, four chopped anchovy fillets, a few capers, salt and milled black pepper. Leave to stand for two hours.

Cook and drain 325g (12 oz) of spaghetti in the normal way. Toss them hot in the salad mixture and serve immediately. No cheese.

SPAGHETTI ALLA MARINARA
Fishermen's spaghetti
In a saucepan, sauté six crushed garlic cloves in a cup of olive oil until golden and then discard. Add 450g (1 lb) of roughly chopped, drained, canned tomatoes, one tablespoon of coarsley chopped parsley, half a teaspoon of oregano, salt and milled black pepper. Cook for ten minutes. If too sharp, then correct with a little sugar. Cook and drain 325g (12 oz) of spaghetti in the normal way. Mix with the sauce. No cheese, but pass the black pepper mill.

SPAGHETTI CON LE POLPETTINE
Spaghetti with meatballs
Strictly speaking, spaghetti served with meatballs or fried veal escalopes garnished with pasta are not part of the Italian gastronomic repertoire. One is an Americanization and the other an 'escoffierization'. However, let me immediately add that I like and approve of both combinations wholeheartedly. I would even go so far as to say that many more American and French ideas could be put to good use in Italian cooking.

You are going to need two quantities of Simple tomato sauce (page 164). Keep it handy or time things so that you finish the sauce at the same time as the meatballs are frying. In a pan sweat one finely chopped, medium-sized onion and two crushed garlic cloves in two tablespoons of lard. Discard the garlic. Drain the onions, reserving the frying fat. Mix them well with 325g (12 oz) of lean, minced beef and pork, one heaped tablespoon of chopped parsley, two whole eggs, two squeezed crustless slices of milk-soaked bread, two tablespoons of grated Parmesan cheese, one dessertspoon of pine nuts, salt and freshly milled black pepper. Form into walnut-size balls. Roll them in flour and brown quickly in the reserved lard (adding more if necessary). Put them into the hot tomato sauce together with a little of the fat and simmer for 20 minutes. Cook and drain 325g (12 oz) of spaghetti and mix with the sauce and the meatballs. Serve with grated Parmesan and black pepper.

SPAGHETTI ALLA PUTTANESCA
Spaghetti with piquant sauce
Sauté three crushed garlic cloves in one cup of olive oil and discard when golden. Add 450g (1 lb) of roughly chopped, drained, canned tomatoes, one tablespoon of rinsed capers, twelve chopped black olives, one crushed chilli, four chopped plump anchovies, one tablespoon of coarsely chopped parsley, one teaspoon of oregano, salt and milled black pepper. Cover and cook briskly for ten minutes. Cook and drain 325g (12 oz) of spaghetti and mix with the sauce. Do not pass cheese but be generous with the freshly milled black pepper. This dish should be piquant, hot and spicy.

SPAGHETTI ALLA ZIMMARO
Spaghetti with tomato and basil
This is one of the simplest and tastiest ways to serve spaghetti. It was a very popular dish at all of my restaurants.

Sauté four crushed garlic cloves in four tablespoons of olive oil until golden. Add 450g (1 lb) of roughly chopped, drained, canned tomatoes, a quarter of a level teaspoon of sugar, salt and milled black pepper. Cook over a brisk flame for ten minutes. Add eight bruised, torn-up basil leaves during the last few minutes. Remove the garlic. Cook and drain 325g (12 oz) of spaghetti and mix with the sauce. Grated Parmesan may be offered, but with this kind of a sauce it is better to rely on milled black pepper. You choose depending on the flavour you require.

TAGLIATELLE ALLA BOLOGNESE (RAGÙ ALLA BOLOGNESE)
Egg noodles in Bolognese meat sauce

Here is a true story that involved some noodles. The Tagliatelle alla Bolognese, in an ornate silver dish, was presented to the customers by the Chef de rang with the exaggerated flair of one who had drunk too much. Indeed he had, it was his birthday! The tray of glistening, coiled egg noodles was placed on the serving trolley alongside the guests' table. The happy waiter proceeded, with the aid of a spoon and fork, to serve the first portion. The requisite quantity of pasta was carefully and deliberately sauced with the luscious ragù and artistically embellished with strategically positioned curls of butter. Primly satisfied and with a final grandiose flourish, he moved to pick up the plate. His indulgent smirk set hard as he found himself groping where the rim should have been. He looked down in disbelief. There never had been a plate at all! The Tagliatelle alla Bolognese, delicately sauced and gracefully adorned, was lying limply, directed on the trolley's serving cloth.

Without a murmur and with a look upwards, he picked up the four corners of the cloth and carried the whole pile out to the kitchen. The amazed customers did not see their waiter again.

Mine was probably the only group of Italian restaurants that always refused to include that particular sauce in the menu. I know of no Italian restaurant in the world, presumptuous as that may sound, where Ragù alla Bolognese is properly prepared. In restaurants everywhere, and even in private homes in Italy, unnecessary and unsuitable ingredients (usually left-over scraps) are employed in the cooking of this sauce, thus creating the most awful culinary deviations. I know that there are no hard and fast rules in Italian cooking, but this is ridiculous, gastronomic murder!

So, if you want to make Ragù alla Bolognese, make sure that the meat is not minced but finely chopped, that both pork and beef are stipulated, and that a little chicken liver and the merest suggestion of fresh cream is included. Do not, no matter who is giving the advice, include mushrooms, lemon juice, mustard, bacon, oregano, basil or peeled tomatoes.

Melt 50g (2 oz) of chopped, streaky, slab lard or real Italian pancetta (both obtainable from Italian food stores) with 50g (2 oz) of butter. Add a small onion, a small carrot, a tender celery stalk (all very finely chopped) and a small piece of bay leaf. Soften but do not let colour. Add 150g (5 oz) each of chopped beef and lean pork. Brown well. Pour in a small glass of red wine and, when evaporated, stir in a cup of strong beef stock mixed with a level dessertspoon of tomato purée. Check the seasoning. Simmer until the ingredients have combined nicely. Lastly, blend in two tablespoons of heavy cream and add a chopped chicken liver (quickly sautéed in a little butter). Cook four portions of fresh or dried tagliatelle. Drain well and mix with the sauce. Serve hot with grated Parmesan cheese and black milled pepper.

TAGLIATELLE CON FUNGHI
Egg noodles with mushroom sauce

My wife Sara still talks with misty eyes of the succulent and tasty fresh noodles with mushrooms that she enjoyed so much at the ultra-smart, smooth and brittle, slightly snobbish, Orsini's Restaurant on West 56th Street, New York. Although I was there at the time and must wholeheartedly agree that they were indeed just fine, I am still firmly convinced that she is really talking about the charmer himself, Orsini.

In a sauteuse or similar pan, gently sweat half of a finely chopped, small onion in two tablespoons of oil and one tablespoon of butter until soft and golden. Add one cup of light stock and let it reduce somewhat.

Chop 25g (1 oz) of Italian dried porcini mushrooms (which have soaked in warm water for ten minutes) and add them with a little of the soaking liquor to the pan. Cook until the onions and mushrooms are combined. Stir in a level teaspoon of tomato purée and a cup of heavy cream. Simmer for a few minutes then, swirling the pan, let the sauce thicken. Check the seasoning. Cook four portions of fresh or dried tagliatelle. Drain well and mix with the sauce. Serve hot with grated Parmesan cheese and some black pepper.

TAGLIOLINI ALLA FRANCO
Thin noodles with seafood sauce
Gently sauté, in a sauteuse or similar pan, 50g (2 oz) each of chopped squid and tentacles, scampi, scallops and crab-claw meat in two tablespoons of butter until cooked. Flame with a small wine glass of brandy. Stir in four ripe, skinned, seeded and sieved tomatoes and a pinch of saffron. Cook for a few moments over a brisk flame. Pour in one and a half cups of heavy cream. Swirl the pan until the sauce thickens. Check the seasoning with salt and cayenne pepper. Cook 325g (12 oz) of fresh tagliolini or dried linguine, drain well and mix into the sauce. Serve hot. Do not pass cheese, but the black pepper mill here is essential.

TIMBALLO DI MACCHERONI AL FORNO
Savoury, baked pasta with egg-plant
I once had a dish, similar to this one, tastily produced by a very deft cook at Matteo's Restaurant in Los Angeles. This remarkable but unassuming restaurant is mostly well known to the movie crowd which refers to the place simply as 'Matty's'. Matty is the genial, happy-go-lucky owner who is quite a character. He is very proud of his fine establishment. It is, as might be expected, a favourite spot of Frank Sinatra and his friends and all the other big movie stars and producers. They flock to Matty's for relaxed, informal dinners, which incidentally are not as wildly expensive as you might suppose.

Cut four ripe egg-plants lengthways into 6mm ($\frac{1}{4}$ in) slices and fry them in oil on both sides until golden. Drain and dry well on absorbent paper, and then flour and dip them in a seasoned mixture of beaten eggs and grated Parmesan cheese. Fry them again until well coloured. Drain and line four larded individual baking dishes with the egg-plant slices. Reserve the rest for 'topping-off'.

Mix 225g (8 oz) of cooked and drained penne macaroni with two recipe quantities of Simple tomato sauce (page 164) reserving a little for garnish. Mix in two fried, crumbled Italian pork sausages, one chopped, cooked chicken liver, two tablespoons of julienned tongue, two of sliced, cooked white chicken meat, 50g (2 oz) of cooked peas, one chopped hard-boiled egg, 25g (1 oz) of chopped Mozzarella cheese and two tablespoons of grated Parmesan cheese.

Fill the lined dishes with the mixture. Cover them with the remaining egg-plant slices. Spread the tops with a little tomato sauce and strew with grated Parmesan. Cover with foil and bake in a moderate to hot oven for 25 minutes. Turn them out and serve as individual portions.

TORTELLINI ALLA PANNA
Stuffed pasta with cream sauce
Mix together 225g (8 oz) of cooked, chopped spinach, 225g (8 oz) of Ricotta or fresh curd cheese, 100g (4 oz) of grated Parmesan, two beaten eggs, a touch of allspice, salt and milled black pepper. Roll out thinly in one sheet, on a floured board, three-quarters of a recipe quantity of Fresh home-made egg-pasta (page 55). Put small teaspoonfuls of the mixture in straight lines about 5cm (2 in) apart on half of the sheet. Fold the remaining half of the pasta over and press, quite firmly, between the mounds of stuffing. Cut them out with a pastry wheel-cutter and allow to stand for a short while. Then cook them in boiling salted water for five minutes or until tender.

Remove the pasta with a straining spoon and place in a serving dish. Cover them with a cream sauce made by swirling and thickening two tablespoons of butter, two tablespoons of grated Parmesan and two cups of heavy cream over medium heat. Serve very hot and pass more Parmesan and black milled pepper at the table.

POLENTA
Maize flour
Polenta – coarse ground maize flour – when cooked used to provide the bulk of the northern Italian manual workers' otherwise meagre diet. This maize-flour-starch diet was partly the cause of the widespread and nasty local affliction in northern Italy, the goitre. But so indispensable was polenta to the needy working population that it was, nevertheless, eaten thrice daily.

Today things have changed. Time dulls pain and softens memories and polenta is remembered more with affection than bitterness by the old people. For the young it has even become almost a chic, fun food. Ideally polenta should be cooked, as is still done in some country houses and in all good northern Italian restaurants and trattorie that specialize in its preparation, in a round-bottomed copper pail known as a *paiolo* which is hung on a chain over the centre of a wood fire in a large, well-ventilated open hearth. The polenta is stirred with a long wooden stick and, when cooked, it is ceremoniously turned onto the boards of the scrubbed kitchen table and there cut into portions. In a restaurant it will be brought to your table on a round wooden tray. Here's how you make it at home.

Let 450g (1 lb) of good quality polenta flour flow in a thin stream into a large saucepan containing 1l 710ml (60 fl oz) of salted, fast-boiling water. Keep the flame medium and constant. Let the polenta amalgamate with the water. I am afraid that, using a long wooden spoon, you must now never stop stirring. When the polenta comes away from the sides of the saucepan, leaving behind a dry crust, it is ready. This will take at least 35 minutes. Now cover the pan for the last couple of minutes and raise the flame fiercely. This is the coup de grace.

Turn the mixture onto a large wooden tray. Cut it into generous portions and serve as you might mashed potatoes with meat, fish or poultry or game stews. When cold it may be cut into slices, golden-fried in butter and oil until crisp and eaten with savoury spreads or as a garnish.

POLENTA PASTICCIATA
Layered and baked polenta

For this recipe follow the directions as for semolina pasticciata al forno at the end of this chapter, substituting polenta for the semolina, prepared as in the preceding recipe.

RISO
Rice

The Pharaohs and the Chinese Emperors knew all about the excellent food values of rice. Indeed, rice was regarded as being almost sacred. The progress of the crop was carefully watched for signs of abundance and thus of good fortune. Today, for the same reason, we still throw grains of rice at the bride who prefers hers that way rather than boiled, fried or in puddings!

Rice is favoured in northern Italy where it is widely grown. Piedmont and especially the province of Novara produce many different kinds suitable for risotti, soups, milk dishes or for plain boiling. It is quite impossible to make a real Italian risotto without using Italian rice of the correct quality. On the other hand, it is just as impossible to prepare a pilau or curry with Italian rice.

FRITTELLE DI RISO
Rice fritters

Mix a couple of tablespoons of thick béchamel sauce and a little grated Parmesan cheese with any sort of cooked savoury rice. Fry spoonfuls of the mixture in hot olive oil, pressing them lightly into round patty shapes. When they are very crisp and golden on both sides, season them with salt and milled black pepper. Serve hot as an accompaniment to a fish or meat course.

RISO PILAFF
Rice pilaff

In a saucepan, sweat a finely chopped onion in oil and butter until soft. Add 325g (12 oz) of thoroughly rinsed long-grain rice. Stir it until it becomes transparent. Pour in enough light, boiling, salted stock to cover the rice by 25mm (1 in). Bring back to the boil. Cover and place in a moderate oven for 15 minutes or until the rice is cooked.

RISO PILAFF ALLA GRECA
Rice pilaff à la grecque

Prepare and cook 325g (12 oz) of long-grain rice in exactly the same way as for Riso pilaff (above). When ready add some cooked, chopped shallots, peas, diced red peppers, chopped spinach, chopped almonds and flavour with coriander and sesame seeds.

RISO AL FORNO
Baked savoury rice

Prepare two quantities of Simple tomato sauce (page 164). Cook 325g (12 oz) of Italian rice in plenty of salted, fast-boiling water for about 12 minutes. Drain. Rinse under cold water. Drain well again. Mix the rice with three-quarters of the tomato sauce. Add three sliced (par-cooked) Italian pork sausages, one small, cubed egg-plant (previously fried in oil), 100g (4 oz) of cooked peas, two sliced hard-boiled eggs, 75g (3 oz) of Fontina cheese, and four tablespoons of grated Parmesan. Mix well but lightly.

Put the mixture into a larded oven pie-dish. Smooth the top carefully without pressing and spread some of the remaining tomato sauce on top. Sprinkle with grated Parmesan and dot with lard. Bake in a moderate to hot oven for 30 minutes or until the rice is well heated through and a crust has formed on top. Pass more tomato sauce and grated Parmesan at the table. You may vary the filling according to the savoury items you have available.

RISOTTO IN BIANCO
White risotto

In a saucepan, gently sweat until soft, but not coloured, one finely chopped small onion in two tablespoons each of butter and oil. Stir in 450g (1 lb) of Italian rice until it is transparent. Add a wine glass of dry white wine and let it reduce. Cover with 1l (35 fl oz) of boiling, strong chicken and beef stock. Cook the rice over a moderate heat stirring now and again until the stock has been absorbed. This will take about 20 minutes. Now mix in one tablespoon of butter and two heaped tablespoons of grated Parmesan. Allow the risotto to settle for a while before serving. Pass more cheese and don't forget to hand around that black pepper mill.

RISO ALLA CINESE
Chinese rice

This rice is ideally suited to accompany pork spare ribs or any other Oriental-style food. Wash 225g (8 oz) of long-grain rice until the water runs clear. Drain it well. Put it into a saucepan and cover by 25mm (1 in) with chicken stock. Cook for 12 minutes and then spread out to cool.

In a heavy pan, slowly melt one generous tablespoon of chicken fat (obtainable from a good delicatessen or, failing that, try a good chicken). Raise the flame and cook four well-crushed garlic cloves for a few minutes, then grind them into the chicken fat quite viciously with a wooden spoon and discard them before they burn. Stir in a tablespoon of shredded raw chicken skin together with half a finely chopped onion. Stir very quickly. As the onions begin to take colour, stir in the cooled rice. Stir quickly again. Now stir in two tablespoons of thin soy sauce and one teaspoon of sugar, salt and milled black pepper. Stir in 100g (4 oz) of cooked peas. Remove the pan from the stove and stir in one whole egg. Give a final stir over a brisk flame and serve this delicious rice hot.

This is Chinese 'stir' cookery. It may sound as though it is hard to prepare, but I assure you that, once you have all the ingredients assembled and are ready to work, and stir fast, it is really quite simple.

RISOTTO ALLA CERTOSINA
Seafood risotto

Have ready 1l (35 fl oz) of boiling, light, vegetable stock. Sauté one finely chopped, medium-sized onion in three tablespoons of oil and one tablespoon of butter until soft. Add 450g (1 lb) of Italian rice and stir, over a medium flame, until it becomes transparent. Cover with the boiling stock and let it simmer, stirring now and then until the stock has been absorbed. Continue to add boiling stock until it is all used up and the risotto is ready. This should take about 20 minutes. Keep warm.

In another pan, sauté 50g (2 oz) each of chopped squid, scampi, shrimp, scallop, crabmeat and two diced white mushrooms in two tablespoons of butter. Flame with a measure of brandy. Stir in four ripe, seeded, skinned and sieved tomatoes and a pinch of saffron. Cook for a few moments. Swirl in one and a quarter cups of heavy cream and let the sauce thicken. Check the seasoning with salt and cayenne pepper. Mix half of the creamed seafood into the risotto. Pour the rest over it and sprinkle with cayenne pepper and chopped parsley.

RISOTTO AI FUNGHI
Mushroom risotto

You will need 1l (35 fl oz) of boiling chicken stock at hand. Sweat one chopped, medium-sized onion in two tablespoons each of butter and oil until soft. Stir in 450g (1 lb) of Italian rice until it becomes transparent. Pour in a small wine glass of white wine and let it reduce. Cover the rice with the boiling stock and let it absorb over a medium heat. Stir occasionally. Repeat this process until the stock is used up and the rice is cooked. This will take about 20 minutes. Mix in 150g (6 oz) of sliced sautéed *cèpes,* field or white cultivated mushrooms. Stir in two heaped tablespoons of grated Parmesan cheese. Serve hot. Pass more Parmesan at the table if needed and the pepper mill too.

This risotto is also very good when

prepared with 25g (1 oz) of Italian dried porcini mushrooms. They should first be washed and then soaked for ten minutes in warm water and added (with a little of the soaking liquor) together with the onions at the start of the proceedings.

RISOTTO ALLA MILANESE
Milanese risotto

This is the greatest risotto of them all, even more famed than the more luxurious Piedmontese counterpart with its glorious white truffles. And yet, even with such a renowned dish, a lot of Italian (and Milanese) cooks do not always agree on the cooking method. Some like to use only butter; others a mixture of oil and butter; some swear that red and not white wine should be added; beef stock, chicken stock or beef marrow-bone fat; Lodigiano or Parmesan cheese. Over the years this recipe has become a highly personalized thing, varying from family to family. But my father, who was a Milanese, liked his cooked in the following way, and this is how I've come to like it too.

Have 1l (35 fl oz) of boiling, strong chicken and beef stock ready. In a saucepan, gently sweat until soft one finely chopped, small onion in two tablespoons each of butter and oil and one tablespoon of beef marrow-bone fat. Stir in 450g (1 lb) of Italian risotto rice until transparent. Add a wine glass of dry white wine and let it reduce. Cover the rice with some of the boiling stock. Cook over a moderate heat stirring frequently until the stock has been absorbed. Add one good pinch of fine quality saffron (previously dissolved in a little stock). Continue to add the boiling stock until the rice is cooked. This will take about 20 minutes. Stir in one tablespoon of butter and two heaped tablespoons of grated Parmesan cheese. Allow the risotto to settle for a while before serving. Pass more grated Parmesan cheese, if required, and freshly milled black pepper at the table to improve the flavour.

RISOTTO CON PISELLI
Risotto with peas

Have 1l (35 fl oz) of boiling, light, chicken stock ready. In a saucepan, gently fry 50g (2 oz) of chopped Italian pancetta or three chopped slices of streaky bacon in two tablespoons each of butter and oil. Add one finely chopped, medium-sized onion and sweat until soft. Add 450g (1 lb) of Italian risotto rice and stir it until it is transparent. Pour in a small wine glass of dry white wine and let it reduce. Cover the rice with some of the boiling stock. Cook over a medium flame stirring occasionally. Add more stock as it becomes absorbed. The risotto will be ready in 20 minutes. Towards the end of the cooking time, mix in 225g (8 oz) of canned or cooked, drained, petits pois. Stir in one tablespoon of butter and two tablespoons of grated Parmesan cheese. Let the risotto stand for a while before serving. Pass more grated cheese and plenty of freshly milled black pepper at the table.

RISOTTO ALLA VENERDI
Friday's risotto

In a saucepan, sauté two crushed garlic cloves with one small chopped onion in three tablespoons of olive oil. Discard the garlic when golden. Coarsely chop and add four raw scampi, two scallops, one squid and the tentacles, eight small shrimps, two tablespoons of small, cooked clams, eight cooked, shelled mussels, 225g (8 oz) of drained, canned tomatoes, four bruised, fresh basil leaves (or a pinch of oregano), salt and milled black pepper. Cook all this for ten minutes over a medium flame. Set aside.

Have 1l (35 fl oz) of light vegetable stock on the boil. Gently soften one small, finely chopped onion in three tablespoons of oil. Add 450g (1 lb) of Italian rice and stir until it becomes transparent. Pour in a small wine glass of dry white wine and let it reduce. Cover the rice with some of the boiling stock. Simmer over a medium flame stirring occasionally. Add more stock a little at a time until it has all been used up and the risotto is ready. This will take 20 minutes.

Mix in half of the shellfish sauce. Pour the remainder over the risotto. Sprinkle with chopped parsley and cayenne pepper. Serve hot.

SEMOLINA
GNOCCHI DI SEMOLINA 'SARA'
Semolina patties with tomato and basil

In a saucepan, bring 1 l (35 fl oz) of chicken stock to the boil. Pour in 225g (8 oz) of medium-fine semolina in a thin steady stream, stirring continually to prevent lumps forming. Cook over a gentle heat for 20 minutes. Remove from the stove and carefully blend in two beaten egg yolks, 25g (1 oz) of butter and four tablespoons of grated Parmesan cheese. Spread the semolina onto a flat, oiled surface to a 12mm (½ in) thickness. Allow to cool. Cut out 5cm (2 in) rounds and arrange them, in slightly overlapping order, in a buttered oven dish. Spoon over a little tomato sauce, top with shredded basil leaves, sprinkle with grated Parmesan cheese and moisten with melted butter. Bake in a fairly hot oven for 20 minutes or until the gnocchi are brown on top. Serve hot.

These may be baked plainly with butter and cheese, or with anything that takes your fancy such as chopped chicken livers, meat sauce, peas or ham. Just use your imagination and your leftovers!

SEMOLINA PASTICCIATA AL FORNO
Layered and baked semolina

Prepare the semolina as for the previous recipe but, when cooked, pour it into a small, deep, oiled dish. Allow to cool. When cold, turn it out and cut it into long slices 6mm (¼ in) thick.

Butter a pie dish and mask the bottom with a little Simple tomato sauce (page 164). Arrange a layer of cold semolina slices on top. Cover this with extremely thin slices of Fontina or, if you have to, Bel Paese. Mask with more tomato sauce. Sprinkle some cooked, crumbled Italian pork sausage, a few chopped, sautéed mushrooms and strew the top with grated Parmesan cheese. Continue in this fashion until the dish is full. Finish with a generous masking of tomato sauce and grated Parmesan. Dot with butter. Bake in a fairly hot oven for 30 minutes or until the dish is heated through and nicely brown on top.

PESCE
Fish

Because of my childhood days in the little fishing village of Minori, on the Amalfi coast of Italy, I will always remember Mediterranean fish with nostalgia. Children and adults alike looked forward to the moment when the local fishermen would arrive at the little houses carrying large, flat, wicker baskets displaying the colourful variety of their night's catch.

None of us ever grew tired of marvelling at the tiny, silver anchovies to be cooked in fragrant *tortiera*-style or opened flat and golden-fried like butterflies; the amazing *cecinielli,* so tiny that they had to be scooped and fried in small exquisite fritters; the long and graceful silver eels; the fascinatingly ugly, stinging *scorfani* so essential to the true flavour of a real Zuppa di pesce; the simmering, squirming *polipo* which would soon end up in a lemon- and oil-dressed salad; small ivory-coloured *totani;* vivid-red prawns and miniature, succulent red mullets; all these decorated with sea-urchins, fresh *vongole* and shiny black mussels and set-off by halves of large, yellow lemons grown right there on the mountain terraces behind the village. A delight to all our eyes which turned our thoughts proudly to the generous sea and then, mundanely, towards the nearest kitchen and the next meal!

Some years after the war we returned with our children to Minori for the holidays. Our bedroom now overlooked the new fishmonger's shop. The fishermen didn't call at the houses any more. Instead, each morning, having unloaded their boats, they would drag the boxes containing the night's haul straight from the beach, all the way up the cobbled street below our now shuddering bedroom. The shattering clatter would, regularly as clockwork, waken us and leave us tensely waiting for each bump as the cases were bounced past. Surely it would have been easier, and quieter, to haul the loaded boats up instead!

At last, having counted the boxes and gone through their beloved price-haggling ritual (I became quite an authority on local fishing yields and wholesale fish prices), the fishmonger and his wife settled to sort out and attractively arrange the day's new stock and to throw the empty fish crates with loud crashes into a far corner of the shop – each crash causing us additional jolts.

Quite soon the sun would emerge and it would be dawn. It was that early and we were all fully awake and twitching! The fishmonger then proceeded to give as good an impression of an English town-crier as I have ever heard. He informed all within earshot of the freshness, beauty and economical price of that day's supplies. We were loudly warned that, unless we hurried, there would be none left. By way of a gratuitous news-extra, he also broadcast various relevant fish recipes. The general cacophony was soon accompanied by fearful thuds and violent cracks which informed us all that the local butcher (another insomniac) was alive and well. Then, almost as though celebrating this fact, the church bells heralding early Mass (taped and electronically amplified because it had become too dangerous to pull the bell-ropes) jealously joined in the din. At this point, most of us would give up the unequal struggle and, muttering darkly, get up.

Each morning I resolved to complain – after all we were on holiday and needed to rest. But each day I would relent, go down to the street, join the rest of the group and silently admire the glorious sight of the magnificent, dazzling display of shimmering, exotic fish. Silver, gold, red, multicoloured – exactly as we remembered them from our early childhood days.

Nevertheless, human nature being what it is, a greedy streak has set in. The highly illegal use of explosive charges, which indiscriminately massacre any living thing, and other forbidden practices, are a common occurrence. The warm, blue, now gravely polluted, Mediterranean is being ruthlessly fished to extinction. In the busy tourist months up to 80 per cent of all fish served in Italian hotels and restaurants is deep-frozen or imported. I have myself seen, in the Rialto and other fish markets, porters humping case after case of squid from Scotland and prawns from Norway which, I am sure, would later in the day be lyrically described as fresh to the romantic sound of strumming guitars and tinkling cash registers.

In Maiori I was once proudly served a fine Dentice al forno (supposedly straight from the beach opposite) seemingly baked to perfection in olive oil, garlic, fresh mint and spiced with a little vinegar. It broke delicately to the touch of my fork which, penetrating further, came to a resolute halt against the still deep-frozen centre. It was taken away with a sigh, an eloquent shrug of Amalfitan shoulders and silently replaced with something less glacial and cold and more honest and warm.

The choice of fish for the following recipes is mostly restricted to that available in local English markets. And what a choice there is! The quality of the fish, shellfish and crustaceans, although admittedly far less colourful than those of Mediterranean waters, is always superb and always fresh. And from what I have seen in New York's famous, bustling Fulton Street fish market, that's true of transatlantic fish as well.

Using only locally bought fish and crustaceans I have prepared and enjoyed many a delicious fish soup both in my restaurants and in my own home which, if not as exotic as a real Bouillabaisse à la Marseillaise, were every bit as good as the Neapolitan Zuppa di pesce with perhaps a little more of the Zuppa part than they provide down there.

I do have a strong liking for Atlantic fish; it seems to me that the flavour is more delicate, more subtle, not as strongly tasting of coral and rock as some of the Mediterranean species. That, however, is strictly a personal taste. Of freshwater fish I have little to say except that I do not like it. I have little regard for trout, ever-popular in restaurants. Today's fish-farm methods have bred all flavour out of them, leaving behind a series of fish-shaped, silver-speckled, stock-control units to be rapidly counted, stored, cooked, sold and quickly entered in restaurants' company ledgers as pure profit.

ASTACO
Lobster

Young lobsters, always so sweet and tender, though expensive, are the perfect size for individual portions. They must be bought and cooked when they are still alive. Your English fishmonger (who is still the most obliging of tradesmen) will usually be of great assistance and cook and clean your lobsters for you.

If possible, the lobsters chosen should be male (they have a better flavour), should always be springy and viciously snappy. Lobsters are always delicious. Whether served hot or cold they instantly provide an air of richness and flamboyant luxury to the table. They are terribly expensive, however. Demand for them has rocketed throughout the world. Their price will never again come down to more reasonable levels. So they will remain a luxury. Of course, the fact that French fishing vessels regularly meet English fishing boats, in the Channel in the dark of night, to buy most of their crustacean catch for much higher prices than the normal person is prepared to pay, does not help matters at all.

Most early mornings at London's Billingsgate fish market, mauled or deformed lobsters (usually the losers in furious undersea battles) are sold at much lower prices than the still unscathed winners. I once knew an Italian restaurant proprietor who, taking advantage of the market commotion, always managed to pick out quantities of badly disfigured lobsters, at really knockdown prices, from increasingly incredulous, perplexed dealers. Unhappily for my usually beaming friend he was finally trapped one morning in the act of adroitly snapping off lobsters' claws left, right and centre. That morning, Billingsgate's choice vocabulary was heavily supplemented by new English words interspersed with quite an amount of hastily improvised Italian ones.

But the lobster I will always remember is the large, cooked four-pounder which I once saw tied from the waist and dangling between the legs of an off-duty, homeward-bound waiter. He had just clocked-off and was about to step out into the cold night (suitably huddled in a long, warm overcoat) when he was stopped by 'Cuddles', a suspicious house detective, whose attention had been alerted by the waiter's strange, side-stepping gait. (I had heard of 'crab-like' walks, but that was ridiculous!) The offender was severely reprimanded, and the lobster confiscated, later to be appreciatively scoffed by the ever-vigilant 'Cuddles'.

ASTACO ALLA FRA' DIAVOLO
Hot, devilled lobster

Mix 225g (8 oz) of butter smoothly with two minced garlic cloves, one pounded chilli, one dessertspoon of dry English mustard, a dessertspoon of chopped fresh tarragon, a small wine glass of brandy and a little salt. Split four 450g (1 lb) live lobsters in half lengthways. (Hold the tail firmly and pierce the indentation on the head with a sharp knife. This kills instantly). Remove the sac and stomach. If you really have to, use four cooked lobsters. Spread them evenly with the mixture. Sprinkle generously with fresh, soft white breadcrumbs. Season with salt and cayenne pepper. Moisten with melted butter and cover with foil and bake in a hot oven for 25 minutes. Crack the claws for easier eating. Serve hot. Pass a mustardy garlic mayonnaise at the table.

ASTACO 'A LA NAGE'
Lobster with beaten butter

Put into a large pot 2l 850ml (100 fl oz) of water, a bottle of light, dry white wine, one sliced, medium-sized onion, six young, sliced carrots, one tender stalk of celery with the leaves, one dessertspoon of crushed black peppercorns, two tablespoons of salt, three torn-up sprigs of parsley, five crushed garlic cloves and a bouquet garni. Bring this to the boil and simmer for half an hour.

Now plunge in four 450g (1 lb) washed, rinsed and live lobsters. Maintain the stock at boiling point for 20 minutes. Remove the bouquet garni and the garlic. Take out, split the lobsters lengthways, and clean thoroughly. Crack the claws to facilitate matters at the table. Serve them in deep soup plates together with the hot cooking liquor and some of the vegetables. Pass some fresh butter which has been spiked with some lemon juice, seasoned with a little salt and black or cayenne pepper and then whipped up lightly. The butter will gently melt into the hot court bouillon and will transform it into the most delicate soup-sauce for you to savour slowly.

INSALATA DI ASTACO 'OFELIA'
Lobster salad
Prepare a salad with crisp Romaine lettuce hearts, watercress, quartered tomatoes, cucumber, thin strips of red pepper, spring onions, sliced celery, radishes and cold, cooked new potatoes. Sprinkle with chopped tarragon and chervil. Cover with a layer of sliced, cold, cooked lobster tails. Decorate with four shelled lobster claws, quartered, hard-boiled eggs, stoned green olives, capers and sliced tomatoes. Serve chilled. Pass a good mustardy vinaigrette sauce or toss the salad well before serving.

MAIONESE DI ASTACO 'PATRIZIA'
Special lobster mayonnaise
While mentally rehearsing his script for the next day Christopher Plummer is standing alone at the bar taking thoughtful sips of chilled white wine. Susannah York comes in smiling cheerfully, blows a kiss over to Christopher, waves eagerly to friends seated in the corner of the bar and goes downstairs to join her waiting party. She is swiftly followed by Françoise Hardy. Later, Henry Ford Jnr, with his charming Italian wife, comes in too. Roman Polanski is cooking up another great movie at the round table. And much later Dudley Moore will sit by the pianist in the intimate bar with friends, drink wine and eat some pasta for a late, late musical snack. Some evening! Christopher Plummer always did like lobster mayonnaise, like this.

Prepare a salad in exactly the same way as the preceding recipe. Moisten it with a little oil and vinegar and toss. Cover with slices of cold cooked lobster tails and the sliced breast of roast chicken. Scatter with chopped, black Umbrian truffles. Mask thickly with mayonnaise and decorate with four shelled lobster claws, quartered hard-boiled eggs, sliced tomatoes, stoned, green olives, capers and anchovy fillets. Sprinkle with lobster coral, chopped hard-boiled egg, truffle shavings, cayenne and chopped parsley. Serve chilled.

BACCALÀ CON LE PATATE
Salt-cod with potatoes
Soak in cold water for 24 hours, four centre-cut, fleshy slices of the finest quality baccalà (salt-cod) weighing in total about 450g (1 lb). Change the water twice. Drain well and lightly squeeze out.

In a saucepan, with one cup of olive oil, sweat one small, chopped onion with two crushed garlic cloves until soft and golden. Remove the garlic. Add the salt-cod together with four cubed, medium-sized potatoes and a whole crushed chilli. Turn these over gently for a few minutes and let them take a little colour. Add 570ml (20 fl oz) of boiling water, one tablespoon of tomato purée, one tablespoon of roughly chopped parsley, salt (remember that the fish will still be a little salty) and milled black pepper. Cover the pan. Simmer until the cod and the potatoes are tender. Add more boiling water, a little at a time, as may be necessary. Check the seasoning. Serve over thick slices of French bread.

BRIOCHE 'TORRE NORMANNA'
Hot brioche filled with seafood
Prepare six heaped tablespoons of mixed, diced and cooked lobster, scallops, scampi, crab claws and quartered white button mushrooms. Sauté all these in a little butter and heat well through. Flame with a small measure of brandy. Add three cups of hot Aurore sauce (page 159), two tablespoons of heavy cream and a dessertspoon of chopped, black Umbrian truffle parings. Check the seasoning with salt and cayenne pepper.

Scoop out four fresh and well-heated Brioches (page 160). Fill them with the creamed seafood and plenty of the sauce. Replace the brioche tops. Place in a hot oven for a few minutes. Pass any remaining seafood and sauce separately at the table.

CALAMARI ALLA LUCIANA
Piquant sautéed squid, Napoli style

Place together in a medium-sized saucepan 900g (2 lb) of small squid cut into ringlets with their tentacles, 900g (2 lb) of un-drained, canned tomatoes, two table-spoons of coarsely chopped parsley, four crushed garlic cloves, six tablespoons of olive oil, salt and freshly milled black pepper. Cover and simmer for 30 or 40 minutes or until the squid is tender. If the sauce appears to be too liquid, remove the cover for the last ten minutes. Eat a few plainly boiled potatoes and lots of crusty or oven-toasted French bread with this.

CALAMARI RIPIENI
Stuffed, braised squid

Their Graces, the Duke and Duchess of Bedford, had dined. They had, in fact, just left – but were soon back. Where could their dark-green American station wagon have got to? I wasn't quite sure but I had a good idea. I telephoned the ever-vigilant traffic department of the Metropolitan Police whose number I knew only too well. Sure enough they had towed the offending car away. So I drove their Graces over to the car-pound.

I went into the shanty-like office and crept unobtrusively past the long queue of muttering car owners, up to the red-faced police sergeant. Very quietly I asked whether he thought it possible to have my two disgruntled customers cleared as quickly as possible as they had a long country drive ahead of them. He must have been as fed-up as the rest for he

looked up and snarled loudly, 'The Duke and Duchess of Bedford will wait and queue just like everybody else.' There was nothing more I could do. I shook hands, left them to deal with the police themselves and perhaps leave their coronets as deposits if they were short of ready cash!

Although this dish is really a main course, the Duchess, a very lively, chic French lady, used to enjoy a small hors d'oeuvre portion of stuffed squid prepared in the following fashion. In a sauteuse or similar pan, sauté four crushed garlic cloves in three tablespoons of olive oil and remove when golden. Add one very finely chopped squid and cook for a few minutes. Mix in four tablespoons of fresh, soft breadcrumbs, twelve stoned, chopped, black olives, one tablespoon of rinsed capers, two dessertspoons of chopped parsley, one dessertspoon of chopped pine nuts, salt and milled black pepper. Cook for a few minutes.

Stuff four squid (weighing just over 450g or 1 lb in total) with the filling. Close up the ends. Now sauté them briskly in the same pan with a little more olive oil and two crushed cloves of garlic. Add 450g (1 lb) of roughly chopped, undrained, canned tomatoes, eight bruised fresh basil leaves, salt and black pepper. Cover and slowly braise for 40 minutes or until the squid are tender.

These may be eaten either hot or cold, as an hors d'oeuvre or as a main course. Reserve some of the sauce and you will have a great spaghetti or linguine condiment.

COZZE AL GRATIN
Gratinéed mussels

Wash and scrub 60 large mussels. Open them raw 'oyster fashion' or steam them open. Discard the top shells. Lay them together with their juice (raw or steamed) in a flat oven tray. Cover each mussel liberally with a mixture of dry breadcrumbs, two finely chopped garlic cloves, abundant chopped parsley, salt and milled black pepper. Douse them with olive oil. Bake in a hot oven for ten minutes. If the bread has not crisped enough, pass the mussels under a hot grill for a couple of minutes. These also make a fine hot antipasto.

GRANDE FRITTO MISTO 'BAIA BELLA'
Crisply fried seafood

The first small restaurant had not yet been opened. The builders were taking their time. But, one day, the time came for the visual work, the decorative touches to be applied. A beautiful mural of the Bay of Naples was commissioned from Polish George. But his price was far too high, and so the colourful Polish-Italian haggling began! After much tearing of hair, beating of breasts, pleading to the Gods, stalking back, forth, away and all the way back again, truculent finger-snapping under each other's noses and other appropriate actions deemed vitally necessary for the satisfaction of both parties' self-esteem, honour and, more important, fast dwindling bank balances, a price was eventually, and thankfully, agreed.

The conditions which Polish George had imposed, apart from the hefty fee, were that he be allowed to work alone through one night, that all materials were to be charged as extra and that he was to be given sufficient brandy for his nocturnal inspiration. All these were agreed, Polish George turned up late one evening with his brushes, colours, and, as the mural was to be in bas-relief, with a large bag of dental cement. He was given his bottle of brandy and was locked in for the night.

Very early next morning I turned up to see the finished result. There, the full length of the wall, was the whole Mediterranean bay. The sea, the waterfront, the city, the pines, the mountains and Vesuvius. They were all there. I looked at it in disbelief! It looked fine, if you were

Norwegian and were feeling homesick. The sea was green, the sky white and the mountains and Vesuvius were, it seemed, snow-capped. Polish George was slumped across a table, head cradled in his arms, dead to the world, the bottle of brandy, now empty, at his side.

That evening Polish George was given a rundown on the glories and colours of the Baia Bella of Napoli and a highly optimistic commercial postcard of the area. He was searched for brandy, given some blue paint and locked in for the night. The next morning I arrived early and very nervous. Polish George was peacefully asleep once more. But this time the view from the terrace was splendid! Here is a suitable recipe.

Assemble shelled and unshelled jumbo-sized scampi, thin squid ringlets, squid tentacles, scallops, prawns, shrimps, whitebait, red or grey mullets, small strips of Dover sole and crab claws. Roll them in flour and fry in small batches in very hot oil until they are golden and well crisped. Drain and dry them on absorbent paper. Keep them warm while further batches are frying. Garnish with fried, crisp parsley and lemon halves. You may serve tartare sauce, but it's not really done.

CONCHIGLIA DI GRANCHIO 'THERMIDOR'
Scalloped crabmeat

In a sauteuse or similar pan, sauté two crushed garlic cloves in two tablespoons of oil and discard when golden. Add a little butter and four cups of diced, cooked king-crab and heat well through. Stir in four teaspoons of strong, made-up English mustard, a few dashes each of Worcester and Tabasco sauces. Now add two cups of hot Aurore or Lobster sauce (pages 159 and 162) and one teaspoon each of chopped fresh tarragon and chervil. Season with salt and cayenne pepper. Fill four warmed scallop shells (previously bordered with piped mashed potato) with the mixture. Sprinkle with two dessertspoons of grated Parmesan and Gruyère cheeses. Brown under a hot grill.

MERLUZZO AFFUMICATO ALLA CREMA
Smoked haddock Monte Carlo

This was a very well-liked dish in the Roaring Twenties, and it has had a revival in the last few years. Today's Bright Young Things have taken a fancy to Smoked haddock Monte Carlo as they have taken to most of our other period favourites. If you ever arrive late, and can get a table, at London's smart Annabel's, do order a dish of marvellously creamy, smoky 'haddie' before you dance to ragtime. Or, if you're at home, then make some yourself. And then wind up the gramophone, put on a wax disc, release the catch, turn the horn around and dance to your supper in the Flapper Style. And don't forget to change the steel needle!

Gently poach 900g (2 lb) of the finest quality smoked haddock in milk for six or seven minutes. Drain well. Discard the skin and all the bones. Arrange the fish in four portions on a hot serving dish. Meanwhile, sweat one finely chopped shallot in butter and oil until soft. Add and cook four seeded, skinned and roughly chopped tomatoes with a dessertspoon of chopped parsley. Season and pile on the centre of each portion of fish.

Mix four tablespoons of thick béchamel sauce with 250ml (9 fl oz) of heavy cream and some of the poaching milk. Heat thoroughly. Check the seasoning with salt and cayenne pepper. Pour the creamy sauce over the smoked haddock. Place a poached egg on top of each. Sprinkle with chopped parsley. Serve very hot.

PADELLE REALI 'BUONA MAMMA'
Scallops in wine sauce

Gently poach, for eight minutes in a covered pan, 12 scallops and four sliced white mushrooms in three cups of fish stock. Drain and set them aside. Strain the cooking liquor and reduce it to the amount of one cup. Add one cup of heavy cream, 50g (2 oz) of butter and a little dry sherry. Season with salt and cayenne pepper. Stir. Bring to the boil and, swirling the pan, thicken the sauce. Pour it over the scallops and mushrooms. Dust with more cayenne pepper. Garnish with triangles of crisp, golden-fried bread croûtes or Puff-pastry crescents (page 163).

PADELLE REALI 'LETIZIA'
Scallops with mushroom, bacon and tomato

Sauté two finely chopped shallots, one crushed garlic clove and four julienned slices of streaky bacon in oil and butter. Remove the garlic. Add and gently cook four thick slices of firm tomatoes and four large mushroom caps. Season with salt and black pepper. Set aside.

In another pan, fry in butter and oil, 12 scallops (halved crossways) previously dipped in milk and rolled in flour. Season. Drain well and arrange on a serving dish. Pour the bacon-shallot mixture over them. Decorate with the tomatoes and mushroom caps. Sprinkle with lemon juice and chopped parsley. Serve hot with crisp, fried, bread croûtes or Puff-pastry crescents (page 163).

SALMONE ALLO CHAMPAGNE
Salmon with champagne sauce

It should be remembered that in 'the bad good-old-days' restaurant employers paid ridiculously low wages, literally only shillings, to their waiters who were forced to depend almost entirely on tips. The real and professional waiters relied solely upon their expertise, hard work, and good service and they earned their money honestly. Others, faithful to the house only part of the time, employed many dubious but highly effective methods to extract the maximum amount from their customers. All had their pet wiles. They were capable of stooping to the lowest of ruses. These tip-artists were very quickly able to weigh up their customers and select the most suitable ploy even as they approached the table. Some waiters would commit minor but obvious errors of service, plaintively justifying themselves by saying that they had been distracted due to a personal worry. It didn't take much prompting from a usually sympathetic customer for them to blurt out sorrowfully (maybe with a few tears) that the bailiffs were being held off by their ailing grandmother; they couldn't afford special milk for the sick baby; or the wife was due in court on a shop-lifting charge.

Whatever deception they resorted to, one thing was sure, they were all experts at the game. They were either cheeky or blatant, whining or professionally majestic. But the result was always the same. The customer, laid bare, was in a corner and regularly paid up.

A long time ago I worked in a restaurant where we had in our team a waiter who possessed none of the above-mentioned vices or virtues. He was completely artless. It was a wonder to us all that he had ever entered a game as difficult as ours. But he was a very good waiter, excellent at his job, and nothing was too much trouble for him. His only problem was that he just did not make good tips. When the daily tronc was opened, the tips counted and the contributors listed, his name was always at the bottom. After a while he hit on an incredible solution. He would add money from his own pocket to the small amounts left officially by his clients. This way at least, he was happier at the tronc opening and tip-counting ritual. Sometimes, being particularly well pleased with his service, he would become quite carried away and would actually over-tip himself.

We never told him that we had discovered his secret, for, as hard-bitten as we were, we all found it quite moving. He left

us after a while for a less expensive job: poorer but, as far as he was aware, his self-esteem, to a large extent, restored.

Here is a grand recipe, a most elegant and delicate dish, one that the 'good tipper' would have served with so much pride and flair. If you are going to make this dish, please do not use frozen salmon. It is not, and I doubt whether it will ever be, up to standard. It is dry, hard, bitter and tasteless – far better to wait until the salmon season starts. Fresh salmon may, of course, be prepared with either red or white wine. If, however, you are going to use a sparkling wine, then you should use the real thing – champagne!

Place four thick, middle-cut cutlets of fresh salmon in a buttered shallow dish together with eight firm button mushrooms and their chopped stalks, one sliced carrot, one sliced, medium-sized onion, one small celery stalk, one bay leaf, a sprig each of parsley and thyme, a teaspoon of black peppercorns and salt to taste. Pour half a bottle of dry champagne into the dish. Cover. Bring to the boil and gently simmer for about five minutes. Remove the salmon and the mushroom caps and set them aside.

Strain the cooking liquor and reduce by half. Whisk in two cups of hollandaise sauce and one cup of heavy cream, 25g (1 oz) of butter, a few drops of lemon juice and adjust the seasoning with salt and cayenne pepper. Simmer and let the sauce thicken.

Mask the salmon cutlets with a little of the sauce. Garnish with the button mushrooms and four fried, breaded scampi. Serve with plainly boiled new potatoes. Pass the rest of the sauce separately.

SCAMPI

Before the war, when scampi were all but unknown in Britain, one of the greatest restaurateurs of them all, Filippo Ferraro (of Berkeley Hotel fame) used to delight in preparing some of his delicious creations at the customers' tables – preferably in front of the windows facing the Ritz Hotel across the road, in an effort to entice away its customers. In one speciality, the Cappuccini cocktail, he used to include a little-known, luscious crustacean that he had discovered accidentally in an exclusive St James's fishmonger's. They were called Dublin Bay prawns.

A few years after the war there was a great scampi boom. A phenomenon no doubt caused by increased affluence and organized cheap foreign travel. From Italy the returning hoards brought back sentiment, smiles, songs, souvenirs, suntans and screams for scampi! But there weren't any in Britain, until chefs de cuisine and their buyers remembered Ferraro's Dublin Bay prawns, and from then on went crazy buying them all up. Soon, gigantic industries trading almost solely on these and, later, other similar prawns, were built up.

Despite what they may claim to the contrary, no English restaurant has ever served a genuine scampi unless, of course, it was smuggled out of Italy. Scampi just never reaches English shores because Italy grimly hangs on to them for her own use. Italy has always been rather short of them herself and so could not possibly sustain an export market.

The Dublin Bay prawn, however, is a perfectly acceptable substitute. Some do maintain, and I am one of them, that its flavour and texture surpasses that of its warm-water cousin. It is possible to buy genuine Dublin Bay prawns in the United States, too. Frozen of course. But if they're left to thaw gently in a refrigerator, they are very good indeed. The States, of course, have a fantastically large and varied selection of their own shrimp, many of which are suitable for the following scampi recipes.

SCAMPI ALLA 'ARMORICAINE'
Scampi with brandy and herbs

Sauté until soft four chopped shallots and two crushed garlic cloves in 50g (2 oz) of butter and three tablespoons of oil. Remove the garlic. Add and cook briskly 36 large, shelled scampi. Flame them with a large measure of brandy. Add to the pan four large, skinned, seeded, roughly chopped tomatoes, one teaspoon of tomato purée, one dessertspoon of chopped fresh tarragon, a tablespoon of chopped parsley, salt and cayenne pepper. Simmer for five minutes, remove the scampi and set aside. Add to the pan one and a half cups of fish stock and reduce by one third. Thicken the sauce by stirring in small pieces of butter. Check the seasoning. Pour the sauce (unstrained) over the scampi and serve with plainly boiled, fluffy rice.

SCAMPI ALLA CERTOSINA
Scampi with cream sauce

In a sauteuse or similar pan, sweat one tablespoon each of finely chopped, tender celery and onion in butter and oil adding a little water to help soften them. Add and cook 36 large, shelled scampi. Flame with a small wine glass of brandy. Season with salt and cayenne pepper. Remove the scampi and keep them warm. Add 450g (1 lb) of skinned, seeded, chopped tomatoes, a dessertspoon of chopped chervil and cook for a few minutes. Swirl in one and a half cups of heavy cream and let the sauce thicken. Strain the sauce over the scampi. Sprinkle with cayenne pepper. Serve with plainly boiled, fluffy rice.

SCAMPI AL CURRY
Curried scampi

Cook a medium-sized, chopped onion and a small, chopped cooking-apple together with a crushed garlic clove in oil and butter until soft. Stir in one teaspoon of tomato purée, a crushed chilli, a heaped dessertspoon of curry powder, a dessertspoon of mango chutney and one and a half cups of vegetable stock. Simmer for ten minutes. Remove the garlic. Check the seasoning. Swirl in one cup of heavy cream and let the sauce thicken.

In another pan, fry 36 floured, shelled scampi in butter and oil until golden. Pour the curry sauce over and serve with plainly boiled, fluffy rice and mango chutney.

SCAMPI ALLA FRANCO
Savoury, deep-fried scampi

Flour 36 large, shelled scampi. Dip them into seasoned, beaten egg and roll them thickly in a savoury mixture of dried breadcrumbs, finely chopped garlic, chopped parsley, grated Parmesan cheese, salt and black pepper. Fry them in abundant, hot, clean oil until golden and crisp. Serve with bunches of crisp, fried parsley, lemon wedges and a good mustardy Tartare sauce (see page 164).

SPIEDINI DI SCAMPI CON PANCETTA
Skewered scampi with bacon

Skewer nine medium-sized scampi alternately with squares of streaky bacon and two small pieces of bay leaf onto each of four grilling skewers. Finish them with a small mushroom. Season with salt and black milled pepper. Douse them with garlic-flavoured olive oil and either grill or sauté until cooked and well coloured. Serve hot. Pass a light Tomato sauce (page 164), Diable sauce (page 161) or garlic Mayonnaise (page 162) at the table. Serve with plainly boiled, fluffy rice.

SPIEDINI DI SCAMPI ALLA PESCATORA
Skewered scampi with mint

Skewer, fairly loosely, nine large, shelled scampi onto each of four skewers. Season lightly with salt and milled black pepper. Douse them with olive oil and grill or sauté until they are evenly cooked and well coloured. Sprinkle with chopped fresh mint and moisten with a well-shaken mixture of three parts olive oil and one of light malt vinegar flavoured with crushed garlic. A few twists of the black pepper mill and serve hot with lemon wedges.

SCAMPI PIRI-PIRI
Spicy, chilli-hot scampi

Here is a scampi recipe which is quite simple to prepare. In fact at Chicago's super exclusive Whitehall Club, where the city's political and business-world high-flyers and jet-set society meet to eat, they serve a similar scampi dish which the chef presents 'snail fashion' in tiny, individual, earthenware crocks. If you do go to the Whitehall Club, order a small portion of these scampi as a first course and then order a helping of their matchless corned-beef hash with a poached egg on top! It's not their most expensive dish nor the most classical by a long chalk but it is one of the very best! You'll never order anything else when you go back there again. Back to the scampi. Here's how they are prepared.

Make a mixture with three finely chopped, hot chillies, tarragon, basil, a pinch of oregano, two crushed garlic cloves, one bay leaf, one and a half cups of olive oil, the juice of half a lemon, 12 crushed black peppercorns, a dessertspoon of crushed sultanas and salt. Whisk together and let stand for about four hours.

Cut and split lengthways 24 jumbo-sized scampi tails, open them out, de vein but do not remove the shells. Range them in an oval dish. Brush them abundantly with the mixture and cover with foil. Place in a moderate to hot oven until nearly cooked. Remove and coat them thickly with fresh, soft breadcrumbs. Drizzle with more of the mixture. Brown them under a hot grill. Serve hot with garlic mayonnaise.

SCAMPI AL WHISKY
Scampi in whisky

Finely chop four shallots, a tender piece of celery stalk, two slices of streaky bacon and sauté in butter and oil with two crushed garlic cloves. Remove the garlic when golden. Add and cook 36 medium-sized, lightly floured, shelled scampi. Flame with a good measure of whisky. Remove the scampi and keep them warm. Add six seeded, skinned and chopped tomatoes and a cup of stock. Cook for five minutes. Thicken the sauce with pieces of Beurre manié (page 160). Return and reheat the scampi. Serve hot with plainly boiled, fluffy rice.

TIMBALLO DI SCAMPI AL CHAMBÉRY
Scampi with Chambéry

Parboil three shallots, two small carrots, a small piece of tender celery stalk and a small red pepper. Chop them very finely, mix with a dessertspoon of chopped parsley and a small sprig of thyme and spread in a liberally buttered oven dish.

Lay 36 medium-sized, shelled scampi side by side on top. Pour in two small wine glasses of Chambéry. Season with salt and cayenne pepper. Cover. Place in a medium to hot oven for 20 minutes or until the scampi are cooked.

Remove the scampi and keep them warm. Discard the thyme. Blend two cups of heavy cream with two egg yolks and swirl them into the dish letting the sauce gently thicken. Return and reheat the scampi. Place them in a serving dish together with the sauce, sprinkle them with butter-moistened breadcrumbs and glaze quickly under a hot grill. Serve plainly boiled rice with this dish.

SOGLIOLE
Sole

There are literally hundreds upon hundreds of different recipes for sole. Cookery books are loaded with them. The sole has been well and truly honoured by the great masters of the kitchen in the past as well as by those of the present. No doubt its glory will not be lost on the great chefs of tomorrow. For the recipes that follow the sole should weigh at least 400g (14 oz). They must be stripped of their black skin. The white undersides should be well scaled or removed altogether. Their heads should be left only if they are to be grilled, deep- or shallow-fried. Side bones should always be trimmed away.

A word of warning! Although it should be kept a trade secret, never compliment the waiter or the restaurant manager on the excellent 'grilled sole' you just ate. For in a restaurant you can be practically 100 per cent sure that your sole will be shallow-fried in oil, patted very dry, then seared expertly with a red-hot iron to simulate the phantom grill's griddle marks.

Dover sole is what the aloof English call them. But the egotistical French insist that they are *soles de Calais*. Whereas they should be called *soles de la Manche* or Channel sole. I have long had visions of French fishing authorities carefully vetting, through a thick blue haze of Gauloise smoke, all the landed soles and, while granting entry permits to some, scornfully refusing others as not being of true Gallic stock.

We can all, if we want, remember either with affection or distaste some sole dish that we have had in the past. But our different memories and ways of seeing things can give contrasting recollections.

My wife Sara, for example, always looks forward to eating sole at the Whitecliffe Hotel in Dover. This is quite possibly because that is where we usually have our last meal in Britain before embarking on the Channel car ferry as we go off on our continental vacation. Apart from that, the soles there are extremely good anyway.

I have spent so many fruitless and chilly hours, however, waiting for my son Nicholas to catch a sole from the far end of Brighton pier, that my reaction has always been of a negative type. I go straight across the road to the Old Ship Hotel and have a roast beef lunch.

Fabio, my youngest son, who doesn't like fish too much, always remembers the small, sweet-tasting Atlantic sole meunière that he relished so much one Easter vacation. He often reminds us of its delicacy. He asks when he could possibly have another just like it, 'After all, it is the only fish that I've ever really liked!' he says rather plaintively. I would like to oblige. I am very fond of Fabio and would do anything for him. But isn't Taroudant, the Berber walled market-town close to the Moroccan Atlas mountains, rather a long way to go for a Friday night's dinner?

FILLETTI DI SOGLIOLA 'CAPRICCIOSA'
Fillets of sole with banana and egg-plant

Flour eight fillets of sole. Fry them gently in oil and butter until barely golden. Meanwhile, fry four thin, floured slices of egg-plant and eight bananas, halved lengthways, in butter and oil. Drain well. Lay them on the sole fillets. Cover them thickly with fresh, soft white breadcrumbs. Moisten well with melted butter. Pass them under a hot grill until nicely crisped on top. Mix some Diable sauce (page 161) and mango chutney and spoon over the centre of each fish fillet.

GOUJONETTES DE SOLE 'MURAT'
Fillets of sole with artichokes and potatoes
Cut eight sole fillets, two medium-sized potatoes and four cooked artichoke hearts (fresh or canned) into uniform, 3cm (1½ in) strips. Flour the fish and fry in butter and oil until golden. In another pan, also in oil and butter, fry the potatoes until soft and coloured and then add the artichokes to heat through. Drain well. Season and mix everything together in a cocotte dish. Pour abundant, foaming, hazelnut-coloured butter spiked with lemon juice and chopped parsley over the dish. Serve very hot.

SOGLIOLA ALLA BELLA MUGNAIA
Sole in butter with tomato and mushroom
Dip four soles in seasoned flour. Fry them gently in butter and oil until cooked and golden. Place them on a hot serving dish. Arrange alternate slices of grilled tomatoes and cooked mushroom caps along each fish. Add three tablespoons of butter, a good squeeze of lemon and a dessertspoon of chopped parsley to the pan juices. Raise the heat and when the butter is hot and foaming, pour it over the soles. Serve hot.

SOGLIOLA ALLA BUONA DONNA
Sole with mushroom and wine sauce
Lay four seasoned soles in two well-buttered oven dishes which have been abundantly layered with sliced white mushrooms. Sprinkle with chopped parsley. Pour in two cups each of fish stock and dry white wine. Season with salt and white pepper. Dot with butter. Cover and place in a medium to hot oven for 15

minutes or until the fish are cooked through. Remove and keep them warm. Reduce the cooking liquor and blend in four tablespoons of heavy cream. Thicken the sauce with a little Beurre manié (page 160). Check the seasoning. Pour the sauce over the soles and pass them briefly under a hot grill before serving.

SOGLIOLA ALLA COLBERT
Deep-fried sole with savoury butter
Make an incision along the backbone of four whole, seasoned soles. With a thin, pliable knife, raise the centre fillets away from the bone. Flour, egg, breadcrumb and fry them in plenty of hot oil until cooked and golden. Now cut out the exposed piece of bone. Fill the gap with chilled, savoury butter mixed with lemon juice, chopped parsley, a few dashes of Worcester sauce and the merest hint of garlic.

SOGLIOLA GRATINATA
Sole au gratin with parsley and garlic
Gently poach four soles in Fish stock (page 162). Remove and drain them well. Brush them with melted butter and cover liberally with a mixture of soft, fresh breadcrumbs, chopped parsley and a finely chopped, large garlic clove. Drizzle with melted butter and brown them under a hot grill. Serve with lemon wedges.

SOGLIOLA ALLA PROVINCIALE
Sole with tomatoes and herbs
My first small Soho restaurant had been open for a short time. Now it was beginning to move. It had built up quite a reputation for itself and had become a well-known happy rendezvous. One evening a large, grey Rolls-Royce stopped in front of the attractive bay-window. The chauffeur held the passenger door open. Out of the car stepped smiling Mr and Mrs Gregory Peck.

The first truly international movie star had arrived at the restaurant. The place was really on its way. A small crowd of local people, who had seen the Rolls arriving, were already rubber-necking the scene from the corner of the street. Within minutes the restaurant was the local rage. Rival restaurateurs, throughout the service of that meal, could be seen strolling, apparently indifferently, past the window but, nevertheless, enviously taking in the gay, colourful scene of the buzzing restaurant.

Gregory Peck and his wife returned time and again throughout the filming of that marvellous epic *The Guns of Navarone*. That first evening, after having enjoyed a plate of pasta, they both ordered and liked this sole dish.

In a frying pan, sweat until soft one finely sliced onion with four crushed garlic cloves in one cup of olive oil. Add 900g (2 lb) of roughly chopped, drained, canned tomatoes, eight bruised basil leaves, a pinch of oregano, a level teaspoon of sugar, salt and milled black pepper. Cook for a few minutes and remove the garlic. Transfer this sauce to two large oven dishes. Lay four seasoned sole on top. Cover and place in a medium to hot oven for 15 minutes or until the fish are cooked through. If the sauce seems too liquid remove the sole and reduce it over a medium flame. Sprinkle with chopped parsley. Serve hot.

SOGLIOLA AL NOILLY PRAT
Sole cooked with dry vermouth
This was always a firm favourite at my restaurants. It is based on a superb sole dish I once had at Maxim's, Paris, and it is a dish well worth trying. It may, of course, also be prepared with sole fillets.

Finely chop four shallots and mix with two tablespoons each of chopped, tender celery heart and mushrooms and one dessertspoon each of chopped parsley and fresh tarragon (or one teaspoon of dried tarragon). Place these ingredients in two large, well-buttered oven dishes. Lay four sole on top. Drench them with melted butter. Coat their top sides only with fresh, soft, white breadcrumbs. Drizzle more melted butter over them and season with salt and white pepper. Pour two cups of Noilly Prat French vermouth around the fish. Cover the dishes and place in a medium to hot oven for 15 minutes or until the soles are cooked. Remove and set aside.

Reduce the cooking liquor a little. Add four tablespoons of hollandaise sauce and one and a half cups of heavy cream. Let this thicken gently. Check the seasoning. Place the sole in a serving dish and strain the hot sauce around them leaving the breadcrumbs exposed and crispy. Serve hot.

SOGLIOLA 'WALEWSKA'
Sole with lobster and cheese sauce

Poach four sole gently in fish stock. Drain well. Arrange a plump, well-heated lobster (or crab) claw on each fish. Strew with chopped, black Umbrian truffle parings. Mask the soles liberally with mornay sauce, sprinkle with grated Parmesan cheese and pass them under a hot grill to brown lightly.

SPIGOLA
Sea bass

Spigola and *cernia* (sea bass and grouper) are indubitably the finest of the many species of Mediterranean fish. Even in Europe a lot of fuss is made whenever these fish appear in the markets or on restaurant menus. Sea bass is the house speciality of Jean Lariaga's New York restaurant Le Mistral on East 52nd Street. Jean, a true Frenchman, is terribly proud of his country's great international reputation for superb cuisine, which is why you regularly find worthy examples of it at his establishment.

SPIGOLA ALLA FIAMMA
Grilled fennel-flavoured sea bass

Slash three deep, diagonal cuts into the sides of two 900g (2 lb) fresh sea bass. Fill each incision with a short piece of dried fennel stalk and place some into the gut opening. Douse liberally with some lightly garlic-flavoured olive oil. Season with salt and freshly milled black pepper. Cook them under a hot grill, close to it at first, then withdraw them for eight minutes or so on each side.

Prepare a bed of dried fennel stalks on a large dish and place the fish on a raised griddle on top. Sprinkle both the fish and the fennel with brandy and a few drops of Pernod and flame. Let the aromatic scent permeate the fish. Fillet them on a separate dish by cutting through the back and gently prising the two sides apart, remove the one, large spinal bone and as many of the smaller ones as you can. Serve with a light vinaigrette, hot melted butter or a simple olive oil and lemon dressing.

SPIGOLA AL FORNO
Baked stuffed sea bass

Mix together a good quantity of fresh, soft breadcrumbs with some grated Parmesan cheese, chopped parsley, a little finely chopped garlic, a touch of allspice, salt and milled black pepper. Moisten the mixture with some melted butter. Stuff the gut openings of two fresh, 900g (2 lb) sea bass with the filling. Sew with thread. Place them in a well-oiled oven dish. Season with salt and black pepper and douse with oil. Bake in a medium to hot oven until they are cooked (about 25 minutes). Remove the fish. Add some butter to the pan juices and heat it through until it foams and turns to a nutty colour. Pour over the fish and serve hot with lemon wedges.

SPIGOLA ALLA MENTA
Sea bass with fresh mint

Place four 450g (1 lb) sea bass in a large frying pan. Strew them with two sliced garlic cloves and eight bruised, fresh mint leaves. Douse them with olive oil. Add a tablespoon each of water and malt vinegar. Season with salt and milled black pepper.

Cover the pan. Place over a moderate heat for 20 minutes or until cooked. Serve hot together with the pan juices.

TRIGLIA ALLA LIVORNESE
Red mullet with tomato and herbs

Sweat one finely chopped, tender celery stalk and the leaves, one small, finely chopped onion, and four crushed garlic cloves in five tablespoons of olive oil until soft. Now add 450g (1 lb) of drained, roughly chopped, canned tomatoes, one tablespoon of coarsely chopped parsley, a little thyme, a small piece of bay leaf, salt and milled black pepper. Cook for about ten minutes. Meanwhile, roll four red mullets (or even better, eight small ones) in seasoned flour. Fry in olive oil. Drain them, add to the sauce and continue to cook for a further five minutes. Remove the garlic and serve hot.

TURBOT 'DUGLERE'
Turbot braised with wine and vegetables

This is one of the finest ways to eat turbot. Try it. Place four suprêmes of turbot (fillets cut from the top of the fish) in a well-buttered oven dish. Add four seeded, skinned, chopped tomatoes, two crushed garlic cloves, two small chopped shallots, half of a small, finely chopped onion, a dessertspoon of coarsely chopped parsley, a piece of bay leaf, one teaspoon of chopped, fresh tarragon, two teaspoons of mixed, chopped chives and chervil, salt and milled black pepper. Pour in a cup of fish stock and two cups of dry white wine. Cover and place in a moderate to hot oven for 20 minutes or until the fish is cooked. Discard the garlic. Remove the turbot and keep it warm until the sauce is ready.

Reduce the pan contents, blend in a cup of heavy cream and swirl in small pieces of butter, letting the sauce thicken. Check the seasoning with salt and black pepper.

This delicious fish dish may be served cold but then oil (not butter) should be used and the sauce thickened with a little flour.

TURBOT POCHÉ HOLLANDAISE
Poached turbot with hollandaise sauce

My first, small restaurant did not have a wine and spirit licence. They were all but impossible to get in those days. The restaurant's solicitor had already refused to make an 'unsupportable' application saying that the demand was still insufficient and that there was no obvious hardship involved in not having a licence.

This being the case, the customers were required to pay for their wines and drinks as they ordered them. A waiter then ran out with the money and bought them from Gaston's French Pub around the corner. According to the elements, this often meant that in the winter the red wines would be too cold, in summer the white ones too warm and, in the long rainy season, the mixed drinks very diluted and way past the legal measure. That, surely, was hardship enough. I therefore consulted the solicitor, David Napley, who was described as being the very best. Satisfied that the small, comparatively new restaurant had merit and was being properly run, David Napley took on the difficult brief.

In court he adroitly dealt with, or nimbly side-stepped, all the usual obstacles placed in the way of new applicants by local rival licensees, restaurateurs, publicans, breweries, a few resident nuts and the ubiquitous and passionate man from the Temperance Society. The brilliant lawyer gave forth with such oratorial eloquence that for a while I was seriously concerned, along with the severe-looking magistrates, that the small fashionable restaurant was indeed carrying the future of the British tourist programme on its shoulders.

The pleas were so efficiently submitted that it really came as no great surprise to hear the Chairman of the bench pronounce those immortal words 'Application granted'.

Sir David Napley likes fish very much. But it has to be rather plainly cooked for his taste. Here is a simple turbot dish that he regularly used to order and enjoy. Put four good *tronçons* (thick slices cut straight through the fish) of a fine turbot in a deep pan together with four slices of lemon. Cover with cold salted water to which a little white wine has been added. Bring slowly to the boil and simmer gently for ten minutes or until the fish is cooked but firm. Lift them out carefully. Drain, sprinkle with chopped parsley and serve with plainly boiled new potatoes. Pass hollandaise sauce or plain melted butter at the table.

TURBOT ALLA SARACENA
Turbot with olives, capers and tomatoes

Gently sweat one sliced, medium-sized onion in six tablespoons of olive oil until soft. Add 450g (1 lb) of drained, roughly chopped, canned tomatoes, 16 stoned, black olives, two dessertspoons of rinsed capers, two dessertspoons of coarsely chopped parsley, one dessertspoon of pine nuts, one dessertspoon of sultanas, a piece of bay leaf, salt and freshly milled black pepper.

Cook for five minutes. Add four generous slices of turbot to the pan, cover and cook for 20 minutes or until the fish is ready. If the sauce seems too liquid, then remove the turbot and reduce it a little. Check the seasoning. Serve hot.

VONGOLE ALLA ALESSANDRIA
Sautéed clams Alexandria style

We recently went to a lovely restaurant in the beautiful, but sadly faded, city of Alexandria. I do not recall its name. We were made most welcome, almost as though we had been expected. The food and the service were superb. Yet I felt faintly disturbed. It was as though we had intruded into their own private memories. The empty restaurant, with its charming fin de siècle décor, still retained a haunting air of past colonial traditions. It almost seemed that the whole setting, together with the old staff, were there just waiting for the old days to return as though nothing had ever changed. We returned often, and each time I had the same feeling.

This is one of the dishes they served us. I brought it back to my own restaurants. Each time I ordered it I could not help but think of that sad, lovely restaurant in Alexandria.

In a sauteuse or similar pan, sweat three finely chopped shallots in 50g (2 oz) of butter until soft. Add 60 clams or the small French clams, *praires,* and cover the pan. Toss them around until they open. Discard those that don't. Add two wine glasses of dry white wine, a tablespoon of chopped parsley, a little salt and cayenne pepper. Cook for a few minutes. Remove the clams, reduce the pan liquor and blend in one and a half cups of heavy cream. Bring the sauce almost to the boil and let it thicken gently. Return the clams to the pan. Sprinkle with chopped parsley and serve hot.

ZUPPA DI PESCE
Fish soup

I have had Bouillabaisse, Zuppa di pesce, Sopa de pescado, Caciucco and a host of other fish soups all over the place, and, as may be expected, I have been either disappointed, indifferent or well pleased. Only a few do I recall with pleasure. But one that has never let me down is the fantastic Cioppino served in such huge and delicious portions at Castagnola's, undoubtedly the best seafood restaurant down on San Francisco's lively, colourful Fisherman's Wharf.

This Mediterranean-style fish soup is quite quickly prepared with ingredients easily obtained from almost any local fishmonger. It will certainly be far better than the ones they are serving in most of those French and Italian quay-side restaurants where the atmosphere is often better than the food.

In a large, wide sauteuse or similar pan, sauté four crushed garlic cloves until golden in one cup of good olive oil. Add two cups of light vegetable or fish stock, 450g (1 lb) of roughly chopped, undrained, canned tomatoes, one heaped tablespoon of coarsely chopped parsley, one dessertspoon of fresh chopped tarragon, salt, and milled black pepper. Cook these for a few moments. Add one squid cut into ringlets, its tentacles, four small hake cutlets (or similar flaky, white fish), two small red (or grey) mullets, four large, unshelled scampi, four small scallops and four crab claws. Cover the pan. Simmer for about ten minutes. Remove all the fish and keep it warm.

Now add 450g (1 lb) each of scrubbed mussels and clams. Cover the pan and shake it over a brisk flame until they open. Discard those that don't. Fish around and remove the garlic. Check the seasoning. If you like a lot of broth you may add a cup of boiling vegetable stock and cook for a few minutes. Return all the fish to the pan and reheat. Do not allow the hake or mullets to break up. Serve in deep soup plates with thick slices of oven-toasted French bread liberally spread with Rouille (page 163). If some of the soup-sauce is left over, it may be reduced and mixed with cooked linguine or spaghetti.

More recipes for fish may be found in the **Antipasti** and **Soup** sections:

Antipasti
BEIGNETS DI COZZE Mussel fritters
CROCCHETTE DI GRANCHIO Crabmeat croquettes
A good main course. Serve with thin fried potatoes and a tossed mixed salad.
CROSTONE DI SCAMPI 'ROTHSCHILD' Scampi-filled croûte
INSALATA DI SCAMPI Scampi salad
INSALATA DI SPIGOLA Sea bass salad
PADELLE REALI 'DONNA LUISA' Sautéed scallops, my Mother's way
PINZE DI GRANCHI FRITTE Cornish deep-fried crab claws
Not really a main course, but there's no harm in trying!
POLIPO ALLA LUCIANA Octopus salad
SOFFIETTI DI LUCCIO ALLA SERPENTARIA Pike quenelles with wine and tarragon sauce
The best quenelles I have ever eaten were not those served to me at the fabulous Laperouse in Paris, but those light, delicious ones at the Mirabelle in London, and those quite stupendous ambrosial creations, so beautifully sauced, that emerged from the superlative kitchens of Ernie's Restaurant in San Francisco, California, were in every way just as delicious. Bravissimi!

Pike quenelles are, of course, normally served at the start of a meal or as a fish course, but many ladies with bird-like appetites do often order and enjoy them as light main courses.

Soup
ZUPPA DI COZZE ALL'AMALFITANA Mussel soup, Amalfi style
Although this is really a first or soup course, it may also be served as a very good main dish. The mussels will not over-fill you but, if the portion is large enough, they might well tire you out!

CARNE, POLLAME E CACCIAGIONE
Meat, Poultry & Game

Italian beef recipes improve dramatically when either British, American or French beef is used. The results are usually excellent. And yet none of the fancy cross-breeds and strains can ever hope to produce that well-loved Neapolitan speciality Carne alla pizzaiola as do those tough, stringy animals raised in the mountains of the Amalfi coast.

Having been accustomed to French butchers' methods which I consider well defined and logical, I am far from impressed by the professional standards of British and Italian butchers. Neither, for example, try to enhance their reputations or satisfy their customers by hanging their beef for the requisite time, at the correct temperatures and under controlled conditions, in order to achieve that perfect balance of tenderness and flavour that is so essential to beef. The three days which normally elapse between slaughter and table are just not enough, especially for beef of mediocre quality.

In Britain it has always been difficult to buy sirloin, porterhouse, T-bone or fillet steak from most local butchers. This lack of variety in steak is partly due to the fact that the British, in general, do not really understand steak cuts and also because of the numbers of rolled-up pieces of beef that British butchers have to prepare at weekends in order to provide an entire nation with a Sunday joint.

In Italy, where the Sunday joint problem does not exist, butchers have an ample supply of suitable beef-steak cuts. But, so that they may extract the maximum yield from the carcases, any part that will lie reasonably flat, regardless of grain direction, and that will slice thinly (preferably with an electric slicer), will be expensive and handed over with the words *Bella e tenerissima*. My wife (or myself) is never quite sure whether they are referring to her or to the steak.

I have had beef and steaks in many places, but the ones I recall with most pleasure are those superbly chosen and broiled sirloins at Gallagher's, that great, old New York restaurant; the prime rib-roasts as prepared at the Pen and Pencil, also in New York, are worth remembering, too.

If you fancy, while in London, a cut or two, thick or thin (do make it plain to the carver that you are going to tip him!) from a real rib-roast from the wing section, crunchy and crusty on the outside, tender, barely pink and progressing to rare towards the centre as perfect roast beef should, with lots of tasty crispy tit-bits, good hot gravy (forget the Yorkshire pudding, it is just as lousy as anywhere else), then you must only go to one place – Stones' Restaurant in Panton Street off Leicester Square.

When it comes to veal there is really not much to say when making comparisons. The argument is finished when it is clearly and quite correctly stated that Italian veal is the best of them all! The others just don't stand a chance against the Italian variety.

I fear that veal eating is an up-hill battle

in Britain. The first problem arises in locating a butcher who stocks it; second, one that stocks a good quality; third, one who says that he understands the various tricky cuts; and, fourth, one who will actually execute the cutting. And all this in a country that generally considers veal to be flavourless food–those are some mighty obstacles!

British lamb, which enjoys a well-deserved reputation abroad, is always of exceptional quality, especially the young and tender lamb from the Welsh hills. I have found that lamb in the United States, at least in the parts I have visited, is also very good. Italian lamb, against which there has been a lot of sales resistance over the years, is now breaking the ice and is making good progress.

Excellent, too, is the sweet and tender *abbacchio* baby lamb from the Roman hills and the equally delicious, perhaps more flavoursome, *pauillac* of France. As there is no English equivalent to these do beware of those restaurants which regularly pass off young kid dressed as baby lamb. Although there is absolutely nothing wrong with that sort of meat (I personally rather like it) I do prefer to be told the truth.

On English chickens I'll waste little time. The battery chickens are the worst of them all. They are generally disgusting, dry, and flavourless too, unless one likes the disagreeable taste of the vile fish-meal they are fed on. Do hunt down those free-range ones instead.

I am afraid that I feel almost as strongly about English pork. The good old-fashioned strong flavour and characteristics have been completely bred out of those poor, artificially fed, commercially reared beasts. Still, if you follow my recipes you will at least be able to add some flavour! With regard to ducks and guinea fowls and game of every sort, they are all without a shadow of a doubt, *meravigliosi*. Now here are the recipes for them.

MANZO
Beef

BISTECCA ALLA FIORENTINA
Florentine T-bone steak

These are steaks cut straight through the sirloin and the fillet leaving a T-shaped bone. They should weigh at least 450g (1 lb) per portion. Anything smaller is not a *Fiorentina!* Brush them with olive oil and grill fiercely at first and then reduce the flame until the meat is cooked to your requirements. Season them with salt and milled black pepper. Pass Choron sauce (page 161) separately at the table.

At my restaurants we sometimes used to cut these steaks nearly three times thicker than usual. They were grilled or broiled in the normal way. Then the station waiter, at the customers' table, cut out the T-bone and carved the meat across the grain into the requisite portions. Watercress salad dressed with a mild vinaigrette and thin fried potatoes were served with it.

BOLLITO MISTO ALL'ITALIANA
Mixed, boiled meats, Italian style

Bollito misto, a sort of Italian *pot-au-feu,* is a northern-Italian speciality. It is much liked in Veneto, Piedmont and Lombardy. In those regions the flavour and texture of the fine quality meats are appreciated and the cooking liquor is almost totally ignored. And that, despite what some cookery books try to tell us, is exactly how it should be for this dish. The resulting stock can always be strengthened later for some other use. Elsewhere in Italy the meats are too often started off in cold water with the intention of extracting as strong a stock as possible. But this drains the meats almost completely of taste and leaves them very dry.

Some restaurant customers who normally eat and enjoy some boiled foods are not too keen to try Bollito misto. It sounds 'flat and uninteresting' and not 'Italian' enough. Perhaps they are secretly annoyed that someone else, besides the New Englanders and the English, have the temerity to produce boiled-meat dinners. I sometimes include this dish on my winter menus. We used to describe the merits rhapsodically and push the sales quite strongly. Once convinced, however, the customers would order it and, indeed, enjoyed it very much–it really is an exceptionally good dish. The quantities are, in this recipe, for ten people. Do remember that you must not use chilled or frozen meats, the result just will not be worth the effort or the considerable expense involved.

Put 10l (350 fl oz) of water into a large pot with two quartered onions, two halved carrots, two celery stalks, two sprigs of parsley, one clove, six crushed black peppercorns and a level tablespoon of salt. Bring to the boil and skim off the froth.

Put in 450g (1 lb) of fleshy shin of beef. Bring the water back to the boil and skim. Simmer for 20 minutes. Add 450g (1 lb) of rump-end of veal and bring back to the boil. Skim off again (this can get monotonous). Simmer for 20 more minutes. Now add a 1kg 350g (3 lb) chicken, bring back to the boil and skim off. Cook for 30 minutes. Join all this with 450g (1 lb) of beef tongue and half of a calves' head (both previously about three-quarters cooked). Simmer for a further 30 minutes or until the meats are tender.

Remove, drain the meats and add a 450g (1 lb) Italian cotechino sausage (boiled separately in order not to ruin the stock and overpower the flavours of the other meats). Pass plainly boiled potatoes and crisply cooked, quartered cabbage hearts.

These quite delicious meats should be accompanied by rock salt and either Salsa verde (page 165), Bagnet'd tomatiche (page 159) or Mostarda di cremona (page 171). Or try all three! After all you've spent a small fortune so far anyway! Reserve the stock for another use. It can provide a delicious basis for soup-making.

BRASATO DI MANZO ALLA GENOVESE
Beef braised in red wine and onions, Genoa style

The word *genovese* to a Neapolitan does not, as might logically be expected, trigger off visions of a gentleman from Genoa or even of the city itself. Instead, it causes him to smile languidly and imagine first, golden, sauced pasta and second, fragrant slices of tender braised beef. And that is exactly how this dish should be served: the sauce forming part of the pasta course and the meat, suitably garnished with creamy mashed potatoes, as the main course.

Despite its name, this particular beef dish is almost totally unknown in Genoa. The marvellous recipe was left to delighted Neapolitan gourmets by Genoese *trattori* who had lived in Naples under King Ferdinand. They had developed the recipe locally themselves, no doubt taking full advantage of the local French influence. The dish became so well liked that it was named after the Genoese themselves and not so much after the method.

Make a hole in and push a crushed garlic clove through to the centre of a 900g (2 lb) piece of fresh silverside of beef. Follow this up with a sprig of parsley, a piece of unsmoked bacon fat and a small piece of Parmesan cheese. In a large saucepan, brown the meat well in 50g (2 oz) of pure lard, then remove and set aside. Add to the lard five large, finely sliced onions and let them colour a little. Return the meat to the pan. Pour in one and a half wine glasses of red wine and reduce. Now add one cup of beef stock, four bruised, fresh basil leaves, salt and milled black pepper. Cover and simmer or braise very gently for at least two hours. Turn the meat fairly often. Make sure that the onions do not stick or burn. The sauce should not be too thick. Reserve some of the sauce for a pasta dish. Let the meat rest for a while to facilitate slicing. Heat the sauce well and pass it separately. This dish may be served with plain polenta or plainly boiled or creamed potatoes.

CARBONATA ALLA FIAMMINGA
Beef braised with beer

Season four thick slices of beef silverside or topside, weighing in total about 675g (1½ lb) with salt and plenty of milled black pepper. Brown them in an oven dish in pure lard. Remove the meat. Add to the dish three finely sliced, medium-sized onions and sweat them until soft and golden. Sprinkle with flour and a level dessertspoon of brown sugar. Add a dessertspoon of tomato purée dissolved in one cup of beef stock, one bay leaf, a clove, salt and black pepper. Return the meat, cover it with the onions and pour in three cups of dark beer. Cover the dish and braise in a slow oven for at least two and a half hours. Serve with new potatoes or buttered noodles.

CODA DI BUE CON FAGIOLI
Braised ox-tail with haricot beans

Try this rich and substantial dish with mashed potatoes or polenta and a good bottle of Barbera. Make it the day before – it really improves.

Brown 2kg (4 lb) of floured ox-tail pieces in 50g (2 oz) of lard in an oven dish. Add two chopped, thick slices of bacon, one sliced medium-sized onion, one sliced leek, one crushed garlic clove, three diced carrots, two chopped, tender celery stalks and the leaves, salt, milled black pepper, and coat well with the lard. Pour in one and a half wine glasses of red wine and reduce a little. Stir in one tablespoon of tomato purée. Cover with light beef stock. Cook covered in a moderate oven for at least three hours or until the meat comes away from the bone. Remove the ox-tail and keep warm. Let the sauce rest for a while. Skim off the risen fat. Strain and reheat. Garnish with white haricot beans (which have been soaked overnight and cooked in salted water with a small onion), glazed carrots and button onions. Pour the sauce over. Serve hot. Dumplings, too, are very good with this.

FILETTO ALLA BOSTON
Fillet steak stuffed with oysters
Slit four 37mm (1½ in) thick fillet steaks. Insert two raw oysters in each. Sew the steaks up with cotton and sauté them in butter and oil until coloured and medium-rare inside. Season, remove and keep them warm. Deglaze the pan with a wine glass of dry white wine and reduce it a little. Add a cup of Veal gravy (page 164) and half a dessertspoon of chopped fresh tarragon. Thicken the sauce by stirring in tiny pieces of butter, check the seasoning and pour it over the steaks.

FILETTO ALLA MASSENA
Fillet steak with artichokes and truffles
Sauté four trimmed, round fillet steaks in butter and oil. Season with salt and milled black pepper. Place them on thick, round, fried bread croûtes, set two slices of poached beef marrow on each steak and surround with sliced, sautéed (fresh or canned) artichoke hearts.

Deglaze the pan with a wine glass of dry Marsala wine and stir in two dessertspoons of chopped, black Umbrian (canned) truffles, some of their liquor and a cup of Veal gravy (page 164). Heat well, reduce, thicken with tiny pieces of butter and pour over the steaks. Serve hot.

FILETTO ALLA STROGONOFF
Fillet strips in paprika and cream sauce
Cut 450g (1 lb) of beef fillet end-trimmings into 5cm (2 in) long, 6mm (¼ in) thick strips. Sweat half a finely chopped, medium-sized onion in butter and oil until soft. Sauté the beef strips very quickly, barely sealing them. Remove and keep them warm. Stir into the pan two level teaspoons of tomato purée. Add two sliced, cooked white mushrooms, one tablespoon of julienned sweet gherkins, two teaspoons of paprika pepper, a few dashes of Worcester sauce, salt and milled black pepper. Return the meat to the pan and cook for a few minutes. Pour in one cup of heavy cream, swirl the pan and let the sauce thicken. Sprinkle with chopped parsley. Serve with plainly boiled, fluffy rice.

FILETTO 'TARTARE'
Raw, spicy, chopped beef
Place three egg yolks in a bowl, season with salt, plenty of black milled pepper and two teaspoons each of English and Dijon mustards. Add olive oil, drop by drop, while constantly stirring with a fork. When the egg mixture begins to resemble a mayonnaise, mix in 550g (20 oz) of finely chopped (not minced), fresh fillet steak. Sprinkle in one tablespoon each of finely chopped shallots, capers, parsley (some like to include anchovies, I don't), two teaspoons of malt vinegar, ten drops of Tabasco and 12 dashes of Worcester sauce. Mix well but lightly. Do not over-work the mixture or mash it. Pile in loose mounds on crisp lettuce. Do not shape or mould. Serve slightly chilled with fried potatoes.

I once introduced a novel and interesting way to serve steak tartare. The prepared steak was loosely piled on top of thick, toasted, buttered farmhouse bread or on hot muffins, topped with light chicken-liver pâté, sprinkled with chopped hard-boiled egg, shallots and parsley. It looked very nice and the twin-taste combination, with the hot crunchy toast, was very good. Served in small neat portions it also became a much requested first course.

FRACOSTA ALLA BOSCAIOLA
Sirloin steak with mushrooms and herbs
Sweat a finely chopped, medium-sized onion and a crushed garlic clove in butter and oil until soft. Remove the garlic. Add five chopped, drained, canned tomatoes, a

dessertspoon of Italian dried porcini mushrooms (soaked in warm water for ten minutes) together with a little of their soaking liquor, a level dessertspoon of fresh, chopped tarragon, four sliced mushrooms, salt and black pepper. Cook for five minutes.

In another pan sauté four 225g (8 oz) trimmed sirloin steaks to the required degree in oil. Season with salt and milled black pepper. Transfer them to the sauce. Deglaze the steak pan with four tablespoons of dry white wine and blend into the sauce. Simmer for a few minutes. Sprinkle with chopped parsley. Serve hot.

FRACOSTA ALLA FIAMMA
Sirloin steak with whisky sauce
Sauté four 225g (8 oz) sirloin steaks in butter and oil to the required degree, season with salt and milled black pepper.

In another pan, gently sweat three finely chopped shallots in butter and oil until soft. Add 25 drained green peppercorns. Cook for a few moments. Flame with a good measure of Scotch whisky. Deglaze the pan with half a cup of beef stock. Reduce and then transfer the steaks to the serving dish. Swirl in one cup of heavy cream and let the sauce thicken and then pour over the steaks. Serve hot, garnish with triangles of fried bread.

FRACOSTA AL MIDOLLO
Sirloin steak with beef marrow
Sweat three finely chopped shallots and two crushed garlic cloves in butter and oil until soft. Discard the garlic. Add and sauté four 225g (8 oz) sirloin steaks to the required degree. Season with salt and milled black pepper. Remove and keep them warm. Deglaze the pan with a wine glass of red wine and pour in one cup of strong beef stock. Let it reduce a little. Check the seasoning. Swirl in a walnut-sized piece of beurre manié and let the sauce thicken. Arrange three slices of poached beef marrow along each steak.

Pour the sauce over, sprinkle with chopped parsley and chervil. Serve hot.

FRACOSTA AL PEPE NERO
Sirloin steak with pepper sauce
Crush four tablespoons of black peppercorns and rub them well into four 225g (8 oz) sirloin steaks which have also been spread with made-up English mustard. Fry them on both sides in butter and oil to the required degree. Season with salt, remove and keep warm. Flame the pan with a good measure of brandy, deglaze and add one cup of Veal gravy (page 164) and six tablespoons of heavy cream. Swirl the pan and let the sauce thicken. Pour over the steaks. Sprinkle with chopped parsley. Serve hot.

FRACOSTA ALLA PIZZAIOLA
Sirloin steak with tomato and oregano
There have been more disasters made and served in the name of the great Neapolitan pizzaiola sauce than I care to remember. And each one has horrified me. Even allowing for the Italian love of change, and despite what any cookery book tells you, there must be no anchovies, capers, pine nuts, onions, shallots, chillies, butter, lard, brandy, wine, carrots, celery or olives. I have seen all of these either used or suggested. Furthermore, the meat is not previously sautéed, broiled or fried. Everything is cooked together, like this.

Put four thin 125g (5 oz) slices of sirloin or rump steak into a large frying pan together with 450g (1 lb) of chopped, drained, canned tomatoes, two large, sliced garlic cloves, one teaspoon of oregano, salt and milled black pepper. Douse liberally with olive oil. Cook briskly over a high flame. When the oil and the tomatoes have combined and turned into a fragrant sauce, it is ready. And that's it! Serve lots of fresh, crusty French bread with this.

By substituting a little meat stock for the tomatoes and in all other ways following the same procedure, you can make a very good and tasty steak dish known as Bistecca alla palermitana. Try that as well.

FRACOSTA AL ROQUEFORT
Sirloin steak with Roquefort butter
Grill four 225g (8 oz) sirloin steaks to the required degree and season them with salt and milled black pepper. Serve very hot. At the table serve a chilled whirl of savoury butter made by mixing together one third of butter with two thirds of Roquefort cheese with some chopped parsley, chopped celery leaves, dry English mustard and a few drops of Worcester sauce to taste.

FRACOSTA ALLA VIGNAIA
Sirloin steak with endives and grapes
Sauté four 225g (8 oz) sirloin steaks to the required degree in butter and oil and season with salt and black milled pepper. Remove and keep warm. Deglaze the pan with a wine glass of red wine and one cup of strong beef stock. Swirl in a walnut-sized piece of beurre manié and thicken the sauce. Decorate the steaks with blanched sprigs of fresh tarragon, garnish with braised Belgian endives and glazed Muscat grapes. Pour the sauce over and serve hot.

FRITTO MISTO ALLA LOMBARDA
A mixture of crispy tit-bits
Read through the following and take your pick. This is a recipe for whatever is available and whatever you wish to spend. It is also one great glorious fry-up!

Small lamb cutlets, small veal cutlets, calves' brains, sweetbreads, kidneys, liver, small sausage-meat patties, beef marrow, veal scaloppines, chicken, egg, rice, potato or mushroom croquettes, savoury fritters of any sort, zucchini, marrow-flowers, young artichokes, bulb fennel, mushrooms, cauliflorets, egg-plant slices, Ricotta balls, and consider anything that I have forgotten but which might go well.

Whatever you have chosen may or may not need blanching. They should all be floured, dipped in egg and breadcrumbs and golden-fried in butter and oil – except the liver, artichokes, zucchini, marrow-flowers and cauliflorets which should be simply egg-fried. While you're about it, why not include apples, pineapple or bananas? They will add even more interest. Serve the whole lot with lemon halves or Tartare sauce (page 164).

GRANATINA DI MANZO 'BAVIERA'
Beef patty
Finely chop (not mince) 325g (12 oz) of sirloin steak together with the strip of fat at the top. Mix it with one egg yolk, one tablespoon of very finely chopped shallots, a little tomato ketchup, a few dashes of Worcester sauce, salt and plenty of milled black pepper. Shape into round patties and flour them lightly. Fry them fairly quickly in oil together with two crushed garlic cloves. Do not turn them more than once. Remove the garlic. Serve them with Barbecue sauce (page 159).

GRANATINA 'PASSI E PINOLI'
Chopped steak with pine nuts and sultanas
Sweat until soft one small, finely chopped onion in a little pure lard. Drain well. Mix with 325g (12 oz) of finely chopped sirloin steak together with the fat at the top. Add two crustless slices of milk-soaked bread, a dessertspoon of grated Parmesan cheese, one egg yolk, one dessertspoon each of pine nuts and sultanas, chopped parsley, salt and milled black pepper. Form into four round patties and flour lightly. Fry them on both sides in the lard used for the onions together with a few fresh sage leaves, which will give this typically southern dish a typically northern flavour – just to be different!

MANZO BOLLITO RIFATTO CON LE PATATE
Rehashed boiled beef with potatoes
When you make beef or beef-chicken soups, or when you serve Bollito misto all'Italiana (page 96), you are almost certainly going to have to find a way to use up the left-over boiled beef. Peel and quarter 450g (1 lb) of potatoes and put them into a saucepan together with one heaped tablespoon of coarsely chopped parsley, two large crushed garlic cloves, four tablespoons of olive oil, salt and milled black pepper. Pour in enough cold water so that the potatoes are three-quarters covered. Cover and cook gently until they are almost tender. Now add the cold, boiled beef (cut into cubes) and continue to cook until the potatoes are soft. Serve with a crisply cooked green vegetable and plenty of crusty bread.

Potatoes cooked in this fashion are very good on their own and will liven any dull fish or meat main course.

MANZO BOLLITO RIFATTO CON POMODORI
Rehashed boiled beef with tomatoes
In a saucepan, sauté a finely sliced, medium-sized onion with two crushed garlic cloves in a little olive oil until soft. Add 450g (1 lb) of drained, roughly chopped, canned tomatoes, four quartered, medium-sized potatoes, one chopped, tender celery stalk and the leaves, four torn-up basil leaves, salt and milled black pepper. Pour in enough cold water so that the potatoes are three-quarters covered. Cook them gently until they are nearly tender, then add the cold beef (cut into cubes) and continue to cook until the potatoes are soft. Season with black pepper if desired and serve hot with plenty of crusty French bread.

MEDAGLIONI DI MANZO ALLA UMBRA
Beef médaillons with truffle sauce
Prepare and fry eight Crocchette di patate (page 143), shaped into round patties, and keep them warm. Sauté eight 18mm ($\frac{3}{4}$ in) thick slices of trimmed beef fillet in butter. Season with salt and black pepper and place them upon the potato croquettes.

Deglaze the pan with half a cup of mixed brandy and Madeira, flame and reduce. Add two dessertspoons of chopped, black, Umbrian (canned) truffles with a little of their liquor, one cup of Veal gravy (page 164) and half a cup of heavy cream. Swirl the pan and let the sauce thicken. Top the beef médaillons with slices of black Umbrian truffles and pour the sauce over them.

PAILLARD DI MANZO
Thinly beaten, grilled steak

Monsieur Paillard was an acclaimed and successful chef-restaurateur who directed, at different times, some of the most famous Parisian restaurants at the turn of the century. He had his last and most impressive establishment especially built in the Champs Elysées at the time of the Paris Grand Exposition of 1900.

Throughout his successful career Paillard invented and devised many new dishes – some of them are still prepared today. Once he had to improvise a quick dish. The result pleased him. It was a thinly beaten beef sirloin steak, oiled, grilled, seasoned, sprinkled with lemon juice and enlivened with a little rich meat glaze. The simple dish also pleased his admirers and it became known as a 'Paillard'. There was nothing at all wrong with his recipe – in fact it was a very good one. But somehow, over the years, the beef became changed to veal, the lemon juice was completely forgotten and so was the meat glaze.

What a shame that such a great restaurateur is now mainly remembered for a dry, acid and flavourless veal parody of a beef dish.

PICKWICK PUDDING
A rich meat pudding

I once worked at Hatchett's, an exclusive restaurant in London's Piccadilly. In the old days it had been an inn and a staging-post for coach travellers bound for the west of England and had been mentioned by Charles Dickens in several of his writings. Each day a different dish was offered to the well-heeled businessmen lunchers. It might be a wing of roast beef or a saddle of Welsh lamb, a boiled leg of mutton with caper sauce or a tasty dish of Irish stew. On Wednesdays it was the robust Pickwick pudding, appropriately served with much dignity by Mr Driscoll, a tall, somewhat aloof, well-bred Englishman.

The Pickwick pudding, however, was not prepared by a white-aproned, plump and jolly lady nor by a portly red-faced English master cook, but by a diminutive Chinese from Vietnam called Chang! Late on Tuesday evenings, Chang would reverently make ready several enormous basins of the pudding and then leave them to simmer gently all through the night. Chang was extremely jealous of his recipe and never divulged it.

On Wednesday mornings the restaurant telephonist was regularly overwhelmed with table reservations and determined demands for portions of Pickwick pudding. Just as regularly, other early and not so prudent lunchers would study the menu and then decide their choice. They, too, always fell for it. 'I'll take today's special trolley dish, please, waiter.' To which, to their amazement, as they looked disbelievingly around the still empty restaurant and then at the still virgin, quietly steaming silver trolley, the reply would be a very matter-of-fact 'I'm very sorry, sir, but the Pickwick pudding is sold out.' Here is a recipe for a meat pudding, however, that Chang would undoubtedly approve of.

To make the crust, mix lightly together 450g (1 lb) of self-raising flour, a good pinch of salt, two teaspoons of mixed herbs and 225g (8 oz) of finely chopped beef suet. Gradually add enough cold water to work into a soft, resilient dough. Knead it smoothly. Roll it out, 6mm ($\frac{1}{4}$ in) thick, on a floured board, to a size that will completely line a 20 cm (8 in) pudding dish. Cut out a round of dough 18mm ($\frac{3}{4}$ in) thick for the topping.

For the filling roll 450g (1 lb) of cubed steak and 225g (8 oz) of well-trimmed calves' (or oxen's) kidney in flour. Add two halved (quickly browned) quails and mix with 50g (2 oz) of chopped onions, two dessertspoons of chopped parsley,

100g (4 oz) of halved mushrooms and season well with salt and white pepper.

Line the basin with the dough. Fill it nearly to the top with filling and pour in enough lightly flavoured beef stock barely to cover the meats. Top with the cut-out round of dough. Press down well and crimp to seal the edges. Cover with greased paper. Tie a dampened, well-floured tea-cloth around the basin, bringing up and tying the four corners at the top of the pudding – or use foil. Stand it in a large saucepan of boiling water. Do not let the water reach the rim. Keep it gently boiling for at least three and a half hours, adding more boiling water if necessary.

When the pudding is ready, untie carefully. Make a small hole in the top crust. Put in twelve shelled oysters together with their liquor and stir in. You may have to add a little plain boiling water to dilute the rich, rich gravy. Serve this fantastic winter dish with mashed potatoes and crisply cooked cabbage. Do not forget the mustard – it is vital.

SPEZZATINO AL CABERNET
Beef stew with Cabernet wine
Some time after my first small restaurant had opened, I began to notice a very pretty girl who used to come in with friends to eat the 'best spaghetti in town'. One evening she came in wearing a green coat and a feathered hat and I spoke to her. Her name was Sara and she was beautiful. Later that same evening I told her that someday I was going to marry her. She didn't take too much notice though, possibly because the spaghetti she was eating claimed all of her attention. I had heard of love rivals, but spaghetti?

Some years later, when we were married, I happened to remind my wife Sara of the green coat and feathered hat. She took me somewhat aback by insisting that she had never owned nor worn any such things. It made me more than wonder. It had certainly been a busy evening! This is one of the recipes she likes to use the most.

In a heavy casserole, sauté 12 new carrots, 16 small mushrooms, 20 button onions and 75g (3 oz) of streaky bacon lardons in lard and oil until coloured. Remove and set them aside. In the same fat, quickly brown 675g (1½ lb) of lightly floured, cubed shin of beef together with three crushed garlic cloves and a bay leaf. Stir in a teaspoon of brown sugar. Pour in three-quarters of a bottle of Cabernet or similar red wine and a cup of vegetable stock. Season with salt and milled black pepper. Bring to the boil. Cover the casserole and cook gently in a moderate oven for two and a half hours. Now return the reserved lardons and vegetables, cover and cook for a further 30 minutes. Skim off much of the fat. Serve with plainly boiled potatoes, lots of crusty French bread and litres of red Cabernet wine.

STEAK DIANE
Minute steak sautéed in piquant sauce
I wonder whether Bette Davis ever remembers the evening when she and three friends ordered Steak Diane in a London late-night club-restaurant quite a few years ago? The Second Head Waiter, swaying happily drunk as usual, insisted on preparing them himself on two spirit lamps as close to her table as possible. Working with exaggerated care, he eventually finished cooking them. They must have looked good to him for he seemed quite pleased. He tried a final flamboyant flourish – which went wrong. He knocked one pan clumsily and, in trying frantically to stop it from tipping, he nudged the other one. Too late! In a flash the two pans and the four steaks were on the carpet in a soggy, unpleasant mess.

Bette Davis, dignified as always, merely raised her eyebrows slightly and calmly carried on talking as though nothing had happened. But she and her party had to make do with four hurriedly grilled entrecôtes.

The only way to cook Steak Diane is as follows. Ask your butcher to flatten four 150g (6 oz) sirloin steaks very, very thinly indeed. Melt a little butter together with a small piece of beef fat in two very hot frying pans. Quickly add the steaks just as the butter is about to take colour. Let them frizzle for a few seconds and turn them over. Keep the flame very high. Season them well with salt and milled black pepper, remove and set aside. Deglaze the pans with a good amount of Worcester sauce and a little stock. Pour the gravy over the steaks, sprinkle with chopped chives and parsley. Serve quickly while still hot.

The essence of this dish is speed and simplicity. Do not, no matter what anybody says, include such things as onion, oil, shallots, garlic, mustard, mushrooms, tomatoes, brandy, whisky, wine, sherry, cream or ketchup. Never!

STRACOTTO ALLA FIORENTINA
Braised beef with vegetables, Florentine style

Make a hole and push a crushed garlic clove through to the centre of 900g (2 lb) of beef silverside and follow up with a sprig of parsley, a piece of unsmoked bacon fat and a small piece of Parmesan cheese.

In a casserole, brown the meat well all over in lard and set aside. In the pan sweat two large carrots, two tender celery stalks and the leaves and four onions, all finely chopped, until soft and golden. Replace the meat. Pour in two cups of red wine and let the liquid become absorbed over a brisk flame. Now add one cup of vegetable stock, one tablespoon of tomato purée, four bruised basil leaves, salt and milled black pepper. Cover and simmer or braise gently for at least two hours or until the meat is cooked through. Turn the meat often during the cooking and see that the vegetables do not stick or burn. Check the seasoning. Let the meat rest awhile to facilitate slicing. Do not strain the sauce. Serve with polenta or boiled or creamed potatoes.

This absolutely fantastic sauce is also very good if mixed with cooked pasta such as penne or rigatoni.

TRIPPA ALLA FIORENTINA
Tripe with tomato and onions

American, English and now even Italian shop-bought tripe unfortunately has had the flavour mostly boiled out of it and is therefore nowhere near as tasty as it used to be. The following recipe though, produces a perfectly acceptable result.

Sweat a finely chopped onion and carrot in butter and oil until soft. Add 675g (1½ lb) of dressed tripe, cut into 12mm (½ in) wide strips, and, letting the moisture dry out over a brisk flame, let it take a golden colour. Pour in a small wine glass of dry white wine and reduce. Add a cup of chicken stock, a heaped tablespoon of tomato purée, a piece of bay leaf, a sprig of fresh rosemary, salt and milled black pepper. Cover and simmer for at least an hour. Serve with thick slices of garlic-spiced, toasted French bread. Pass creamed or boiled potatoes. It is absolutely essential to sprinkle grated Parmesan cheese over this dish.

VITELLO
Veal

ANIMELLE DI VITELLO ALLA KING
Creamed calves' sweetbreads

Soak three calves' sweetbreads in cold water for at least three hours. Change the water, season, bring to the boil, remove from the stove and allow the sweetbreads to cool in their cooking liquor under a weight. Cut away the tubes, membranes and gristle. Rinse well (this is preliminary procedure for all sweetbread dishes).

Cut the sweetbreads into thin slices, dip them lightly in flour and sauté in butter.

Season with salt and milled black pepper. Arrange them in slices on crisp, fried bread croûtes. Cover them with sliced sautéed mushrooms and criss-cross with thin strips of cooked or canned red peppers. Set aside.

Deglaze the pan with a little medium-dry sherry and add half a cup of thick Veal gravy (page 164). Blend in a cup of Béchamel sauce (page 159) enriched with an egg yolk. Swirl in four tablespoons of heavy cream and gently heat through. Check the seasoning. Pour over the sweetbreads. Sprinkle with cayenne pepper and chopped parsley. Serve immediately, do not let the croûtes become soggy!

ANIMELLE DI VITELLO ALLA NORMANNA
Calves' sweetbreads with calvados
Prepare and parboil three pairs of calves' sweetbreads as in the preceding recipe. Cut them into 12mm (½ in) slices. Flour, egg, breadcrumb and fry them until golden in butter and oil. Drain and keep them warm on a serving dish. Meanwhile, in another pan, gently fry six halved slices of bacon and twelve thin, floured slices of cooking-apple. Set them on top of the sweetbreads. Deglaze the second pan with a good measure of calvados or applejack. Add a dessertspoon of chopped chervil, a cup of lightly flavoured stock and reduce well. Swirl in six tablespoons of heavy cream and thicken the sauce gently. Pour it over the sweetbreads. Sprinkle with chopped parsley. Serve hot.

ANIMELLE DI VITELLO 'VICTORIA'
Calves' sweetbreads with scampi and lobster sauce
Prepare twelve slices of calves' sweetbreads as in the previous recipes. Flour and fry them in butter. Season with salt and milled black pepper and set aside. Meanwhile, sauté in butter and oil 12 quartered button mushrooms and 12 scampi, halved lengthways. Season and set aside. Deglaze the pans with a small amount of Madeira wine and transfer everything to one pan. Blend in one cup of heavy cream and half a cup of Lobster or Aurore sauce (pages 162 and 159). Check the seasoning. Garnish the sweetbreads with the scampi and the mushrooms and cover with the sauce. Serve hot with plainly boiled rice.

VOL-AU-VENT DI ANIMELLE ALLA CREMA
Vol-au-vent with creamed sweetbreads

Modestly speaking, my restaurant generally triumphed when it came to honours and mentions in most of the restaurant guides current at the time, so I don't have too many complaints to make on the subject. In any case I've always taken those publications and their effect on trading with an appropriate pinch of salt.

I have, however, often wondered where on earth some authors of those slightly patronizing, always pompous books, get their remarkable catering experience and technical expertise. Why on earth don't they open their own restaurants and make a fortune for themselves and, whilst they're about it, show us all how things should be done. Or is it comparable with the theatre critic writing his own play situation? I rather fancy it is.

I have long noticed that one of the food guides has particular admiration for those gayer establishments that will make sure that their contrived speciality dishes are always baked in 'delicate, light-as-air pastry'. That is almost certain to notch a few extra marks. Whenever a new precious edition of that particular book is published, I always feel slightly cheated to see that it has not been perfectly baked in an oven and is not offered for sale to the public suitably presented in a golden and feather-light puff-pastry wrapper!

Prepare two calves' sweetbreads as in the previous recipes. Cut them into cubes and mix with two tablespoons of cubed, white mushrooms, four tablespoons of diced tongue, four fresh, cooked (or canned) cockscombs and a thinly sliced, black Umbrian truffle. Sauté in butter and season with salt and milled black pepper. Flame with a small wine glass of brandy, pour in a little Madeira and reduce. Add a cup of thick Veal gravy (page 164) and six tablespoons of heavy cream and heat gently through. Season again if necessary.

Fill four fresh, warmed Vol-au-vent cases (page 165) with the mixture. Replace their tops and set them in a hot oven for a few minutes. Serve them hot.

CERVELLA DI VITELLO AL BURRO NERO
Calves' brains with black butter sauce

Wash four sets of calves' brains well and soak them for at least two hours, changing the water several times. Skin them and wash away all the blood. Simmer them gently for 15 minutes in salted water containing some sliced onion, a bouquet garni and a little vinegar. Drain and place in a serving dish. Heat 75g (3 oz) of butter together with a heaped tablespoon of rinsed capers and one of chopped parsley to a deep hazelnut colour. Pour it, while still foaming, over the brains. Deglaze the pan with two tablespoons of malt vinegar and add to the dish. Serve very hot with plainly boiled new potatoes.

CERVELLA DI VITELLO ALLA MONTEVERDE
Calves' brains fried in savoury batter

Soak, prepare and cook three sets of calves' brains as in the previous recipe and let them cool in their own cooking liquor. Cut lengthways into uniform slices. Flour and dip them into a mixture of seasoned, beaten eggs flavoured with two crushed garlic cloves, chopped parsley and two tablespoons of grated Parmesan cheese. Fry them in olive oil until golden. Serve with crisp fried parsley sprigs and lemon halves or a light tomato sauce.

COSTOLETTA DI VITELLO ALLA MILANESE
Veal cutlets fried with Parmesan cheese and breadcrumbs, Milanese style

Chartered accountant and company chairman, Christopher Armstrong came over after his lunch and joined me for a drink.

He idly asked how much profit the restaurants were making. When he heard the figure he widened his eyes, ordered another brandy on the house, drank it down, made a rapid calculation and worked out that in four years the restaurants could apply for a stock-market quote on the London Exchange. And do you know? He was right!

Apart from being able to give good advice, Chris always liked to munch anxiously on breaded veal cutlets while watching the racing from his private box at Ascot. This is how they were prepared for him.

Trim and flatten four veal cutlets on the bone. Flour, dip them in seasoned beaten eggs to which a little grated Parmesan cheese has been added and coat them well with fine dry breadcrumbs. Fry them gently in hot oil until cooked and golden. Drain well and serve with lemon halves.

FEGATO DI VITELLO ALLA LIONESE
Sautéed calves' liver with onions

In my opinion calves' liver cooked this way is superior to the rather vinegary Venetian version of which so much unnecessary fuss is made.

Slowly sweat two very thinly sliced, medium-sized onions in butter and oil until soft and golden. Season with salt and milled black pepper. Remove from the pan and set aside. Flour 12 thin slices of good calves' liver and fry them in butter and oil in the same pan for no more than 15 seconds each side. Remove, place on a serving dish and smother them with the onions. Deglaze the pan with a little stock and pour the gravy over the liver. Sprinkle with chopped parsley, serve quickly and hot.

FEGATO DI VITELLO ALLA SALVIA
Sautéed calves' liver with fresh sage

I include this ridiculously simple dish because it is a very tasty way to prepare liver. Quickly sauté 12 lightly floured, thin slices of good calves' liver in a mixture of oil and butter together with eight fresh sage leaves. Season with salt and milled black pepper and transfer to a serving dish. Deglaze the pan with a little stock, pour the gravy around the liver and serve immediately.

NODINO DI VITELLO ALLA BUONA DONNA
Veal chop with wine and vegetables

Sauté in an oven casserole 50g (2 oz) of unsmoked bacon lardons and two crushed garlic cloves in butter and oil. Remove the garlic when golden. Add and brown four floured veal chops. Pour in one cup of chicken stock together with 12 par-cooked new potatoes, eight par-cooked button onions and six quartered mushrooms. Season with salt and milled black pepper. Cover and cook in a moderate to hot oven for an hour or until the veal is tender. Arrange the veal and the vegetables on a serving dish. Skim off some of the fat and deglaze the casserole with a small wine glass of dry white wine. Reduce well and pour the gravy over the chops. Sprinkle with chopped parsley. Garnish with triangles of crisply fried bread.

NODINO DI VITELLO ALLA SASSI
Sautéed veal chop with potatoes and rosemary

Sauté four seasoned veal chops in butter and oil together with two small sprigs of rosemary until well coloured and cooked through. Meanwhile, fry four potatoes cut into the tiniest of cubes with two crushed garlic cloves until cooked and crispy. Remove the garlic and pile the potatoes in small mounds on top of each chop. Add a little more butter to the pan, slightly brown it and pour, together with the pan juices, over the chops. Sprinkle with chopped parsley and serve hot.

OSSO BUCHO ALLA MILANESE
Braised shin of veal

Flour four thick pieces of veal shin-bone cut from the meaty part of the leg and brown them in an oven dish in butter and oil. Add and sauté, all chopped, one medium-sized onion, one carrot and a celery stalk and the leaves. Pour in half a wine glass of white wine and let it reduce. Stir in a tablespoon of tomato purée. Season with salt and milled black pepper. Add a bouquet garni and a bay leaf. Barely cover with lightly flavoured chicken stock. Place in a moderate oven and braise covered for at least two hours. Remove the meat. Skim off as much of the risen fat as possible. Pour the sauce over the *ossi buchi*. Serve with Risotto alla Milanese (page 75), Risotto in bianco (page 73), mashed creamy potatoes or smother the veal pieces with lots of tender and tiny buttered peas.

PICCATINE DI VITELLO ALLA MINORESE
Veal scaloppines with fresh peppers

Piccatine are small, thinly beaten, tender escalopes of veal. Allow three to the portion. They should be nicely trimmed into regular round shapes.

Prepare a quantity of Peperonata (page 30). Sauté 12 lightly floured veal piccatine in olive oil until nicely coloured. Season with salt and milled black pepper. Combine them with the hot Peperonata and let them absorb some of the flavour. Serve hot.

PICCATINE DI VITELLO 'PALAZZO DI CRISTALLO'
Veal scaloppines with brandy and cream sauce

My wife and I once flew back from our vacation in Amalfi to London just to see Crystal Palace, our favourite football team, play its first match in the English First Division. They played Manchester United who did score two goals – but, so did we! A great, honourable draw. I devised this dish after that grand match.

Flour and fry 12 seasoned, thin, small veal scaloppines and eight slices of tongue in butter and oil until golden. Place on a serving dish and set aside. Add and sauté eight sliced white mushrooms and sprinkle with four teaspoons of finely chopped, black Umbrian truffles. Flame with brandy, add a small wine glass of sherry and four tablespoons of veal gravy. Reduce slightly. Swirl in a cup of heavy cream and let the sauce thicken. Pour over the scaloppines and serve with golden-fried, milk-bread croûtes.

ROGNONCINI TRIFOLATI CON CIPOLLA
Calves' kidneys sautéed with onions

Soak two large calves' kidneys in slightly salted water for two hours. Wash, skin and quarter them lengthways. Remove the centre core. Slice them fairly thinly.

Gently sweat two finely sliced, medium-sized onions in olive oil and a little water until soft. Raise the heat and reduce any moisture. Add the kidneys and sauté briskly until barely pink inside. Pour in half a wine glass of dry white wine and reduce. Season with salt and milled black pepper.

Serve immediately with plainly boiled and buttered new potatoes.

ROGNONCINI DI VITELLO ALLA RICCA
Calves' kidneys with foie gras and cream sauce

Prepare two good-sized calves' kidneys as in the preceding recipe. Season them well with milled black pepper. In a frying pan, sweat one finely chopped shallot in butter and oil until soft. Add four thinly sliced, white mushrooms and the kidneys and sauté briskly until they are barely pink inside. Season with salt. Remove the kidneys and the mushrooms and keep warm. Deglaze the pan with a small glass of port and reduce. Stir in a cup of heavy cream. Add two tablespoons of diced foie gras. Swirl the pan and thicken the sauce gently. Pour the sauce over the kidneys and serve with fried croûtes or plainly boiled rice.

ROGNONCINI DI VITELLO AL VINO ROSSO
Calves' kidneys with red wine sauce
Prepare two good-sized calves' kidneys as in the two preceding recipes. In a frying pan, sweat a small, finely chopped onion and one crushed garlic clove in butter and oil. Discard the garlic. Add and quickly sauté the kidneys until barely pink inside. Season with salt and milled black pepper. Remove and keep them warm together with 16 thin slices of poached marrow-fat. Deglaze the pan with a wine glass of red wine and half a cup of Veal gravy (page 164). Reduce a little and sprinkle lightly with sugar and chopped parsley. Thicken the sauce with a walnut-sized beurre manié. Return the kidneys to the pan and reheat quickly. Serve with fried bread croûtes or plainly cooked rice.

SAUTÉ DI VITELLO ALLA MARENGO
Veal sautéed in white wine
Who was that tall, attractive, loose-limbed man entering the London restaurant? Forks, spoons, napkins, glasses were delicately poised in mid-air. Some seemed to recognize him but weren't too sure. It was Ronald Reagan, the movie star and ex-Governor of California. He was in London, on a European tour, and having lunch with the American Ambassador who regularly came into my Mayfair restaurant for quiet, informal meals when he wanted to get away from it all.

But the effect on the ladies! Gregory Peck, Paul Newman, Tony Curtis, Henry Fonda, Roger Moore, David Niven, and old granite-face himself, John Wayne, all had the same effect on the girls each time they walked into that restaurant. Ronald Reagan ordered the lunchtime trolley dish that day, it was prepared like this.

Lightly flour 450g (1 lb) of shoulder of veal cut into fairly large cubes. Brown well in butter and oil with one chopped onion and three crushed garlic cloves. Pour in a wine glass of dry white wine and reduce. Mix in 450g (1 lb) of roughly chopped, drained, canned tomatoes, one cup of chicken stock, a piece of bay leaf, a little thyme, a few fresh sage leaves, salt and milled black pepper. Cover and simmer for an hour or until the meat is tender. Garnish with four fried egg yolks, season with black pepper and triangles of fried bread croûtes.

This dish is said to have been improvised by Napoleon's batman on the field of battle at Marengo in Italy. The original recipe calls for the inclusion of a few cooked crayfish. These are difficult enough to obtain in big cities let alone on a battlefield. In any case how did they ever find time to go fishing? So just leave them out altogether or perhaps add a few sweet-tasting boiled scampi or shrimps.

SCALOPPA DI VITELLO FARCITA
Stuffed veal escalope
Sauté a finely chopped shallot and four finely sliced mushrooms in butter and oil with two tablespoons of chopped ham and one dessertspoon of chopped parsley. Blend in two tablespoons of very thick Béchamel sauce (page 159). Season with salt and milled black pepper. Chill.

Place the filling in the centre of four thinly beaten veal escalopes and cover with four similar ones. Seal the edges well, flour, egg and breadcrumb and then fry them gently in butter and oil. Drain well. Mask with a mixture of one third Béchamel and two thirds Hollandaise sauce (pages 159 and 162). Sprinkle lightly with grated Parmesan cheese. Glaze quickly under a hot grill and surround with Veal gravy (page 164).

SCALOPPA DI VITELLO ALLA 'ORLOFF'
Veal escalope with onion au gratin

Sweat 450g (1 lb) of chopped onions in butter until soft but not coloured, add a little water to help them along. Sieve them together with enough milk-soaked bread to make a thick purée. Return to the pan, add one teaspoon of tomato purée, half a teaspoon of castor sugar, salt, white pepper and bind with a little heavy cream. Simmer for a few minutes. Set aside and let cool.

Sauté four seasoned veal escalopes in butter and oil. Remove and spread them lightly with canned, Piedmontese, white truffle paste. Cover them fairly thickly with the cooled onion purée and mask with mornay sauce. Sprinkle with grated Gruyère cheese and heat through in a hot oven. Give a finishing glaze under a grill. Surround with Veal gravy (page 164), sprinkle with chopped parsley and serve hot.

SCALOPPA DI VITELLO 'SAVOIARDA'
Veal escalope with wine, cream and cheese sauce

This recipe was brought back from Switzerland and introduced to my restaurant by Carlo Avogadri, who was my executive chef for some years. Carlo is a

truly great Maître Chef de cuisine. We opened many restaurants and designed many kitchens together.

Sauté four floured, thin, seasoned escalopes of veal in butter and oil until golden. Cover them with thick slices of good cooked ham. Remove and set aside. In the same pan sauté three very finely sliced, firm, white mushrooms. Season with salt and milled black pepper. Pile them onto the escalopes. Deglaze the pan with a glass of Chambéry and a little chicken stock and reduce. Thicken with a cup of heavy cream and pour over the escalopes. Sprinkle with grated Emmenthal cheese. Warm through in a hot oven and brown lightly under a grill.

SCALOPPA DI VITELLO ALLA VALDOSTANA
Veal escalope with tongue and cheese
This is my personal variation of this dish. Sauté four thinly beaten, floured, seasoned veal escalopes in butter and oil until golden. Spread them liberally with canned white Piedmontese truffle paste – or, better still, shavings of white truffles. Place a slice of cooked tongue on each and cover with the thinnest possible slice of Fontina cheese. Dot with butter and place under a hot grill until the cheese has melted. Surround the escalopes with Veal gravy (page 164). Sprinkle with chopped parsley and serve hot.

SCALOPPINE AL LIMONE E CAPPERI
Veal scaloppines with lemon and capers
Try these tasty scaloppines the way they make them at the small, bright and easy-going Ristorante Girasole which is run so well by my old friend, Otello Scipione. It's in London's Fulham Road.

Sauté 12 thin, floured and seasoned veal scaloppines in butter and oil until golden. Add two tablespoons of well-rinsed, roughly chopped capers (or use the infinitely better salted ones), a large dessertspoon of chopped parsley and cook briskly. Place the meat on a serving dish and keep warm. Deglaze the pan with a little chicken stock and the juice of half a lemon. Pour over the scaloppines. Decorate with thin, peeled slices of lemon. Sprinkle with parsley and serve very hot.

SCALOPPINE ALLA PARTENOPEA
Veal scaloppines with tomato and cheese
Flour and fry 12 thin, seasoned veal scaloppines in butter and oil until golden. Spread them thinly with mashed anchovies. Cover them with thin slices of sautéed tomatoes, sprinkle lightly with oregano and top with thin slices of Mozzarella cheese. Place a stoned black olive on top and heat under a hot grill until the Mozzarella softens. Sprinkle lightly with chopped fresh basil.

TENERONE DI VITELLO ALLA RUSTICA
Braised breast of veal, country style
This is a winter dish. I often had it prepared at the restaurants and enjoyed watching the customers' faces as the silver domes of the carving trolleys were rolled back releasing the rich aroma. Lorenzo and Mara at their fabulous, smart San Lorenzo in Beauchamp Place, London, one of the very best Italian restaurants in London today, quite often prepare a hearty dish of rich and savoury *teneroni*.

Have ready four, 75mm (3 in) wide, pieces of veal (including the bones) cut straight across the breast. In a large heavy casserole, sauté two chopped white leeks and a crushed garlic clove in oil and butter. Remove the garlic, add the veal and brown it well. Pour in a wine glass of dry white wine, a cup of chicken stock and add a bouquet garni, one dessertspoon of tomato purée, salt and milled black pepper. Cover and braise gently in an oven for an hour.

Now add (all parboiled) eight small onions, eight whole small carrots, 50g (2 oz) of green bacon lardons. Cover and continue to simmer for up to 40 minutes. Add more stock a little at a time if necessary. Remove the meat. Skim off the risen fat from the casserole and pour the rich sauce and vegetables over the meat. Garnish with fried croûtes and serve with Risotto in bianco (page 73), buttered noodles or plainly boiled new potatoes.

VITELLO TONNATO
Cold sliced veal with tuna fish sauce
First roll and tie a 900g (2 lb) piece of leg of veal. Then pour into a saucepan a measured amount of water which will eventually cover the veal and add two wine glasses of dry white wine, one halved medium-sized onion, one cut-up celery stalk, one sliced carrot, one bay leaf, two cloves, salt and milled black pepper. Bring to the boil, skim off the froth and add the meat. Bring back to the boil, cover and simmer for two hours or until the veal is tender. Let it cool in the cooking liquor.

For the sauce mash 100g (4 oz) of tuna fish with two chopped anchovies and the yolks of two hard-boiled eggs. Sieve and drizzle in half a cup of olive oil 'mayonnaise' fashion and stir until thick. Add a teaspoon of rinsed capers, a tablespoon of lemon juice and thin the sauce with a little of the cooking liquor. Check the seasoning and add black pepper if required. The consistency should be creamy enough to mask a spoon.

Slice the veal fairly thinly, arrange it on a serving dish, cover liberally with the sauce, decorate with sliced gherkins, capers, thin lemon slices and dust with cayenne pepper. Serve with a new potato salad, sliced cucumber and radishes if in season.

Sliced cold pork and cold, boiled chicken may also be successfully served with this kind of sauce and are delicious on a hot summer's day.

CIMA DI VITELLO ALLA GENOVESE
Cold veal with savoury stuffing
This is the very good Italian stuffed-veal dish which should always be served cold. Soak, clean and cook a calves' sweetbread and brain as in the previous recipes. Chop them roughly and put them into a bowl with 100g (4 oz) of cooked peas, 25g (1 oz) of finely chopped pork fat, 25g (1 oz) of pistacchio nuts, 75g (3 oz) of cooked and drained, roughly chopped spinach, one milk-soaked, crustless slice of bread, one whole egg and one tablespoon of grated Parmesan cheese. Sweat a finely chopped, medium-sized onion and two crushed garlic cloves in oil and butter until soft, add and quickly sauté 50g (2 oz) each of minced pork and veal with a little thyme and fresh sage. Season. Discard the garlic and the herbs. Add this to the mixture in the bowl, season with salt and milled black pepper. Mix well but lightly.

Stuff the filling into a 900g (2 lb) piece of breast of veal (shaped and sewn with kitchen thread like an open bag) and insert two hard-boiled eggs down the centre. Sew up the open end. Put the veal in a large saucepan and cover it with boiling, salted water. Cover the pan and simmer gently for two hours. Skim as necessary. Let the meat cool in its own liquor under a heavy weight. Chill. Slice and serve cold. Absolutely delicious!

AGNELLO
Lamb

AGNELLO IN CASSERUOLA
Lamb casserole
Chop up two medium-sized onions, two garlic cloves, two young carrots and one tender celery stalk with the leaves. Soften them in a large casserole together with a bay leaf and a sprig of rosemary in a little lard and oil. Add 900g (2 lb) of lamb cutlets and brown them well. Stir in a

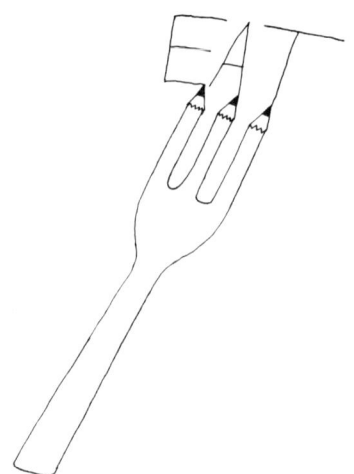

tablespoon of tomato purée and sprinkle with a dessertspoon of flour. Add 450g (1 lb) of small new potatoes, one cubed turnip and 450g (1 lb) of peas. Season with salt and milled black pepper. Pour in one and a half cups of vegetable stock. Cover the casserole and cook gently for one hour. Check the seasoning, skim off the fat and serve hot with plenty of crusty farmhouse bread.

AGNELLO ALLA ROMANA
Lamb casserole, Roman style

Some restaurant customers can be very difficult indeed. They can make the already sensitive job of a Maître d'hôtel quite impossible at times. One such customer was not only difficult, he was thoroughly unpleasant and rude, too. He was also stone-deaf. The Maître d' was fed up with him. He felt like turning the tables and making life miserable for him for a change. Without being too obviously rude, of course!

Inspiration came as the customer in question approached his table with usual bad temper. The Maître d's seemingly clear, well-mannered 'Good morning, sir' as he respectfully pulled out the chair, was totally ignored. As were the rest of his verbal preliminaries. And not only because of downright rudeness either! The grouchy old man just stared at him – a little puzzled at first. Then he angrily rapped his antique deaf-aid and, glaring, thrust it even more brusquely under the Maître d's nose, the Maître d' obligingly repeating, apparently quite distinctly, what he had just said. But it was no use.

The old man made various adjustments to the thing and, after a battery change, he totally dismantled it and eventually, as a last resort, battered it on the table. But nothing helped. He stopped and gave up the struggle. With some amount of difficulty he ordered his meal and settled back to a hateful lunch. Merely picking at his food, he was reduced to lip-reading as he looked up mystified, somewhat forlornly, at all the other waiters who had delightedly decided to increase his discomfiture by making improper inquiries after his health, his deafness, his deaf-aid and his ancestors.

At the end of that rotten meal he rose from the table and walked the gauntlet past the assembled waiters. Their 'Good day, sir', this time not silently mouthed but chorused loud and clear into the deaf-aid, must have made him jump, and wonder at his deaf-aid's abrupt return to efficiency.

I remember that old gentleman well and I recollect that his favourite luncheon dish was Irish stew spiked with pickled red cabbage. I don't have that recipe unfortunately, so here is a typical Neapolitan lamb dish instead that would have surely put that old man into a receptive mood.

Have your butcher cut a leg of very young lamb into 37mm (1½ in) thick pieces, straight through the bone. Place the meat in a baking dish with three crushed garlic cloves and dot with pure lard. Add two broken-up sprigs of rosemary. Douse with olive oil and season with salt and milled black pepper. Place the baking dish in a hot oven for 15 minutes or until the lamb has coloured well. Then add 450g (1 lb) of new potatoes and 225g (8 oz) of small peas. Moisten with a little stock. Cover and continue cooking in a moderate to hot oven for 75 minutes. Uncover for the last 20 minutes. Check the seasoning.

CARRE D'AGNELLO ALLA LIGURE
Roasted rib of lamb with Ligurian herbs

Season two nicely trimmed racks of young lamb with salt and black pepper. Dot with lard and sprinkle them with oil. Place in an oven dish containing some diced celery, carrots and onions. Moisten with a little stock and roast in a hot oven for half an hour. Spread the cutlets fairly thickly on the outside with a moist mixture of soft, white breadcrumbs, butter, chopped parsley, finely chopped shallots, thyme, rosemary and marjoram. Brown under a hot grill. Deglaze the roasting pan with half a cup of stock. Strain and pass the gravy with the lamb which should be cut into separate cutlets at the table.

COSTOLETTE D'AGNELLO IN TORTIERA
Baked lamb cutlets with potatoes

A shipment of young, tender and succulent Roman baby lamb had been ordered direct from Italy for trial in the restaurants. In no time at all a call was put through from the Air-Cargo Terminal at London's Heathrow Airport. Could the shipment please be acknowledged?

Once signed for, that was it! The authorities pulled out the regulation book and pointed out that because the lamb came from Italy it could not, under any circumstances, be released. No amount of pleading, praying or cajoling could sway the stern officials. Even bribery was briefly considered. The white-wrapped lamb was just across the counter – it looked so good, so tantalizing. The meat could either be flown straight back to Rome (at the customer's expense) or it would be burnt in the cargo terminal's own incinerator. A decision was reluctantly taken. A little later an appetizing smell of roasting baby lamb came wafting around the airport perimeter. Perhaps a little rosemary and touch of garlic would have been an improvement, but it was a good effort! What the airport personnel, whose food must be at least as abominable as that served to the paying flight passengers, thought when they smelled the delicious aroma, I don't know. But I'm sure that they were more than disappointed not to find Costolette d'agnello in tortiera on their canteen menu that lunchtime. You can, however, for here is the recipe. It's a sort of Neapolitan Lancashire hot-pot.

Liberally strew a larded oven dish with half of a mixture of one sliced, medium-sized onion, one chopped leek, one chopped garlic clove and five chopped, drained, canned tomatoes. Arrange twelve young lamb cutlets on top. Sprinkle with a little more of the vegetable mixture. Season with salt and milled black pepper. Cover the lamb with six medium-sized potatoes cut into 6mm (¼ in) slices and add the rest of the vegetable mixture. Sprinkle with a little oregano, salt and milled black pepper. Dot with lard, Add half a cup of lightly flavoured stock, cover with foil and cook in a moderate to hot oven for 45 minutes. Uncover and cook for 15 minutes more.

SCOTTADITI SACROMONTE
Grilled, marinated lamb cutlets

This is a very simple dish to make. As the Italian name implies, the cutlets may be eaten with the fingers and, indeed, if you are to enjoy the sweet meat close to the bone, they should be!

Marinate, for at least two hours, 12 small, trimmed and tender lamb cutlets in a mixture of olive oil, two crushed garlic cloves, two crushed chillies, a little bruised mint, a sprig of rosemary, one bay leaf, a little lemon juice, salt and some crushed black peppercorns. Pat the cutlets dry. Grill them until they are pink inside under a hot grill. Reserve the marinade for future use.

SPIEDINI D'AGNELLO ALLA RODIGIANA
Skewered lamb, Italo-Greek style

A famous English newspaper, the *Daily Sketch,* once canvassed some of London's so-called 'in' restaurants. One of mine won hands down! Between the hours of six thirty and midnight, the following celebrities were seen to dine there at different times: Ingrid Bergman, Leslie Caron, Danny Kaye, David Niven, Gregory Peck, Laurence Harvey, Sammy Davis Jnr, Michael Caine, Julie Christie, Terence Stamp, Carl Foreman, Pietro Annigoni, David Bailey, Jean Shrimpton. Surprisingly they missed out Ari Onassis! He was quietly sitting in an alcove with a beautiful woman, a flask of Chianti and a large can of olive oil. But maybe he preferred not to be noticed while he was enjoying a rich dish of lamb kebabs.

Marinate for at least two hours (the same marinade as in the preceding recipe) 450g (1 lb) of tender shoulder of lamb cut into medium-sized cubes. Remove and drain the pieces well. Start off four skewers with a cube of stale bread and then alternate with the lamb, pieces of peppers, blanched onion slices, bacon squares, pieces of fennel and small mushrooms. Finish with a cube of bread. Drizzle the kebabs with olive oil and cook them under a grill until the lamb is nicely pink inside. Season with salt and milled black pepper. Baste occasionally with a little of the marinade. Serve with Riso pilaff alla greca (page 73).

MAIALE
Pork

CASSEOLA ALLA MILANESE
Pork ribs and cabbage casserole

This is a typical dish from Lombardy, strong and robust as the people from that region are. It could be called a sort of 'sweet-sour kraut'. If it's a cold day outside and you have the ingredients handy, try it.

In a casserole sweat a medium-sized, chopped onion in oil until soft. Stir in four roughly chopped, drained canned tomatoes and add four pork cutlets, 450g (1 lb) of pork spare ribs and a quartered (parboiled) pigs' trotter. Now mix in a Savoy cabbage cut into wide strips, a bouquet garni of rosemary, bay leaf, a clove, dried basil, crushed garlic, salt and milled black pepper. Cook all these for a few minutes over a brisk flame. Pour in one cup of lightly flavoured vegetable stock, cover and cook slowly for one and a half hours. Add two parboiled Italian pork sausages during the last 15 minutes. You will need plenty of crusty bread or toasted French bread with this one.

COSTATA DI MAIALE CON CAVOLI ROSSI
Sautéed pork chops with red cabbage

Gently sauté four pork chops in pure lard until they are cooked and well coloured. Season with salt and black pepper and sprinkle them with the merest suggestion of fennel seeds. Remove the chops. Deglaze the pan with a little stock and red wine. Reduce and pour it over the chops. Serve them with Red cabbage (page 136) and plainly boiled potatoes.

COTECHINO CON LENTICCHIE
Boiled Italian pork sausage with lentils
Cotechino is a rather rich, pure pork sausage which needs to be boiled. It may be bought at any Italian, good continental or gourmet store. Buy one weighing just over 450g (1 lb). Soak it in abundant water for not less than three hours. Simmer it gently in plenty of water for about two and a half hours. Do not prick at any time. Let it cool slightly in the cooking liquor before slicing. Serve with Zuppa di lenticchie (page 46) which has been drained of its broth or, if you prefer, with creamy mashed potatoes or crisply cooked spinach.

Zampone, a stuffed pigs' trotter, is very similar to cotechino and should be cooked and served in a similar manner.

'KEBAB' DI MAIALE
Barbecued pork kebabs
Make a marinade with six tablespoons of liquid soy sauce, three tablespoons of oil, three level dessertspoons of brown sugar, two crushed garlic cloves, two crushed chillies, one bay leaf, salt and milled black pepper. Mix in two cubed pork fillets. Marinate them, turning often, for at least two hours. Skewer them alternately with small squares of green bacon. Grill them until nicely coloured and tender. Serve with crisp, thinly sliced cucumbers which have been salted under a heavy weight for an hour and then squeezed dry. Accompany the kebabs with Riso pilaff alla greca (page 73) or Riso alla cinese (page 74). Pass Saté dip (page 164) so that both pork and cucumber may be dunked.

MAIALE AL LATTE
Pork cooked with milk
In a large saucepan, seal 900kg (2 lb) of boned loin of pork in four tablespoons of olive oil with a crushed garlic clove and a sprig of rosemary. Season with salt and milled black pepper. Remove the garlic and the rosemary. Pour in 570ml (20 fl oz) of hot milk. Cover and simmer for one and a half hours or until the meat is tender. Let the pork rest a while before slicing. Serve with the rich gravy.

Mashed potatoes go well with this dish.

SALSICCIE CON SPINACI
Italian sausages with spinach
Michael Caine likes English banger-style sausages very much, fried and served with mashed potatoes, especially before a Chelsea home-match. I never included them on my menus so he used to order Italian sausages instead.

Italian sausages are made of 100 per cent pure pork and are therefore liable to contain quite an amount of fat. So it is advisable to prick them slightly before placing them in the frying pan. Add only a little oil, enough to start them off, as they will make their own fat. Fry them gently until nicely coloured and cooked inside. Do not season them. Serve with Spinaci passi e pinoli (page 148) or Cime di broccoli (page 134) or Patate alla Contadina (page 143).

SATÉ ALLA MALESIANA
Skewered pork strips, Malayan style
Make a marinade with six tablespoons of liquid soy sauce, three tablespoons of oil three level dessertspoons of brown sugar, two crushed garlic cloves, two crushed chillies, one bay leaf, salt and freshly milled black pepper. Cut two pork fillets lengthways into strips 10cm (4 in) long and 12mm ($\frac{1}{2}$ in) wide. Mix them into the marinade and leave for at least two hours. Turn them often. Thread the strips onto wooden Chinese saté sticks or thin metal skewers. Grill them under (and fairly close to) a hot grill. Two minutes each side will be more than enough. Do not fry or cook them on a solid broiler as this will make the saté bitter. They should be a golden colour and still moist inside. Serve with Riso alla cinese (page 74) and Saté dip (page 164). Pass a cucumber salad.

Other recipes for meat can be found in the **Antipasti** and **Pasta** sections:

Antipasti
COSTE DI MAIALE 'MARCO POLO' Barbecued spare ribs

Pasta
SALSICCIA CON POMODORI Italian sausages with tomato sauce
See Mezzani con la Salsiccia.
POLPETTINE DI MANZO AL SUGO Meatballs in tomato sauce
See Spaghetti con le Polpettine. These meatballs are quite delicious. They may be served as a substantial main course with lots of creamily whipped potatoes to soak up the marvellous sauce.

POLLAME
Poultry

ANITRA 'CESARE PIZZALA'
Duck in port and cream sauce
This dish was especially created for London's 1958 Olympia Culinary Exposition by my good friend Cesare Pizzala, Maître chef de cuisine. It won the Silver Medal of Honour. This is the first time that Cesare has allowed the recipe to be published.

Cut a 2kg 250g (5 lb) duck into eight pieces. Season with salt and black pepper. Gently cook them covered in a little butter until coloured and tender. Remember that the thighs and drumsticks will take a little longer. Set aside.

Skim off some of the fat from the cooking pan. Add a piece of bay leaf and 50g (2 oz) of chopped shallots and sweat them until soft. Pour in a quarter bottle of Pinot Grigio or any similar dry white wine and reduce it by a third. Stir in three-quarters of a cup of Veal gravy (page 164) and one and a half cups of heavy cream. Return the duck pieces together with a small teaspoon of sugar and three tablespoons of port wine. Let the sauce thicken gently.

Arrange the duck on a serving dish and cover with the sauce. Garnish with fried bread croûtes, seedless Muscat grapes, small, glazed onions and braised button mushrooms. Sprinkle with chopped parsley.

ANITRA ALLA CONCA D'ORO
Roasted honeyed duckling with oranges and chestnuts
We were all looking forward to an early night. The late-duty waiters were just itching to finish serving the few lingering parties and then get on with the whole boring *fermature* or closing-up process. Suddenly, and much to everyone's annoyance, in walked a party of four for a very late meal! It was left to the cheekiest Maître d', the one with the most experience at manoeuvring inconsiderate latecomers, to take the supper order. He must have used all his guile for, with a triumphant look, he indicated that the food order was not too complicated either for the waiters or for the one remaining, very bad-tempered French cook, of whom we were all mortally terrified in these late situations.

The waiter had convinced the late guests that their digestion and pleasure would benefit if they left the choice of the menu to him. This they had done with some reluctance. And so, whether they liked it or not, they would be eating smoked salmon and braised duckling with orange sauce to follow.

The order was taken to the kitchen with trepidation by a young hesitant Chef de rang, fearful of the customary vile-tempered reaction he was sure to receive. The late cook was, as usual, quite drunk. Tomorrow's plat du jour was probably at that moment marinating minus most of the red wine that had been left out for the purpose.

The first course was comparatively simple to produce. The duck, though, was more difficult. The two cooked and semi-frozen ducklings, as icy-looking, hard and tough as any I had ever seen, were taken from a refrigerator. With a screech of rage, the cook threw them passionately at the waiters standing curiously by the hotplate. The ducks bounced from a tiled wall with such force that they rebounded from corner to corner. They landed back at the cook's feet, as though tormenting him. He picked them up from the floor and plunged them, roughly wiped, into the boiling spluttering oil of the deep-fryer. For a few seconds they frizzled convulsively and were then finally laid to rest under the red-hot salamander. Masked with warmed-up sauce, highlighted with oranges and liqueur, they were sent out to the restaurant.

We all watched with undisguised interest from a distance. To our astonishment, to the carver's relief, and to the customers' delight, the duckling pieces fell in light, tender portions onto the dish. I swear that even the band played an exultant chord! The whole meal was pronounced to be excellent by the contented clients who sent their compliments to the kitchen. To this day I am sure they still remember those two mouth-watering Canetons à l'orange. I know that I do! Here's how you can cook your ducklings, if you are relaxed and in a good mood.

Rub two well-dried ducklings with salt, black pepper and a little oil. Roast them in the usual way in an oven dish containing some chopped onion, carrots and celery. Brush the ducks with warmed honey 15 minutes before they are ready. Remove and keep them warm.

Skim the fat from the oven pan. Sprinkle in three tablespoons of sugar and one tablespoon of malt vinegar and simmer for a few minutes. Deglaze the pan with two cups of Veal gravy (page 164). Strain the gravy and add the juice of one orange, four tablespoons of Cointreau (or Grand Marnier), one tablespoon of brandy, one tablespoon of redcurrant jelly and the blanched, finely shredded peel of one orange. Bring to the boil, thicken with a little arrowroot and simmer the sauce until the flavours are well combined. Check the seasoning. Decorate the ducklings with segments and slices of orange and eight glazed (canned) chestnuts. Pour a little of the sauce around the ducklings and pass the rest separately.

CHICKEN PIE ALL'INGLESE
English chicken pie

Whenever I used to put these marvellous individual chicken pies on my menu, I used to make sure that they went into the ovens at twelve o'clock so that they would be ready just as the majority of the main courses were being called for. The customers really loved them and they sold out in a flash. This recipe will make just one large pie for four people.

Prepare a forcemeat with eight tablespoons of fresh breadcrumbs, three tablespoons of finely chopped ham, one tablespoon of grated Parmesan, a little melted butter, one egg, a dessertspoon of chopped parsley, a little nutmeg, salt and milled black pepper. Mix well, form into little balls and roll them lightly in flour. Prepare a mixture of one finely chopped onion, one finely sliced leek, 100g (4 oz) sliced mushrooms and coarsely chopped parsley. Cover the bottom of a pie dish with half the vegetables. Wrap four whole chicken legs in thin slices of unsmoked bacon and lay them in the dish. Add the forcemeat balls and strew with the rest of the chopped vegetables. Season with salt and milled black pepper. Pour in enough chicken stock to reach three-quarters of the way up the dish and half a cup of heavy cream. Cover with your favourite pastry. Brush with beaten egg and make two slits in the centre. Bake in a moderate oven for an hour and a quarter or until the pastry is cooked and the chicken is tender.

CRESPELLE DI POLLO ALLA FIORENTINA
Chicken pancakes on spinach with mornay sauce

Make eight thin, unsweetened Pancakes (page 163) and set aside. Mix together some sliced, cooked, white chicken meat, diced ham, sautéed sliced white mushrooms, a few tablespoons of heavy cream, a little strong Veal gravy (page 164) and season with salt and milled black pepper. Heat well through. Spoon the filling onto each of the pancakes. Roll them up. Place in a well-buttered oven dish on a bed of crisply cooked spinach flavoured with softly sweated onion. Cover with Mornay sauce (page 163), sprinkle with grated Parmesan cheese and glaze in a hot oven until brown on top.

CROCCHETTE DI POLLO
Chicken croquettes

Finely chop three firm white mushrooms and sauté them in oil and butter with a little chopped shallot. Add to the pan 225g (8 oz) of cooked, chopped, white chicken meat, 150g (6 oz) chopped ham, one chopped hard-boiled egg, one dessertspoon of parsley, one tablespoon of grated Parmesan, a few dashes of Worcester sauce, salt and cayenne pepper. Cook for a few minutes.

Add enough thick, hot béchamel sauce (enriched with two egg yolks) to make the mixture just moist. Mix well and spread it onto a flat surface. Let this chill in the refrigerator for at least two hours. Form quickly into cork-shaped croquettes, flour, egg and breadcrumb them. Fry in oil until golden and well heated through. Serve with bunches of crisply fried parsley and a light tomato sauce.

FEGATINI DI POLLO ALLA SIRACUSA
Skewered, grilled chicken livers
Skewer the following onto four grilling skewers: halved chicken livers, small mushrooms, squares of streaky bacon, slices of blanched onion and small pieces of bay leaf. Finish with a small whole mushroom. Sprinkle with olive oil. Grill or sauté them slowly until nicely cooked. Season with salt and plenty of milled black pepper. Serve with Riso pilaff alla greca (page 73) and pass some Diable sauce (page 161) at the table to make them even more delicious.

FRITTO DI POLLO
Southern-Italian fried chicken
Prepare a marinade with olive oil, one bay leaf, two crushed chillies, one small sliced onion, two crushed garlic cloves, two tablespoons of lemon juice, a level dessertspoon of dry English mustard, rosemary, thyme and a few sage leaves. Mix well. Joint a young frying chicken into eight portions. Marinate for three hours, turning them often. Pat dry, flour, egg and roll them in breadcrumbs seasoned with sesame seeds and paprika. Shallow fry them slowly in oil until golden and well cooked through. Serve with Diable sauce (page 161) or a light Tomato sauce (page 164).

FRITTO DI POLLO RIFATTO
Left-over chicken fried in batter
Cut left-over cooked chicken into small uniform pieces. Flour and dip them in a light Beer batter (page 160). Shallow-fry gently in olive oil flavoured with two crushed garlic cloves, a few fresh sage leaves and a sprig of rosemary. Garnish these tasty, crisp morsels with fried bacon and potato croquettes and serve with Barbecue sauce (page 159) or a plain Tomato sauce (page 164).

GIAMBONETTO DI POLLO CON PORCINI
Braised, stuffed chicken leg
Cut through four chicken legs with a very sharp knife and remove the bones completely. Open them out flat, cut away all the sinews and nerves and beat them out slightly. Do not remove the skin. Mix together some finely minced pork, veal, ham, milk-soaked breadcrumbs, one chopped, sweated shallot, brandy, grated Parmesan, a little grated lemon peel, salt and milled black pepper. Bind moistly with a little heavy cream. You will have to decide the proportions yourself as it all depends on the size of the chickens. Stuff the chicken legs with the filling, roll and tie them tidily with kitchen twine.

In a sauteuse or similar pan, cook a little chopped onion, carrot, celery and leek in butter and oil until soft. Add and brown the stuffed chicken legs. Pour in half a cup of chicken stock and simmer or braise gently for 30 minutes. Remove the chicken and keep it warm. Deglaze the pan with a wine glass of dry white wine. Stir in a dessertspoon of tomato purée dissolved in a cup of chicken stock. Reduce a little. Check the seasoning. Thicken the sauce by stirring in small pieces of beurre manié.

Arrange the chicken legs on a serving dish. Cover them with sliced sautéed *cèpes* (or large cultivated mushrooms). Strain the sauce over them.

INSALATA DI POLLO
Chicken salad

Prepare a salad in a bowl with crisp Romaine lettuce hearts, watercress, quartered tomatoes, sliced cucumber, chopped endives, spring onions, sliced tender celery with the leaves, radishes, cold new potatoes and some cooked French beans. Sprinkle with chopped chervil and tarragon. Add thin sticks of Gruyère cheese and cooked tongue and ham. Cover with sliced cold chicken breast. Decorate with sliced hard-boiled eggs, tomatoes and cucumber. Pass or mix in a good mustardy vinaigrette. Serve chilled.

MAIONESE DI POLLO
Chicken mayonnaise

Prepare a salad in the same way as for Insalata di pollo and moisten with a little vinaigrette. Sprinkle with chopped chervil and tarragon. Cover with sliced, cold chicken breast. Mask generously with mayonnaise and decorate with sliced hard-boiled egg, tomatoes and cucumber. Sprinkle with cayenne pepper and chopped parsley.

PETTO DI POLLO SORPRESA
Rolled and stuffed chicken breast

This is, of course, nothing more than my own personal variation of that classic and famous Russian speciality with the French name Suprême de volaille à la Kiev.

The first London restaurants to feature and popularize this marvellous dish were those owned or operated by ex-Polish Army personnel who had decided at the war's end, and quite rightly, that there was no point in returning to a homeland for which they had fought so fiercely and valiantly but was now, once again, subjected to another country. Seigi's Club, Les Ambassadeurs, immediately spring to mind and, later, the Mirabelle Restaurant and the original River Club followed in the presentation and promotion of this great but comparatively simple to prepare dish.

I always considered chicken Kiev to be almost perfectly conceived. The service of it particularly intrigued me. The carefully staged incision of the plumply rolled breast almost became a 'show-biz' performance. Fascinated guests watched with delight as the hot liquid butter was suddenly released

and gushed forth. But something nagged at me. The dish, to my Italian mind, missed out on something. Could it need foie gras? White truffles, or black? Exotic Oriental spices? Suddenly, one day, it came to me. It needed garlic!

I mentally perfected the new recipe. The dish would be transformed to an Italo-Russian style. After all they renamed one of their cities 'Togliattigrad'.

My partner and I had opened our first restaurant only a short while when I asked the chef to prepare a few sample Italian chickens Kiev which were to contain the new and heathen ingredient. He, being a strict traditionalist, and one who firmly believed in never allowing progress to get in his way, flatly refused. We had a few strong words. My partner, who was not short of a few strong words of his own, chose a well-selected few, rushed to my defence and in doing so, also rushed the chef out of the kitchen and off our payroll.

The next chef was more co-operative and at last the first Italianate 'Kievs' emerged from our kitchen. They were a smash with our customers.

What to call the crispy, golden and succulent portions was my next problem. The new-style 'Kievs' were rather difficult to make at first. Their success rate was not high. I had noticed that whenever they turned out well the chef was particularly pleased. Also a little surprised. And that was it! If he was surprised then so would the chickens be! And so I baptized the now famous Petto di pollo sorpresa, nowadays so frequently copied by most other Italian restaurants.

Always try to follow a few fundamental rules when you are served a Petto di pollo sorpresa. The first is to let the waiter take command – and the risks. Let him perform, no matter how strong the temptation, the 'cutting-open' ceremony. The second is to insist on checking the keenness of his knife. The third is to be prepared to shield yourself hurriedly behind your dinner companion. If, however, you really do wish to try it yourself, then always point the breast away from yourself – or if you don't like the look of your neighbours at the next table, towards them. You will notice that they, too, when the hot molten

yellow stream of fragrant parsley-speckled butter hits them full in the face, will be just as surprised as you, the waiter, the chef and chicken have been.

This is how you can prepare the gorgeous chicken breasts. Have your butcher cut and skin four tender breasts of young chicken leaving the wing tip bone. Or you may, of course, buy them ready prepared. Carefully, without breaking the flesh, flatten them with a flat-sided mallet-cleaver – very, very thinly. Place a 50g (2 oz) conical-shaped piece of well-chilled butter which has been mixed with a little finely chopped garlic and parsley, a teaspoon of grated Parmesan cheese, salt and milled black pepper, in the centre of each piece of chicken. Roll them up tightly leaving the bone exposed rather like a handle. Seal in the butter by pressing the edges very firmly. Roll them in flour, dip in seasoned beaten egg and then carefully breadcrumb them. Deep-fry the chicken breasts in hot oil until they are cooked and golden outside with the now melted, savoury butter bursting to be released from its moist and tender prison. Serve them with Crochette di patate (page 143) or plain mashed potatoes.

PETTI DI TACCHINO ALL'EMILIANA
Turkey escalope stuffed with Parma ham

Slit four turkey-breast escalopes and insert thin slices of Parma ham into them. Flour, egg and breadcrumb them and seal well. Fry gently in butter and oil until they are cooked and golden. Remove and drain on absorbent paper. Mask with a little tomato sauce and sprinkle liberally with grated Parmesan cheese. Brown under a hot grill.

POLLASTRINO IN TEGAME
Split, sautéed baby chicken

Get your butcher to split four baby chickens from the back, cut away the whole of the backbones and flatten them slightly. Season well with salt and milled black pepper. Rub with olive oil and place them in a large, heavy, oiled pan. Brown quickly on both sides, then place a piece of wood (such as a small breadboard) over them with a very heavy weight on top. Continue to cook for about seven minutes each side over a moderate heat. Remove the chicken. Deglaze the pan with a little light chicken stock and a few dashes of Worcester sauce. Pour the gravy over the chickens. Sprinkle with chopped parsley. Serve hot with whirls of savoury butter spiked with chopped parsley, Dijon mustard, Tabasco, garlic and lemon juice.

POLLO ALL'ASTIGIANA
Chicken with cream sauce, truffled rice and grapes

Place four chicken breasts in a deep, buttered sauteuse or similar pan together with a cup each of strong chicken stock and dry white wine. Add a few slices of onion, a clove, a piece of bay leaf, salt and white pepper. Cover. Poach gently until the chicken is cooked. Remove it and keep warm.

Make a béchamel sauce, using the strained pan juices as well as milk. Smoothly blend in two egg yolks and four tablespoons of heavy cream. Heat through well. Check the seasoning. Place the chicken breasts on individual mounds of Risotto in bianco (page 73) which has been mixed with diced foie gras and chopped, black Umbrian truffles. Garnish with glazed, peeled white Muscat grapes. Mask with a little of the sauce and serve the rest separately.

POLLO AL BAROLO
Chicken in red wine sauce

Cut 100g (4 oz) of salt pork into lardons and brown them gently in oil and butter in a heavy casserole with three crushed garlic cloves. Add 16 firm button mushrooms, 16 small onions, a sliced, tender celery stalk and slowly let them colour. Remove everything and reserve for adding later.

Add eight tender chicken portions to the fat, sprinkle them with a teaspoon of sugar, add a bay leaf and a little rosemary and brown them all over. Season with salt and black pepper. Flame with a good measure of Italian grappa. Stir in a tablespoon of flour. Pour in half a bottle of Barolo red wine or any good red wine. Cover the casserole and cook for 25 minutes. Return the reserved vegetables and lardons and continue to cook, uncovered, for a further 20 minutes. Remove the chicken pieces. Skim off any excess fat. Pour the sauce and garnish over the chicken. Serve with fried bread croûtes.

POLLO ALLA CACCIATORA
Sautéed chicken with mushrooms and tomatoes

Bettina, the hat-check girl, took the telephone message and passed it to the Restaurant Manager. After some confusion in the busy kitchen, a large hamper was brought out and placed in a waiting limousine. It sped away through the dense London traffic, south towards Gatwick Airport. A private executive jet needed victualling. The owner had requested that appropriate Italian fare be served to his friends and himself during the long flight to the United States – final destination Palm Springs. I briefly considered the possibility of entering the airline catering business. I turned it down. There is only one Frank Sinatra.

Among the dishes that went aboard that plane was a large casserole of Pollo alla cacciatora. There are many different versions of this dish. Practically every Italian community has its favourite. Here's how I used to like mine.

Put into a heavy sauteuse or similar pan four portions of jointed, young, frying chicken, 25g (1 oz) of pure lard, two tablespoons of olive oil, one sliced medium-sized onion, one sprig of rosemary, four sliced mushrooms, salt and freshly milled black pepper. Toss over a brisk flame until everything has taken on a good colour. Add a wine glass of white wine and let it reduce. Now mix in 450g (1 lb) of roughly chopped, drained, canned tomatoes, half a cup of chicken stock and five bruised basil leaves (or a good pinch of dried). Stir well. Cover and simmer for 40 minutes or until the chicken is cooked. Skim off some of the risen fat. Check the seasoning. Serve with crispy, fried bread croûtes.

This is one of Italy's best known dishes. But it has always puzzled me why, instead of a nobler, more befitting game bird, the docile and rather stupid farmyard chicken was chosen by the ardent and excitable Italian hunter to be so gastronomically honoured and forever immortalized. I know that in Italy, during the game season, anything that moves lives in dire peril of never seeing the following dawn, but surely there must have been something more valid around the day that they invented this delicious dish!

POLLO ALLA LIVORNESE
Casseroled, lemon-flavoured chicken

Stuff a 1kg 350g (3 lb) roasting chicken with half a good-sized lemon, 50g (2 oz) of butter, salt and milled black pepper. Rub the outside with salt and black pepper. Brown it quickly all round in a casserole in butter and oil together with two crushed garlic cloves. Add a cup of chicken stock with just a squeeze of lemon added, and a tablespoon of chopped parsley. Cover and cook for 40 minutes or until the chicken is tender. Baste occasionally. Remove the garlic. Carve the chicken into portions. Skim off the risen fat and serve the pan juices just as they are.

POLLO ALLA MAYFAIR
Chicken, cream sauce and rice fritters

In a sauteuse or similar pan, sauté 225g (8 oz) of sliced, new carrots and two sliced white parts of leeks in butter and oil until lightly coloured. Remove the vegetables and set aside. Add four chicken portions to the pan and colour well all over. Pour in one cup of chicken stock. Return the vegetables with a small piece of bay leaf and half a teaspoon of grated lemon rind. Season with salt and milled black pepper. Cover and simmer for 30 minutes or until the chicken is tender. Remove the chicken pieces and set them on crispy Fritelle di riso (page 73). Skim off the fat, reduce the pan juices and press through a sieve. Blend in a cup of Hollandaise sauce (page 162) and two tablespoons of heavy cream. Check the seasoning. Heat the sauce well and pour over the chicken. Serve hot.

POLLO ALLA SERPENTARIA
Chicken with brandy and tarragon sauce

We called him Josh. He was the First Head Waiter, second-in-charge to the Restaurant Manager. And he drank a lot. He was nearly six feet tall, with a head that was curiously too small for his large frame. He seemed to have no neck at all, just a large, round, white, stiffly starched wing-collar and black bow tie. His face was quite red, tinged with purple. As though he was constantly under a blinding light, his eyes were permanently screwed into a fierce squint – and he had the flattest feet that I have ever seen.

While leading customers to their tables, he would, stiff-fronted shirt bulging, ponderously sway from side to side like some enormous duck. And having completed the journey, with a grunt of satisfaction, he would turn, give a few gruff instructions to the waiter and slowly retrace his steps to his reception desk. There, more parties would be waiting their turn for the solemn pilgrimage to their table.

Despite his somewhat bad-tempered appearance, Josh was a kindly man. He was always prepared to raise anonymously the meagre wage of a young, hard-working commis or to lend a few pounds to someone in need; to scrutinize severely but fairly the tronc share-out, generously arranging a few more points here and there, stoutly defending the weaker ones from the bullies; generally to try to make life easier all round. Contrary to the selfish habits of most of the other first head-waiters who preferred to snigger at the misfortunes of a station in trouble with its service, Josh would always give a helping hand. Quietly and unobtrusively, he would serve some complicated dish or other and, with a grunt, would quietly sway away. But one never thanked Josh for his help. He would have been terribly embarrassed, as though these acts of kindness belied his supposed toughness.

The effects of the bottle of gin that he always brought to work would, as time passed, inevitably begin to make themselves felt. His reflexes would slow to such an extent that his physical and oral capabilities would start to resemble those of a slow-running sound film. When he reached this stage and, for some reason, was obliged to take a party's dinner order personally, he would recommend not a dish that he was particularly fond of himself, nor indeed one that was a house speciality, but a dish that he found phonetically more convenient to articulate. His favourite (he had only a few at that time of night) was Poulet de grain à l'estragon. This one he had practised over the years and had mastered the syllables. He would pronounce the name slowly and deliberately and follow it up with a carefully rehearsed, memorized narration of the ingredients and method of preparation, suitably accompanied by eloquent gestures.

It sometimes became awkward for Josh when an inattentive customer would casually ask him to repeat what he had just said. He would break into a cold sweat, his carefully composed façade crumpling. Squinting frantically, he would mutter thickly to the host that he had just remembered something important (probably his bottle of gin) and hurriedly signal one of us over to take charge of the situation.

Towards the end of the dinner service, his bottle nearly empty, he would stand by his now peaceful reception desk and settle contentedly to sway back and forth while waiting for closing time. His eyes narrowed to focus for the bare three or four feet necessary to recognize the departing guests to whom he would mumble a sincere good night.

The rhythmic ebb and flow of his swaying was a tremendous aid to Josh, for it helped to create the illusion that not only was he murmuring a polite good night but, at the same time, was also actually bowing them out. His pendulum-like movements could be a little tricky on occasions, especially if a departing group consisted of more than six people. His oscillations, as the guests passed him, became more pronounced and more and more perilous. We always watched with some amount of concern. We needn't have worried! Josh, with the experience of many bottles of gin behind him and countless nights like these, had learned to defy gravity – never did we see him lean past the point of no return.

Josh became my good friend. Many were the glasses that we took together as we came to know each other better. He has been dead for many years now. As one would expect, he died from excessive drinking. But he is still well remembered and that's some consolation. I raise my glass now to an unforgettable character and gentleman – Josh! He would appreciate that.

Here is the recipe for his so well-pronounced chicken dish. It is really a very good way of preparing chicken and is not as expensive as it might sound. In Italian it is known as Pollo alla serpentaria.

Spread an oven casserole with three chopped shallots, a small piece of chopped leek and a small piece of chopped celery with the leaves. Pour in one cup of chicken stock. In a separate pan season the inside of a 1kg 350g (3 lb) chicken with salt and

freshly milled black pepper and colour it well in butter and oil. Pour off the fat into the casserole. Stuff the chicken with a 50g (2 oz) piece of butter mixed with a dessertspoon of chopped tarragon. Transfer the bird to the casserole. Flame with a good measure of brandy. Cover and place it in a moderate to hot oven for 40 minutes or until the chicken is cooked and tender. Baste it fairly often.

Remove and keep the chicken warm. Skim off the fat and strain the pan juices, pressing out the vegetables gently. Add another dessertspoon of chopped fresh tarragon and four tablespoons of good strong Veal gravy (page 164). Let the sauce reduce a little. Thicken it with a good-sized walnut of beurre manié. Decorate the chicken with a blanched sprig of tarragon and mask it with a little of the sauce. Serve the rest at the table separately.

Serve with tiny, plainly cooked, buttered new potatoes and a crisp, Belgian endive salad with a light vinaigrette.

POLLO 'VIA APPIA'
Split, grilled and flamed chicken
Sam Spiegel, that great movie producer with all the Academy Awards, had just finished dinner. He was talking business with his guest and was waiting for coffee to be served. A young couple decided to wait for their table downstairs instead of at the bar. I gave them a couple of complimentary drinks and left them at the bottom of the spiral staircase. A while later I went back down. There was Sam Spiegel, his spectacles characteristically perched high on his brow, talking and drinking coffee in the most relaxed and natural way while sitting with his guest on the staircase. The two young people he had so generously ceded his table to were raising their glasses and smiling over to a real gentleman. Mr Spiegel is fond of grilled chicken. This is how I prepared it for him.

Get your butcher to split a 1kg 350g (3 lb) chicken from the back, cut away the whole backbone and flatten the bird well. Marinate it for at least two hours in the same marinade as for Fritto di pollo (page 121). Drain it. Place it in an oven dish. Seal each side under a very hot grill. Lower the heat and cook for 20 minutes each side or until the chicken is tender, golden and crisp. Place it on a large serving dish and surround it with a large crown made of bay leaves. Sprinkle both the chicken and the leaves with Italian grappa. Flame it at the table. Let the aromatic fumes penetrate the bird. Extinguish the flames, carve into suitable portions and serve with Diable sauce (page 161).

SOVRANA DI POLLO 'BELGRAVIA'
Chicken with whisky and cream sauce
In a sauteuse or similar pan, gently sweat, in butter and oil, six heaped tablespoons of mixed, very finely chopped celery, carrots, shallots, cucumber and leeks. Add four skinned, slightly flattened chicken breasts. Season with salt and white pepper. Pour in a cup of chicken stock and cover. Poach them slowly, adding more stock if required, until cooked. Remove the chicken and set aside. Reduce the pan juices and flame with a liberal measure of Scotch whisky. Swirl in one cup of heavy cream and let the sauce gently thicken. Check the seasoning. Pour it, unstrained, over the chicken. Serve with fried bread croûtons.

SOVRANA DI POLLO 'MARC ANTONIO'
Curried chicken with egg-plant
Sweat one chopped, medium-sized onion and half of a chopped cooking-apple in butter and oil until soft. Mix in a tablespoon of curry powder, a level dessertspoon of flour and a teaspoon of tomato purée. Pour in two cups of chicken stock and add a dessertspoon of dessicated coconut. Season with salt and milled black pepper. Simmer for 20 minutes. Blend in two tablespoons of heavy cream.

Meanwhile, gently fry four floured, seasoned, skinned and slightly flattened chicken breasts in butter and oil until tender. Place in a serving dish and cover them with curry sauce. Serve with fried egg-plant and Riso alla cinese (page 74) or Riso pilaff (page 73). Pass mango chutney at the table.

SOVRANA DI POLLO ALLA VESUVIO
Chicken escalope with egg-plant
I devised this dish on the spur of a desperate moment. The restaurant was crowded with early pre-theatre diners and I was trying to take the dinner order from a young couple who just could not make up their minds. An idea struck me. I had just placed on the bay-window buffet a large platter of Melanzane alla Parmigiana, layered egg-plant 'Parma' style. I told the would-be diners that I would prepare something new and entirely original for them.

I took the dish back into the kitchen and asked the chef to golden-fry two breaded chicken escalopes. These I topped with similarly shaped slices of the savoury egg-plants, moistened them with a little more tomato sauce, sprinkled over some shredded basil leaves and grated Parmesan. Gratinéed under a hot salamander, the result was very appetizing indeed. This, after all, was merely a simple marriage of two popular Italian dishes. The young customers found it quite delicious. They asked me what I would call this new dish. As I could see a reflection in the long mirror opposite me of the glowing mural of the Bay of Naples, I replied unhesitatingly Sovrana di pollo alla Vesuvio.

Flour, egg and breadcrumb four skinned, flattened chicken breasts. Fry them in butter and oil until golden. Drain well. Cover them with egg-dipped, fried slices of egg-plant and strew with torn fresh basil leaves. Cover with tomato sauce. Top with thin slices of Mozzarella and sprinkle with grated Parmesan. Place under a hot grill until the cheese begins to melt. Serve very hot.

This dish may also be prepared with veal escalopes, de-nerved and flattened chicken drumsticks, slices of turkey breast, pork cutlets and young, tender lamb steaks.

CACCIAGIONE
Game

CAPRIOLO AL PEPE
Venison with pepper sauce
Marinate eight 12mm (½ in) thick slices of venison fillets for 48 hours in red wine, brandy, one chopped onion, a celery stalk, two carrots, thyme, one bay leaf, one clove, one crushed garlic clove, salt and a dessertspoon of crushed black peppercorns.

Pat the fillets dry and rub them well with crushed black peppercorns and a little thyme. Sauté them to the required degree in butter and oil. Season with salt, remove and set them on fried, crisp croûtes. Deglaze the pan with half a cup of the strained marinade, a small wine glass of Madeira wine and reduce a little. Add a dessertspoon of malt vinegar and one of redcurrant jelly. Swirl in one cup of heavy cream and gently let the sauce thicken. Check the seasoning. Pour the sauce over the venison, sprinkle with chopped parsley and serve hot.

COSTOLETTE DI CAPRIOLO CON CAVOLI ROSSI
Venison cutlets with red cabbage
Como is the old capital of the rich, northern Italian province of the same name. Magnificently surrounded by mountains, it is splendidly situated on the shores of beautiful Lake Como itself. Ask anyone living in Como whether they know of the Pizzala brothers and you will almost certainly detect a flicker of recognition. The same will happen in Spotorno, the attractive Ligurian beach resort

where they ran the very successful Villa Teresina. For wherever they go, they leave the indelible stamp of their personalities. That's the kind of people they are.

I have known the brothers for many years and had worked with Antonio at Hatchett's Restaurant, in London's Piccadilly. I was pleased, therefore, when they decided to come to London to open a restaurant and join the vibrant Sixties scene. They took over the Mitre, a famous old City of London pub, and entrusted the design work to Enzo Apicella who, using his rare talents with much imagination, gave the premises such an elegance that I have always considered it to be his best work.

The grand opening of the smart new Ristorante Pizzala was an important event as it marked the establishment of the finest eating-house in that part of London. The Ristorante Pizzala as such is no more. The brothers sold out and returned to their beloved Lago di Como for a well-earned rest.

Here is one of the dishes that their clients loved. Sweat 75g (3 oz) of chopped bacon in lard together with an onion (studded with five cloves) and two whole carrots. Stir in 1kg 575g (3½ lb) of julienned, cored red cabbage with a chopped cooking apple and a bouquet garni. Season with salt and milled black pepper. Add a 225g (8 oz) piece of bacon, half a bottle of red wine and one cup of vegetable stock. Cover and cook for 45 minutes. Discard the onion, the carrots and the bouquet. Slice the bacon and set aside with the cabbage.

Marinate 12 well-trimmed venison cutlets in the same marinade as in the preceding recipe for at least 48 hours. Pat dry and flour. Brown them in oil in a casserole with the drained marinade vegetables. Pour in two cups of the strained marinade and half a cup of vegetable stock. Season with salt and milled black pepper. Cover and simmer for an hour or until the meat is tender.

Arrange the cutlets on a serving dish together with the sliced bacon and surround with the red cabbage. Press the casserole contents through a sieve. Return to the casserole and add a dessertspoon of arrowroot dissolved in a small wine glass of Italian grappa. Simmer until the sauce thickens and serve it separately at the table.

FAGIANO ALL'ITALIANA
Pheasant Italian style

Cut two young pheasant (reserve the drumsticks for another use) into portions. Brown them in butter and oil together with a chopped medium-sized onion, a chopped carrot, two chopped slices of streaky bacon, salt and milled black pepper. Sprinkle with flour, add a wine glass of red wine and a cup of vegetable stock. Stir well. Cover and simmer for 40 minutes or until tender over a medium flame. Arrange the pheasant portions on slices of crispy fried bread croûtes. Reduce the pan juices. Check the seasoning and pour the sauce over the pheasant. Sprinkle with parsley.

FARAONA ARROSTO
Roasted guinea fowl

Rub a good-sized guinea fowl well with salt and plenty of milled black pepper. Put 100g (4 oz) of butter, a few juniper berries, a crushed garlic clove and a little rosemary inside the bird. Cover it with thin slices of green streaky bacon. Roast it with butter and oil for about 50 minutes or until cooked. Remove the bacon 15 minutes before the end. Keep the bird warm. Skim the fat from the pan and add a small wine glass of dry Marsala and half a cup of chicken stock. Bring to the boil. Strain and thicken the gravy by stirring in a small piece of beurre manié until smooth. Pass the hot sauce separately at the table.

FARAONA ALLA SMITANA
Guinea fowl with sour cream sauce

Season a good-sized guinea fowl with salt and milled black pepper. Put a large piece

of butter and half a lemon inside the bird. Brown it well in butter in a heavy casserole. Cover and cook for 30 minutes, basting often. Add four sliced, firm, white mushrooms and continue to cook for a further 15 minutes or until the bird is tender. Remove it together with the mushrooms and set aside.

Skim off most of the fat and sweat one large, finely chopped onion in the casserole juices until soft. Pour in a wine glass of dry white wine and reduce it well. Blend in one and a half cups of heavy cream and sharpen with lemon juice. Check the seasoning and press through a sieve. Mask the guinea fowl with a little of the sauce.

PERNICE CON CAVOLI
Partridge and cabbage casserole

It is strange that it was the Neapolitans, who, in general, neither like nor appreciate most game dishes, who introduced, the partridge to France.

Flour two plump partridges and brown them quickly in lard in an oven casserole together with two coarsely chopped slices of unsmoked bacon. Meanwhile, parboil a young cabbage, drain and quarter it and place it in the casserole around the two birds. Add two sliced carrots and a bouquet garni made with a piece of celery, a clove, a bay leaf and parsley. Season with salt and milled black pepper. Pour in one cup of red wine and one cup of vegetable stock. Cover the casserole and cook gently in a moderate oven for an hour. Then add a 450g (1 lb) piece of parboiled unsmoked bacon and two good-sized pieces of Polish garlic sausage. Recover the casserole and continue to cook for a further hour. Remove the bouquet garni.

Cut the birds in half, slice the bacon and the sausage and arrange them with the cabbage piled high in a serving dish. Deglaze the casserole with a little stock and pour the gravy over the dish.

QUAGLIE DI VIGNA 'BACCHUS'
Split cooked quails

The young commis, bearing an enormous silver domed dish, staggered out of the kitchen and over to Gene's crowded station. The main course for an important party of eight seated at the large round table had arrived, at precisely the wrong moment! Gene, his mind a crazy whirl of different orders, was very busy. While he blessed the fact that the guests at the large table had considerably helped matters by deciding to order the same main course, he wished that his commis had delayed things.

Gene was forbidden, as we all were, to serve the food from the silver 'flats' directly onto the customers' plates. That was considered to be an inferior form of service. And yet the main course had to be served. His commis was beginning to wilt at the knees under the heavy burden and the food wasn't getting any warmer.

Firmly settling the monstrous dish along his left arm, Gene ordered his commis to place the hot dinner plates in front of each guest. House Rule Number One was duly broken. With an extravagant flourish Gene removed the silver cover and presented the eight dark and beautifully roasted grouse to the host who, deep in conversation, nodded his approval. Gene shot a final glance around the restaurant. Reassured, he proceeded to break Rule Number Two by serving the plump birds in the prohibited manner. He swiftly served first the guest of honour, a lady, and then the others. He soon completed the full round of the table. So far so good. He hadn't been spotted. When he reached the host, his spoon and fork, which had been moving mechanically and rapidly from dish to bird to plate, faltered. At first his reaction was one of disbelief. The last grouse was no longer there! Gene stood his ground. There had been eight grouse for, following routine, he had automatically counted them.

Gene pulled himself together. He shot a panoramic glance at the floor around him. It wasn't there. Then, by pure chance, he happened to peer down the back of the guest of honour's chair. And there it was, nestling comfortably in the lush folds of the silk evening-coat. Gene moved in with the speed of a hawk. His pincered spoon and fork descended and scooped the grouse back onto the dish. With a graceful movement, he served it to the still talking, unsuspecting host.

The mutinous bird, now resting safely on a crispy croûte, suitably garnished with watercress, was none the worse for its experience. The fact that it had left a greasy stain on a very expensive coat and that it had, in the space of a few seconds, considerably aged Gene was of no importance now.

As I rarely served grouse at the restaurants (I personally hate them), no relevant recipe follows. Here is a simple recipe for grilled quails instead. Stuff eight small quails with a piece of butter, a tip of garlic, a little rosemary and season them with salt and milled black pepper. Wrap them in thin slices of lard or unsmoked bacon and skewer together. Place them under a moderately hot grill or in a moderate to hot oven and turn them evenly until they are cooked. Remove the lard or bacon towards the end of the cooking time and let them brown nicely. Serve on fried polenta or crispy, fried, bread croûtes together with Insalata alla Cesare (page 140).

LEGUMI E VERDURE
Vegetables & Salads

Vegetables are grown with extraordinary care by almost the entire British nation. They are planted, watched and tended with loving dedication. Their progress is followed with interest by passersby and neighbours. They are discussed at home or in the pub at length, comparisons are made and bets wagered. At last they are picked or cut and taken proudly home where they are promptly destroyed by appalling cooking, regardless of all good advice.

Of necessity, the British, who do not usually have a pasta or substantial first course at meals, invariably rely on a regular root and green vegetable garnish for bulk and so still retain the traditional 'two-veg' mentality. Italians, therefore, as they do not seem to place vegetables in any particular menu order, may sometimes be considered by the Anglo-Saxons to be rather casual vegetable consumers.

Vegetables are well loved, however, in Italy. The dishes are so well prepared and so versatile that, at meals, they are eaten before, in the middle, at the end and even instead of! This can be confusing to explain, especially when compiling an Italian vegetable recipe index. The various dishes can often be equally suitable as antipasti, first courses, mixed with pasta or rice, as garnishes, accompaniments, substantial main courses and, raw or cooked, in salads.

Italy abounds with splendid, beautifully tended vegetables and herbs that constantly fill the bustling, glowing markets. It is always a grand sight to see the seasonal selection loaded onto carts and stalls or proudly displayed in the covered market arcades or open-fronted shops – an almost bewildering profusion of shape and beauty in many different colours.

You will find that some of the recipes in this book call for the use of truffles and, because they come from the ground, I have included them in this section. Fresh truffles are very, very expensive, and often unobtainable. But do try to buy black Umbrian truffle parings or delicious white Piedmontese truffle paste which are both available in small cans. They are fairly expensive but are good and do retain some of the elusive, tantalizing truffle flavour.

Brillat Savarin, the famous French gourmet and author of the classic *La physiologie du goût,* once mortally wounded Italian pride by relegating the divine Piedmontese white truffle to second place behind the French black variety – which, in my opinion, is coarser and inferior – having detected, as though he were the first, a faint hint of garlic in its taste and perfume. He was indeed quite right. There is that faint hint of garlic. But – he should have awarded extra marks for an additional fragrant quality! Neither did he consider the theory that Piedmontese white truffles, along with artichokes, asparagus, caviar, oysters and zabaglione, are supposed to have potent aphrodisiac properties. But then I suppose Brillat Savarin was only interested in food!

I personally find the flavour of vegetables and salads prepared *all'italiana* so good that I very often ask for extra helpings and find myself almost completely ignoring the accompanying meat. As vegetables contain all the essentials for a well-balanced diet, I do believe that I could very easily become a vegetarian, especially if I could find a vegetarian restaurant that offered properly prepared Italian-style vegetable and pasta dishes.

CIME DI BROCCOLI
Broccoli leaves

Cook 900g (2 lb) of young broccoli leaves in very little salted, boiling water until barely tender. Drain well. Sauté, in a deep pan, three crushed garlic cloves in four tablespoons of olive oil until golden. Plunge in the broccoli tops (stand back from any spitting and spluttering) and add two roughly chopped chillies, salt and milled black pepper to taste. Toss for a few minutes, remove the garlic and the chillies and serve hot.

Broccoli (or turnip) leaves prepared this way are very good when served with plainly cooked fish or meats and more especially with pork sausages.

CARCIOFI ALLA APPIANA
Fried globe-artichokes

For this method you can only use very young, early season artichokes. These can often be so tender that they may be eaten raw. So if you are reading this recipe in the autumn and you have an irresistible urge to eat artichokes in this way, I am afraid that you will have to wait for spring to come and when it does, to the relief of us all, this is how you can prepare them.

Cut the stalks and part of the bottoms from eight small spring artichokes. Ruthlessly pull off all the outside leaves until you come to the really tender inner ones. With a sharp knife cut off their tops, trim all round and cut away any choke there may be. Slice them lengthways into thin segments. Soak for an hour in cold water to which you have added the juice of half a lemon and mixed in a tablespoon of flour. Drain and dry well. Flour and dip the artichokes in seasoned, beaten eggs and fry them slowly in olive oil until golden. Drain well on absorbent paper.

CARCIOFI ALLA 'CESARA'
Sautéed globe-artichokes

Prepare eight young spring artichokes in the same manner as for Carciofi alla appiana. Quarter them and rub well with the cut side of a lemon. Place them in a heavy sauteuse together with two chopped garlic cloves, one tablespoon of coarsely chopped parsley, salt and milled black pepper. Douse them abundantly with olive

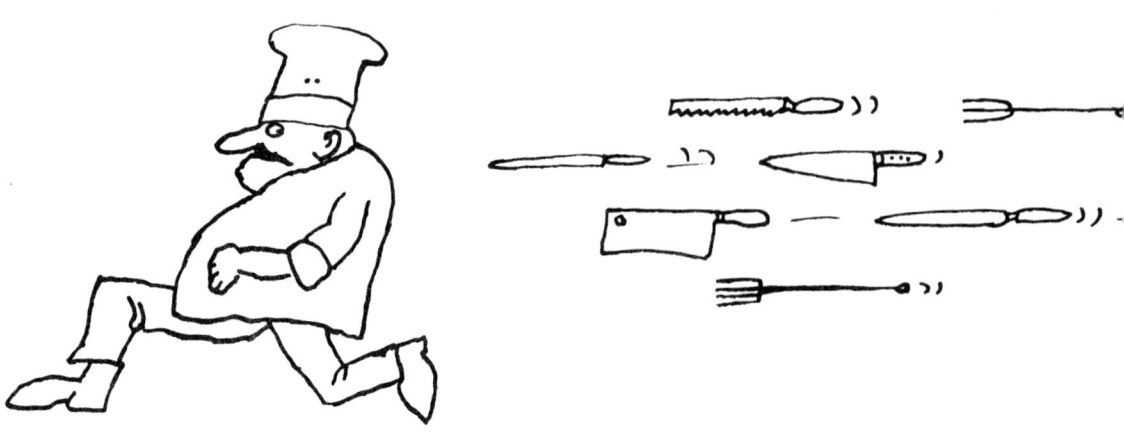

oil and cook slowly until tender. Should they run dry during cooking or begin to stick to the pan, add a little hot water and olive oil.

SAUTÉ DI CARCIOFI E PATATE
Sautéed globe-artichokes with potatoes
This is a great dish—artichokes and potatoes are perfect when cooked together. Follow the directions for Carciofi alla Cesara but add 450g (1 lb) of small new potatoes (or cut some down to size) and a cup of cold water at the start and double the quantities of parsley, garlic and olive oil. Should they run dry or stick to the pan, add a little hot water and olive oil.

CAROTE ALLA CREMA
Carrots in cream sauce
Cut 450g (1 lb) of young carrots into 6mm ($\frac{1}{4}$ in) slices. If they are old, parboil them first, or if they are really tiny leave them as they are. Place them in a heavy sauteuse or similar pan with one tablespoon of butter, one level dessertspoon of sugar, salt and milled black pepper and barely cover them with water. Cover the pan and simmer for 20 minutes or until the carrots are tender and the liquid is opalescent and syrupy. Blend in four tablespoons of heavy cream, gently reheat and serve hot.

CAROTE ALLA VICHY
Carrots Vichy style
These are cooked in precisely the same way as Carote alla crema (above) but this time omit the cream and, if possible, use genuine Vichy water for the cooking. Sprinkle with chopped parsley before serving.

BEIGNETS DI CAVOLFIORE
Fried cauliflorets
Cook the florets from a medium-sized cauliflower in boiling, salted water until barely tender and drain well. Dip them into a light Beer batter (page 160) and fry them in hot oil until golden and crisp.

CAVOLFIORE AL FORMAGGIO
Cauliflower with cheese
Don't worry. I wouldn't presume to bring 'coals to Newcastle' by giving another version of the British cauliflower cheese. It is so beloved all over the country that I am quite sure that everyone knows the recipe. But do take note of these cauliflower recipes: they are different and do make a change!

Parboil the florets from a medium-sized cauliflower. Drain them well and sauté in 50g (2 oz) of butter until golden. Season with salt and black pepper. Sprinkle two dessertspoons of grated Parmesan cheese over the dish and serve hot.

FRITTELLE DI CAVOLFIORE
Cauliflower fritters
Parboil the florets of a medium-sized cauliflower. Chop them roughly, put them in a bowl and add one whole beaten egg and one egg yolk, a tablespoon of flour, one tablespoon of grated Parmesan cheese, salt and milled black pepper. Mix well. Spoon the mixture into hot oil and fry slowly in small fritter shapes until golden. Drain well and serve hot.

CAVOLINI DI BRUXELLES CON LA PANCETTA
Brussels sprouts sautéed with bacon
Cook 450g (1 lb) of small young Brussels sprouts until barely tender and drain them well. Sweat two chopped slices of streaky bacon together with a small, finely sliced onion in oil until soft. Add the sprouts and toss them around until they glisten with the bacon fat. Season with salt and milled black pepper. Serve hot.

CAVOLINI DI BRUXELLES AL SALTO
Brussels sprouts sautéed with garlic
Cook 450g (1 lb) of young Brussels sprouts until just tender in salted, boiling water. Drain them well. Sauté two crushed garlic cloves and one crushed chilli in four

tablespoons of olive oil until golden. Add the cooked sprouts and toss them until they glisten. Season with salt and milled black pepper. Remove the garlic and serve hot.

CAVOLO ALLA LOMBARDA
Cabbage Lombardy style
Discard the outer leaves and the core from a medium-sized Savoy cabbage and cut it into wide strips. Sweat a finely sliced, medium-sized onion and two crushed garlic cloves in olive oil until soft. Add 450g (1 lb) of drained, roughly chopped, canned tomatoes, four bruised basil leaves, one roughly chopped chilli, salt and milled black pepper. Stir in the cabbage. Cover the pan and simmer for about 40 minutes. Check the seasoning. If it appears to be too liquid, cook uncovered for the last ten minutes.

If you add a piece of Polish ring sausage, some Frankfurters and a few slices of boiled bacon in the last ten minutes, and if you serve the result with plainly boiled potatoes, you will have a delicious and easy main course.

CAVOLO ROSSO AL VINO
Red cabbage with apples and wine
Discard the tough outer leaves and core of a young red cabbage and cut into wide strips. In a saucepan, heat two tablespoons of lard and toss the cabbage until it glistens. Add half a wine glass of red wine, two tablespoons of sugar and one sliced cooking apple. Season with salt and milled black pepper. Cover and cook gently for about 40 minutes. Remove the cover for the last ten minutes.

This cabbage is very good with roast pork, pork chops and sausages. Indeed, it gives a tremendous lift to any plain meat dish.

CETRIOLO ALLA CREMA
Cucumbers in cream sauce
Cucumbers always remind me of two things: the flavour and moist crispness of sandwiches at tea-time and the quite incredibly delicate Poulet aux concombres that is prepared at Maxim's restaurant in Paris. But if you can't make it to Paris, then try these cucumbers in cream sauce with some plain roast chicken instead.

Peel and slice, not too thinly, two medium-sized cucumbers. Cook them gently in a large pan in butter until tender. Season with salt and milled black pepper. Swirl in a cup of heavy cream and let the sauce thicken. Sprinkle lightly with chopped tarragon or dill. Serve hot.

CICORIA BELGA ALLA CREMA
Belgian endives in cream sauce
Cook eight trimmed, medium-sized Belgian endives in salted water and a little lemon juice until tender. Drain well. Season with salt and black pepper. Range them in a serving dish and cover with a hot béchamel sauce blended with five tablespoons of heavy cream and a pinch of dill. Serve hot.

CICORIA BELGA ALLA MUGNAIA
Belgian endives sautéed in butter
Place eight trimmed, medium-sized Belgian endives in a large frying pan with two tablespoons of butter and sprinkle with lemon juice. Season with salt and milled black pepper. Cover and simmer, turning often, until tender and golden coloured. Sprinkle with chopped parsley. Surround with Veal gravy (page 164) and serve hot.

CIPOLLE AL FORNO
Baked onions
Remove the dry flaky leaves from four medium-sized onions, wipe them clean and place them in a very slow oven for about two and a half hours (or you may cook them in foil as you might baked potatoes). When the onions are tender, remove the outer skin layers and serve them hot on side plates. Pass a dressing of olive oil, malt vinegar, salt and freshly milled black pepper.

CIPOLLE GRATINATE
Onions au gratin

Peel three very large Spanish onions and cut them into 18mm (¾ in) thick slices. Range them in a heavy pan, season with salt and milled black pepper and cover with a little lightly flavoured vegetable stock. Dot with butter and simmer until tender. Lift them out carefully and arrange in a gratin dish. Swirl one cup of heavy cream into the pan juices and let the sauce thicken. Check the seasoning. Pour the sauce over the onions. Sprinkle with mixed grated Parmesan and Cheddar cheeses. Glaze under a hot grill. Sprinkle with chopped parsley for decoration and serve immediately.

CIPOLLE ALLA RONCHESE
Baked onion and beetroot salad

Bake two large onions as for Cipolle al forno. Peel off the outside skins and cut them into neat segments. Mix with an equal quantity of sliced cooked beetroot. Season with salt and milled black pepper and dress with olive oil and vinegar. Allow to stand for a while before serving. Serve warm or cold.

FAGIOLI ALLA ETRUSCA
Haricot beans with sage

With my first small restaurant doing capacity business, more help was required, and quickly. Of the right calibre too! Alvaro Maccioni, who had been a commis waiter at London's exclusive Mirabelle Restaurant, was at that time employed as Manager of the Café Royal, Wimbledon Common. He was in the habit of coming in with his wife for a meal and a chat on his day off.

One evening, rushed as I was, I half-seriously asked him whether he would take a step-back and become a plain waiter once more. At first he merely smiled his toothy grin and didn't even bother to consider my offer. But when I told him how much my table waiters were making a week, Alvaro, being a good mathematician, made a rapid calculation and an even faster decision. He got up, took off his jacket, cleared his own table, stood to attention and asked 'When do I start?' The very next day he was wearing the restaurant's distinctive T-shirt and waiting at the tables.

Alvaro didn't, I am glad to say, last very long as a waiter. Within a matter of weeks he was promoted to the position of Manager (the restaurant's first) and he stayed for some years. Later he left to open a small, very popular restaurant in swinging King's Road, Chelsea, made a small fortune, opened a large private members' club, did marvellous business and then sold the whole lot. Only to open two more! – I Paparazzi in Soho and La Famiglia in Chelsea, and both very good they are too. This is a recipe that Alvaro, a true Tuscan, often likes to serve as an accompaniment to some of his main courses.

Soak 225g (8 oz) of white Italian cannellini beans overnight. Drain, rinse well and simmer them in unsalted water for two hours or until tender. In a separate saucepan, sauté four crushed garlic cloves in six tablespoons of olive oil until they are a light golden colour. Stir in one tablespoon of tomato purée and add the cooked beans together with a little of their cooking liquor and ten fresh bruised sage leaves. Season with salt and milled black pepper and simmer gently for 20 minutes. Stir often. Discard the garlic. If it is too sharp, sprinkle in a little sugar. Serve hot.

FAGIOLINI ALL'AGLIO
French beans sautéed with garlic

Cook 450g (1 lb) of topped and tailed young French beans until barely tender. Drain well. Sauté two crushed garlic cloves in six tablespoons of olive oil until golden. Add the beans and toss them until they glisten and have absorbed the flavours. Season with salt and milled black pepper. Remove the garlic. Serve very hot.

FAGIOLINI FRITTI
Crisp, fried French beans
Top and tail 450g (1 lb) of very young French beans and cook in a little salted boiling water until barely tender. Drain well and cool. Dip them in milk and in seasoned flour, shake off any excess and deep fry in very hot oil until crisp. Sprinkle with salt. Serve immediately.

FAGIOLINI ALLA PANCETTA
French beans with bacon
Cook 450g (1 lb) of French beans until barely tender and drain them well. Divide into small bunches and wrap each bunch up in a thin slice of blanched streaky bacon. Place in a baking dish. Season with salt and milled black pepper, dot with butter, cover with foil and finish cooking in a medium to hot oven. Serve hot.

FAVE STUFATE
Sautéed broad beans
Cook 675g (1½ lb) of young, shelled broad beans (or frozen ones) in unsalted boiling water. Drain them well. Sweat one finely chopped, medium-sized onion together with two chopped slices of streaky bacon in butter and oil until soft. Add the broad beans, season with salt and freshly milled black pepper and heat gently through. Serve hot.

FINOCCHI FRITTI
Fried fennel
Trim the tops and bottoms and remove the outer layers from four medium-sized fennels. Cut them lengthways into eight segments and cook in boiling, salted water until nearly tender. Drain well, cool and pat dry. Flour, dip in beaten seasoned egg and fry in hot oil until golden. Drain well and serve hot.

FINOCCHI ALLA MUGNAIA
Fennel sautéed in butter
Prepare four fennels as in the previous recipe. Cut them lengthways into eight segments. Parboil, drain and cook gently in a heavy frying pan with two tablespoons of butter until soft. Season with salt and milled black pepper. Place them in a serving dish. Pour hot foaming, hazelnut-coloured butter spiked with lemon juice and a dessertspoon of chopped parsley over them. Serve very hot.

FINOCCHI AL PARMIGIANO
Fennel with Parmesan cheese
Prepare and cut four fennels as in the previous recipes. In a heavy frying pan, cook them gently in two tablespoons of butter until they are soft (you may need to help them along with a little stock). Season with salt and milled black pepper and add two dessertspoons of grated Parmesan cheese. Toss until the cheese has melted and the fennel is well coated. Sprinkle with chopped parsley and serve hot.

INSALATA DI FINOCCHI
Raw fennel salad
Top and tail two medium-sized raw fennel. Remove the tough outside layers and wash well. Cut them into fairly thin slices. Dress simply with three parts of olive oil, one part of mild malt vinegar, salt and milled black pepper. Serve chilled.

FUNGHI
Mushrooms
Wild mushrooms are obviously much tastier than cultivated ones. Most people like mushrooms and buy them fairly often. But there are others who not only enjoy eating them but are also positively obsessed with finding the wild ones.

True mushroomers never pull fungi from the ground: they cut them just above the root, thus ensuring continuing growth. To them there is no more stirring sight than unexpectedly coming across a glorious profusion of plump, orange and brown-capped, firm and tender moon-struck *boletus* or *cèpes* . . . mushrooms to us. But unless you know your mushrooms, do not pick or eat any unless you have taken good, knowledgeable local advice. Some are very pretty – as well as dangerous.

Probably, however, you will have to go out and buy your mushrooms from the local greengrocer, usually a down-to-earth chap used to calling 'a spud a spud' who will generally be able to offer you only the cultivated button, medium and cap variety – and very good they are too! The small button ones are better employed as garnishes or prepared as Funghi sott'olio (page 20); the older and larger kind have much more flavour and are acceptable in all types of cooking. Here are just a few recipes which I believe you will like as much as my customers did.

FUNGHI ALLA CREMA
Mushrooms in cream
Wipe 450g (1 lb) of firm mushrooms with a damp cloth, slice and sauté them for a few minutes in butter. Flame and deglaze the pan with a small wine glass of brandy. Season with salt and milled black pepper. Swirl in one cup of heavy cream and gently thicken the sauce. Sprinkle with chopped parsley and serve hot.

FUNGHI GRATINATI
Mushrooms au gratin
Clean and sauté 12 large mushroom caps in butter and oil, keeping them quite firm, and set aside. In the same pan, sweat one tablespoon of finely chopped shallots, one minced garlic clove and the finely chopped mushroom stalks. Mix in four tablespoons of fresh breadcrumbs, one dessertspoon of chopped parsley, salt and milled black pepper. Cook gently and bind with two tablespoons of heavy cream. Stuff the mushroom caps with the filling. Glaze quickly under a hot grill.

FUNGHI ALLA MILANESE
Mushrooms in breadcrumbs
Clean 12 large firm mushrooms. Dip them in flour, egg, breadcrumbs flavoured with

grated Parmesan cheese and then fry in hot oil until golden and crisp. Serve hot with lemon wedges.

FUNGHI ALLA PROVENZALE
Mushrooms with tomato and herbs
Wipe with a damp cloth and slice 450g (1 lb) of large fleshy mushrooms. In a heavy pan, sweat three finely chopped shallots and two crushed garlic cloves in olive oil. Add the mushrooms and sauté them briskly. Remove the garlic. Mix in four large, skinned, roughly chopped, ripe tomatoes, one heaped teaspoon of fresh chopped tarragon, two teaspoons of chopped parsley, salt and milled black pepper. Cook for a further five minutes and serve hot.

FUNGHI TRIFOLATI CON ACCIUGHE
Garlic and anchovy sautéed mushrooms
Wipe and slice 450g (1 lb) of fleshy mushrooms. Sauté them briskly in olive oil. Stir in a finely chopped mixture of parsley, four anchovies, one garlic clove and capers. Season with salt and milled black pepper. Cook for just a few moments and serve quickly.

INSALATE
Salads
Almost all of the vegetables listed in this section may be served either raw or cooked as salads. Italian mixed or tossed salads are never fussy or over-complicated, but they are carefully thought out. The ingredients are well balanced in respect of colour, shape, texture and taste.

Remember that when serving cooked and cooled broccoli leaves or spears, turnip tops or leaves, escarole or spinach as salads, you must never use vinegar: just olive oil and lemon juice. And, please, never vinegar or lemon juice with tomatoes, just good olive oil, unless of course they are part of a combination salad. With cold or hot potato salad always use vinegar, never lemon juice.

There is no such thing as an 'Italian' salad dressing. If anyone tries to sell you a bottle, ignore it! It doesn't exist. Italians usually dress their salads very simply with enough good olive oil to coat, a little vinegar or lemon juice to sharpen and salt and milled black pepper to taste. The salads are tossed very thoroughly but always lightly.

CECI ALLA SARACENA
Chick-pea salad
Chick-peas, so beloved by the Arabs, are almost as well liked by the Neapolitans and all southern Italians. This particular dish may be served, either hot or cold, as a vegetable garnish, as a simple first course or as a salad or side-dish.

Soak overnight 325g (12 oz) of young stock chick-peas in cold water to which a tablespoon of flour has been mixed in. Rinse well and cook them until tender in unsalted water. Drain and return them to the saucepan together with a cup of hot water. In a separate pan, sauté four crushed garlic cloves, six chopped anchovies and a dessertspoon of chopped parsley in a cup of olive oil and add to the chick-peas. Season with salt and plenty of milled black pepper. Remove the garlic and serve them either warm or cold.

INSALATA ALL'ALBESE
Lettuce and truffle salad
Mix sliced Romaine lettuce, watercress, tender celery hearts, thin strips of Fontina cheese and white truffle shavings with an olive oil and lemon-juice dressing blended with a little single cream.

INSALATA ALLA CESARE
Caesar salad, Mayfair style
Dress crisp Romaine lettuce hearts garnished with sliced avocados, fresh pineapple chips, hearts of palm, orange slices and watercress with a mild vinaigrette.

LATTUGA ROMANA ALLA CINESE
Romaine lettuce, Chinese style

Remove the outer leaves and cut the bottoms from two large, crisp Romaine lettuces. Wash and dry them very well. Cut them across into three parts and pat dry with a cloth.

Heat two tablespoons of oil in a very deep pan and gently brown four large, crushed garlic cloves and then discard them. Raise the flame to very high and toss in the lettuce, stirring it rapidly with a long spoon. It will frizzle a lot, so be careful. Stir in two dessertspoons of mild soy sauce, salt, milled black pepper and a level teaspoon of sugar. Keep the lettuce on the move all the time. Serve very hot and crisp.

MELANZANE D'AMATO
Egg-plants, Salerno style

Cut two ripe, unskinned egg-plants in half lengthways and remove some of the seeds. Sprinkle with salt and let stand for an hour. Drain and pat dry. Fry quickly in hot olive oil until golden, drain well and set aside.

Mix eight dessertspoons of soft breadcrumbs, two of olive oil, one of capers, one of chopped parsley, eight stoned, chopped black olives, four chopped anchovies, six chopped basil leaves, salt and milled black pepper. Top the egg-plants with this filling. Range them in a baking dish, sprinkle with olive oil and pour a little into the dish. Cover with foil. Bake in a moderate oven for an hour. Serve hot or cold as a vegetable accompaniment, side-dish, light main course or hors d'oeuvre.

MELANZANE FRITTE
Fried egg-plants

Cut three ripe, unskinned egg-plants into slices about 6mm ($\frac{1}{4}$ in) thick, sprinkle with salt and leave them for an hour. Drain and pat dry. Flour and dip them into a light Beer batter (page 160) and fry until golden in hot olive oil. Drain well and serve hot.

MELANZANE AL FUNGHETTO
Egg-plants cooked as mushrooms

Enzo Apicella, charming, intelligent, slim in places, freelance journalist and boulevardier, had become a regular customer at my first small restaurant. In no time at all he had become a good friend. Enzo always had his own very definite ideas on how Italian restaurants abroad should look and feel. For this reason he was given the chance to design a new basement dining-room. It was very successful.

Encouraged by this, it was decided to give Enzo a free hand in the development and design of my company's second, more luxurious restaurant in Mayfair. And was he enthusiastic! Here was his great chance. Enzo put his preliminary ideas forward, not, as one might normally expect, on paper but in felt-tip outlines on my pink damask tablecloths. His suggestions were many. The talks went on and on, notions developed, ideas were kicked around, enthusiasm took hold and increased tremendously and so did the bills from the laundry, which daily became more frantic and short of unmarked pink damask blue-prints, sorry – tablecloths!

The building works to the new restaurant eventually were given the official go-ahead and Enzo dived into the fray. But, with all his virtues, he could be a little absent-minded at times. Once, delayed badly for a working lunch with the architect-in-charge whom he had met but once, he arrived breathless and terribly late. He joined the lone, very polite gentleman, mumbled his apologies, ordered himself a large drink and an even larger lunch.

The opening conversation went along the usual lines. The weather, the terrible traffic, the day's news. Enzo finished off the pasta course with his customary gusto. But half-way through the main course he began to look around uneasily, to mop his suddenly moistened brow and to loosen the tie he always wore in those days. Their conversation was no longer making too much sense. His companion was looking at him rather worriedly.

Enzo's worst fears were confirmed when the restaurant doors were abruptly crashed open and the very late, real architect puffed his way in. Enzo straightened his tie, picked up his plate and glass and, muttering apologies, backed away from the very astonished gentleman and over to his new table and luncheon partner.

Of course there was a certain amount of preliminary work to carry out before the conversions could start in earnest. But they did eventually commence. I could describe in detail, but won't, how all of us would solemnly and silently stand round a hole which daily became deeper and deeper; how one day Enzo, in the deep basement gloom, forgot where the hole was and found it unexpectedly with a crash; how he consequently supervised a lot of the work while hanging from a door frame because of his rediscovered slipped disc; how the bank across the road took out, and then hurriedly withdrew, a work-stopping injunction on discovering that the noisy works were being financed by its own Head Office; how a workman zealously smashed a beam-supporting hole straight through the basement of the startled bank next door, setting off the alarms; how an enormous, red-tinted, fabulously expensive Belgian perspex sheet was gingerly carried in, meticulously poised, only to be promptly splintered to smithereens by a passing trolley-truck; how we had to send a small waif-like child, in true Dickensian style, crawling through the maze of overhead ducts to retrieve obstacles left inside by diligent workmen; how we nearly lost the child...

After a lot of work, hilarious situations, laughs, incidents and time – nine months – at last the restaurant was ready.

Enzo is an aficionado of egg-plants. He particularly likes the way my mother prepared them. Her recipe for this method, which I used in the restaurants, goes like this and you will particularly like it too!

Cut four ripe, unskinned egg-plants into 12mm ($\frac{1}{2}$ in) cubes. Fry them until golden in plenty of hot olive oil. Drain well on absorbent paper and set aside. In the original oil, sauté four crushed garlic cloves until golden and add six drained, roughly chopped, canned tomatoes, eight bruised basil leaves, salt and milled black pepper. Cook briskly for a few minutes stirring all the time. Mix in the egg-plants, sprinkle with one teaspoon of sugar and discard the garlic. Cook for a further minute.

This is a well-known Neapolitan way of preparing the versatile egg-plant. When cold, it is a perfect antipasto dish. It also makes a good accompaniment hot, warm or cold, to plain main courses.

MELANZANE IN LIMOUSINE
Sandwiched, fried egg-plants

Cut eight 6mm ($\frac{1}{4}$ in) thick slices of ripe, unskinned egg-plants, sprinkle with salt and let them stand for an hour. Drain and pat dry. Fry briskly on both sides in hot olive oil. Drain well on absorbent paper. Lay a 6mm ($\frac{1}{4}$ in) thick slice of Mozzarella cheese on four egg-plant slices, sprinkle with chopped fresh basil and top with the remaining slices. Seal them as firmly as possible with flour, beaten egg and bread-crumbs and fry them in shallow, hot olive oil. Serve as hot as you can so that the cheese gently oozes out when the crisp outside is cut through.

PATATE
Potatoes

Where have all the beautiful varieties of the English potato gone? I cannot answer that, but I can tell you what is mostly being sold in their place as a result of computerized agriculture: the 'Majestic'! The British potato has been most definitely rationalized. It is now of uniform size, colour, shape, weight, texture, bulk and taste.

Conversely in Italy, where the Americas are still constantly blessed for the wondrous gift of the tomato (especially by the Neapolitans), the potato, another gift from over there, cuts no ice at all. The Italians can take it or leave it. And yet they grow a superb potato themselves and they also have a number of remarkably good recipes for their use. Here are some of them.

CROCCHETTE DI PATATE
Potato croquettes
Boil 450g (1 lb) of potatoes in their skins, peel and mash. Place in a bowl and cool. Mix well with one tablespoon of lard or butter, one beaten egg plus one extra yolk, two tablespoons of grated Parmesan cheese, one dessertspoon of chopped parsley, salt and milled black pepper. Allow to cool. Roll into cork-shaped croquettes and flour, egg and breadcrumb them. Let them chill and then fry in hot oil until golden.

A small piece of Mozzarella cheese may be inserted into the centres at the time of rolling (in which case leave out the parsley). Served very hot they are then called Crocchette con il filo because of the hot cheese strands that form.

FRITTELLE DI PATATE
Potato fritters
Peel and coarsely grate four potatoes. Wash under water until it runs clear. Squeeze out all the moisture in a cloth. Put them in a bowl and mix with one heaped tablespoon each of finely chopped onion and the white part of a leek, one beaten whole egg plus one extra yolk, two tablespoons of flour, salt and milled black pepper. Spoon into a heavy frying pan and fry gently until golden in fritter shapes in lard, bacon fat or mixed butter and oil.

GATEAU DI PATATE
Savoury potato cake
Prepare exactly the same mixture as for Crocchette di patate (above) with the addition of two tablespoons of diced ham. Ideally, the potatoes should be well pounded in a mortar rather than merely mashed.

Lard a round oven dish liberally and dust with dried breadcrumbs. Spoon in half of the potato mixture. Cover this with thinly sliced Fontina, Mozzarella or mild Cheddar cheese. Top with the rest of the mixture and smooth the top lightly. Dust with more breadcrumbs. Dot with lard and bake in a fairly hot oven until well heated through and golden on top.

Provolone cheese may be used and chopped salami may be substituted for the ham. In my opinion, however, they both impart a much too powerful flavour.

INSALATA DI PATATE
Hot or cold potato salad
Cook 450g (1 lb) of new potatoes and skin them while still hot. Cut them into 6mm ($\frac{1}{4}$ in) slices. Mix with two very finely sliced shallots and dress with three parts of olive oil, one of malt vinegar, a pinch of oregano, salt and milled black pepper. Toss very gently to prevent the potatoes from breaking up. Serve hot or cold.

PATATE ALLA CONTADINA
Potatoes, farmer's wife style
In a saucepan, sweat a finely sliced, medium-sized onion in lard until soft. Add four medium-sized, cubed potatoes, two small chopped, tender celery stalks with the leaves and stir until well coated. Stir in a dessertspoon of tomato purée. Half cover the potatoes with water. Season with salt and milled black pepper. Cover and cook gently for 30 minutes or until the potatoes are tender. If necessary, add more hot water during the cooking. The potatoes should be beautifully soft and moist.

PATATE 'FONDANT'
Potatoes fondant
Place four peeled, medium-sized potatoes in a small oven dish and pour in enough chicken stock to reach them three-quarters of the way up. Dot with butter. Season

with salt and milled black pepper. Cover with foil. Cook in a moderate oven for about an hour, uncover for the last 15 minutes. When ready, the potatoes will have completely absorbed the stock, will be golden coloured and *fondant* inside.

PATATE ALLA PIZZAIOLA IN BIANCO
Potatoes, white pizzaiola style
In a large frying pan, place four cubed medium-sized potatoes, one chopped garlic clove, two dessertspoons of chopped parsley, four tablespoons of olive oil, one cup of water, salt and milled black pepper. Cover and simmer for half an hour or until the potatoes are cooked. Add more hot water if necessary. The potatoes should be nicely moist.

PATATE ALLA 'SARLADAISE'
Sliced, baked savoury potatoes
Peel and slice very, very thinly 450g (1 lb) of potatoes. Rinse them well under running water until it runs clear. Dry well in a cloth. Butter liberally a dariole mould or a shallow round baking tin. Cover the bottom with a slightly overlapping layer of potatoes. Sprinkle with melted butter, strew with very finely chopped mushrooms or chopped, black Umbrian truffles and season with salt and milled black pepper. Repeat this process, finishing with a layer of potatoes. Season and sprinkle with more melted butter. Bake in a hot oven for 20 minutes. Now comes the difficult bit: you have to turn the potato cake over (with a dariole mould it is easy). Replace in the oven and cook for a further 20 minutes or until the potatoes are cooked. Serve very hot. This is a famous French potato dish and is an ideal accompaniment for roast lamb.

ROESTI
Swiss potato pancakes
The basement room in the small restaurant had become fashionable. I first really realized this when the late Laurence Harvey set his official seal of approval by bringing down a large party one evening. In his inimitable way he demanded, and I gave him, the very best table. I had served him many times in the past at other restaurants. I remembered something that he particularly liked and sent a commis to a nearby Angus Steak House for a quantity of plainly baked potatoes, which I did not keep at that time. The cook removed all the pulp (to be later served as small bacon-fried patties), thoroughly scraped the skins and then crisped them in a hot oven.

When Laurence saw his favourite potatoes presented to him under a serviette, just as he liked them, peasant style, he was quite moved. Here is a potato dish that he also liked to order on occasions.

Coarsely grate four medium-sized, cold, boiled potatoes. In a frying pan, gently sweat a finely chopped onion with two chopped slices of streaky bacon in oil and butter. Mix the potatoes in lightly. Season with salt and milled black pepper. Shake the mixture well and let it settle into the pan. When a crust begins to form, turn it over so that the crunchy pieces go to the centre and keep doing this until both sides are crusty and golden and the centre is full of crispy bits. A little warmed heavy cream may be poured over. Serve very hot.

TORTA DI PATATE
Another kind of potato cake
Cut four medium-sized, peeled potatoes into tiny cubes. Rinse them well under running water until it runs clear. Dry them in a towel. Mix them thoroughly with two well-crushed garlic cloves, salt and milled black pepper. Wrap in a dry cloth and leave for five minutes so that they may absorb the flavour. Discard the garlic. Heat some lard in a heavy frying pan, add the potatoes and press them down well. Cover and cook gently over a low heat. Turn the cake over (with the aid of a plate) when a golden crust has formed. It is ready when

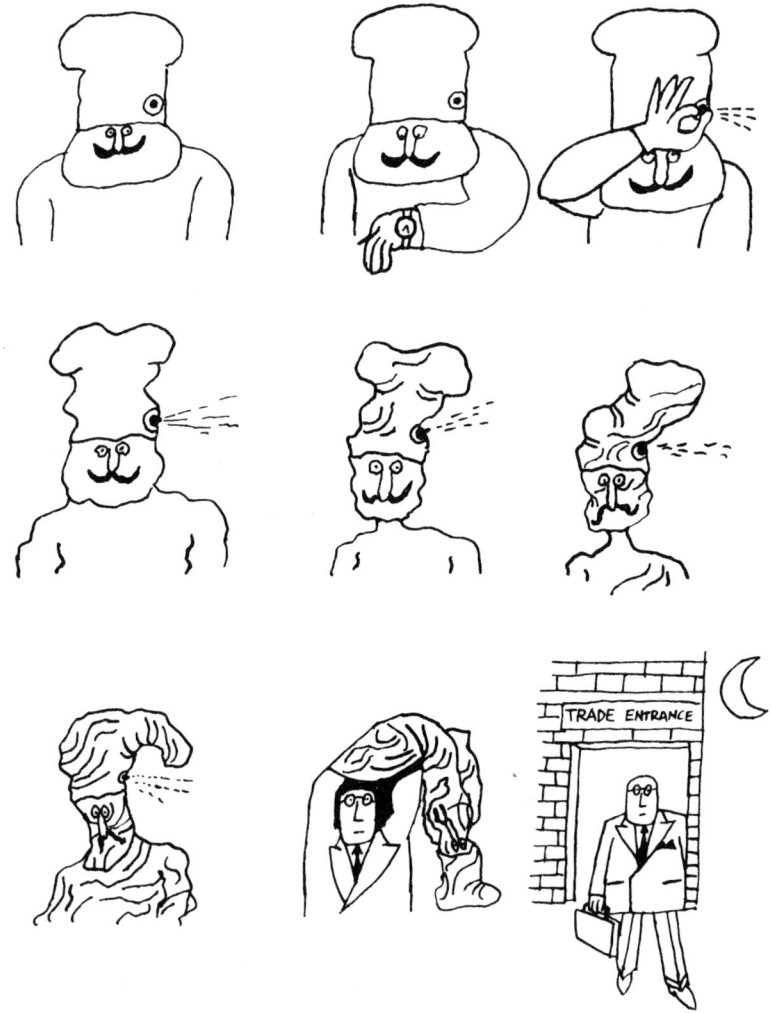

both sides are crisp, crunchy and golden and the inside is tender and moist. Send it to the table proudly, stand back and wait for the compliments to fly.

If you have some fresh green onion or garlic shoots, do chop and add them.

TORTIERA DI PATATE
Hot-pot potatoes

Cut four peeled potatoes into 6mm ($\frac{1}{4}$ in) round slices. Cover the bottom of a well-larded pie dish with a layer of potatoes. Sprinkle liberally with a mixture of finely sliced onions and the white part of leeks. Strew generously with chopped ripe tomatoes. Season with salt and milled black pepper, a pinch of oregano and dot with lard. Continue in this fashion until the potatoes are used up. Finish with a layer of potatoes. Dot the top with lard, season with salt, black pepper and just the tiniest touch of oregano. Cover and bake in a moderate oven for 45 minutes, and then remove the cover for the last 15 minutes.

PEPERONI AL GRATIN
Gratinéed peppers

Put six large, fleshy, red or yellow peppers (not green) under a hot grill. The thin skin will bubble, burst and burn a little. Peel while they are still hot. Core, seed and cut them into 12mm ($\frac{1}{2}$ in) wide strips. Range them side by side in a small baking dish. Strew with a mixture of chopped parsley, garlic, capers, two anchovies, fresh breadcrumbs, salt, milled black pepper and a little oregano. Douse with olive oil. Build up layers until the peppers are used up. Top with soft fresh breadcrumbs and sprinkle with olive oil. Bake in a hot oven for half an hour. Serve hot or cold.

PISELLI STUFATI AL PROSCIUTTO
Peas with ham

In a saucepan, slightly colour two chopped slices of Parma ham or streaky bacon together with a small, finely sliced onion in butter and oil. Add 450g (1 lb) of shelled, small, fresh peas, half of a shredded lettuce heart and enough water to reach the peas three-quarters of the way up. Cover and simmer gently until the peas are tender. Season with salt and black milled pepper.

INSALATA DI POMODORI
Tomato salad

Tomatoes, when used in salads, should never, never be skinned. The perfect tomato needs no impregnation whatever by invading, overpowering flavours. There is only one way to enjoy and appreciate a real tomato salad – the Neapolitan way, like this.

Either slice or quarter eight medium-sized, firm but ripe.tomatoes, season with salt and milled black pepper, strew with torn-up, fresh basil leaves (or a pinch of the finest oregano), drench with olive oil and trickle a little cold water over them. Turn them over just once. Do not wait for any absorbing nonsense and never murder them with lemon juice or vinegar. Eat with lots of crusty French bread and do a lot of dunking into that marvellous olive oil. That's the way to enjoy a tomato salad! Some like to scatter a few thin slices of fresh garlic over the salad. That's just about, but only just, okay by me too.

POMODORI ALLA CREMA
Tomatoes in cream sauce

Place four halved, large, ripe tomatoes in a frying pan, season with salt, milled black pepper and sprinkle with a little sugar. Cook them, covered, in butter and oil. Spoon off most of the fat, swirl in one and a half cups of heavy cream and let the sauce thicken gently. Correct the seasoning if necessary and serve hot.

POMODORI AL FORNO
Baked tomatoes

Cut the tops from four large, ripe tomatoes and scoop out the seeds. Place the pulp in a bowl with six dessertspoons of soft breadcrumbs, one dessertspoon of chopped parsley, one finely chopped garlic clove, a teaspoon of chopped basil or a pinch of oregano, salt and milled black pepper. Mix, moisten with olive oil and stuff into the tomatoes. Sprinkle with olive oil, cover with foil and bake in a moderate oven for 20 minutes or until the tomatoes are cooked through.

POMODORI ALLA PIZZAIOLA
Tomatoes with garlic and herbs

Put four large, ripe, halved tomatoes in a frying pan. Sprinkle them with thin slices of garlic, six torn-up basil leaves or a pinch of oregano, salt and milled black pepper. Douse them with olive oil. Cover the pan and cook gently until they are tender. Serve hot together with the pan juices and correct the seasoning if necessary.

PORRI AL BURRO
Leeks with butter sauce

Clean and prepare eight leeks and cook in salted boiling water. Drain well. Serve them hot with cool butter whipped up lightly with salt, white pepper and lemon juice or plainly with hot, clarified butter and season with black pepper if desired.

PORRI ALLA CREMA
Leeks in cream sauce
Clean and prepare eight leeks and parboil them in salted, boiling water for five minutes. Range them in a large frying pan, dot with butter, season with salt and milled black pepper. Cover and simmer until tender. Add two tablespoons of Veal gravy (page 164) and swirl in a cup of heavy cream letting the sauce gently thicken. Serve hot.

PORRI ALLA MUGNAIA
Leeks in butter
Proceed in exactly the same manner as in the above recipe but, instead of the veal gravy and cream, sprinkle the cooked leeks with lemon juice and chopped parsley. Thicken the pan juice by swirling in very small pieces of fresh butter. Serve hot.

PORRI ALLA PARMIGIANA
Leeks with Parmesan cheese
Clean and prepare eight leeks and parboil them in salted, boiling water for five minutes. Drain them well. In a frying pan, sauté three julienned slices of streaky bacon in oil and butter. Range the leeks in the pan, season with salt and milled black pepper. Cover and simmer until tender turning frequently to prevent burning or sticking. Sprinkle with two dessertspoons of grated Parmesan cheese. Serve hot.

PORRI ALLA VINAIGRETTE O OLANDESE
Leeks with vinaigrette or hollandaise sauce
Clean, prepare and cook eight leeks and drain them well. Serve them hot or cold with a mustardy vinaigrette or hot with hollandaise sauce.

CIME DI RAPE
Turnip tops
These are prepared in exactly the same way as Cime di broccoli. The recipe is on page 134 in this section.

SCAROLA 'PASSI E PINOLI'
Escarole with pine nuts and sultanas
In a heavy frying pan, sauté four crushed garlic cloves in four tablespoons of olive oil and discard when golden. Add and sauté four well-trimmed young escaroles or broad-leaved, non-curly endives (previously cooked until almost tender). Sprinkle with one dessertspoon each of pine nuts and sultanas. Season with salt and milled black pepper. Continue to cook gently for a few minutes.

FRITTELLE DI SEDANO
Celery fritters
Remove the outer stalks and wash four hearts of young, tender celery. Cut them in half lengthways and cook them in boiling, salted water. Drain well and pat dry. Chop them up roughly, place them in a bowl and mix with one whole, beaten egg plus one extra yolk, one tablespoon of grated Parmesan cheese, one tablespoon of flour, salt and milled black pepper. Fry fritter-shaped spoonfuls in hot oil until golden and cooked inside. Drain well. Pour a little Veal gravy (page 164) over them and serve hot.

SEDANO ALLA MUGNAIA
Celery braised in butter
Prepare four young, tender celery hearts as for Frittelle di sedano (above) and parboil in salted boiling water for five minutes. Drain well. Range them in an oven dish with a cup of chicken stock, dot abundantly with butter and season with salt and milled black pepper Either cover and simmer, or braise in the oven until tender. Sprinkle with lemon juice and chopped parsley.

SEDANO AL PARMIGIANO
Celery with Parmesan cheese
Proceed exactly as in the above recipe but remove the cover when the celery is almost tender, allowing the liquor to dry out slightly and the celery to take on a good

golden colour. Sprinkle with two tablespoons of grated Parmesan cheese. Check the seasoning and serve hot.

SPINACI ALL'AGLIO
Spinach tossed in olive oil and garlic
Wash 900g (2 lb) of very young spinach thoroughly. Place it in a saucepan, cover tightly and cook gently without adding any water. Drain well. In a frying pan sauté two crushed garlic cloves in four tablespoons of olive oil until golden. Add the spinach and toss it around until it shines with the flavoured oil. Season with salt and milled black pepper. Discard the garlic and serve hot.

SPINACI ALL'AGRO
Spinach with lemon dressing
Cook 900g (2 lb) of young, tender spinach as in the previous recipe. Drain well. Serve hot or cold dressed with olive oil, seasoned with salt and milled black pepper and spiked with lemon juice – never vinegar with this spinach dish.

SPINACI AL BURRO E PARMIGIANO
Spinach with Parmesan cheese
Prepare and cook 900g (2 lb) of young, tender spinach. Drain well. Sauté in two tablespoons of butter in a frying pan until it glistens. Sprinkle with grated Parmesan cheese and season with salt and milled black pepper. Serve hot.

SPINACI CRUDI ALL'INSALATA
Raw spinach and bacon salad
This is a variation of the famous French *pissenlits* salad. It is possible to find the very young, tender leaves of the wild dandelion, but it can be a lot of trouble. Try this unusual salad, instead, with spinach. You will need 450g (1 lb) of the youngest, most tender leaves of spinach that you can buy (otherwise don't bother). Wash them in plenty of water. And when you're satisfied that they are clean, do it again – spinach can be treacherous and make you very ill.

Rub a large salad bowl with garlic, add the spinach, season with salt and milled black pepper. Sauté six julienned slices of streaky bacon gently in a very little olive oil until the bacon fat has melted. Pour it boiling hot, with the bacon, over the spinach and immediately sprinkle with light malt vinegar. Toss quickly and thoroughly and serve immediately.

SPINACI PASSI E PINOLI
Spinach with pine nuts and sultanas
Proceed in precisely the same way as for Scarola passi e pinoli on page 147. Note, however, that the spinach should be cooked without water as indeed it should always be.

FRITTELLE DI FIORI DI ZUCCHINE
Zucchini-flower fritters
It is impossible to buy these delicious little yellow zucchini flowers, but you may be able to gather them from your own kitchen garden plot or from those of your neighbours.

Remove their pistils and stems and wash and dry them thoroughly. Dip them into a light Beer batter (page 160) and fry them, a few at a time, in hot oil until crisp and golden and cooked inside. Drain well and serve hot.

ZUCCHINE BOLLITE
Poached zucchini
Trim the ends from eight small zucchini and gently poach them in salted, boiling water until tender but not soft. Drain them well and cut in half lengthways. Serve hot on side plates with cool butter whipped up with lemon juice, salt and milled black pepper or with melted clarified butter, hollandaise sauce or a light olive oil, vinegar or lemon dressing. Alternatively, serve these zucchini cold with mayonnaise or vinaigrette sauce to which a little chopped dill has been added.

ZUCCHINE FRITTE
Crisply fried zucchini
Cut four medium-sized, unpeeled zucchini into 3cm (1½ in) long sticks. Soak them in milk, roll in flour, shake off any excess and fry in hot oil until they are golden and crisp. Sprinkle with salt and serve very hot.

ZUCCHINE ALLA PROVENZALE
Zucchini with tomatoes and herbs
Cut eight medium-sized zucchini into 6mm (¼ in) slices. Sweat a sliced, medium-sized onion in a frying pan together with two crushed garlic cloves in four tablespoons of olive oil and discard the garlic. Add the zucchini and cook gently for 15 minutes. Mix in 225g (8 oz) of roughly chopped, drained, canned tomatoes, six bruised basil leaves, a little chopped tarragon, a light sprinkling of oregano, salt and freshly milled black pepper. Continue to cook gently until the zucchini are tender and the sauce has amalgamated. Serve hot or, even better, cold.

ZUCCHINE ALLA SCAPECE
Sweet and sour zucchini
One evening Princess Margaret stood up and led a friend to the dance floor in the dimmed restaurant. She didn't realize and nor did he that the bongo player was performing a spot-lit speciality number. All the room watched fascinated as the lovely Princess danced. I hurriedly gave orders. The spot beams were slowly faded down, then out. And the performer, fingers still jumping, retreated to the bandstand. The music quietened and changed gear smoothly. Other dancers joined the floor. And the Princess, not realizing that she had just starred in a West End cabaret, danced on.

Apart from that incident, I remember quite clearly, that amongst a variety of southern-style vegetable specialities, the chef had prepared a dish of these zucchini. And I remember, too, that Princess Margaret had a second helping of them.

Cut eight medium-sized, firm zucchini into thin slices. Pat them dry. Fry them, a few at a time, in very hot olive oil until golden on both sides. Be careful not to burn them. Repeat until all the zucchini are fried. Drain and dry well on absorbent paper. Lay them in a flat dish, strew with one very thinly sliced garlic clove, a few torn-up mint leaves, salt and milled black pepper. Sprinkle with castor sugar and then with a little mild malt vinegar. Build similar layers until the zucchini are used up. Do not allow the sharpness of the vinegar or the sweetness of the sugar to predominate; it must be in perfect balance.

This is the best loved of all the Neapolitan ways of preparing the small and tender zucchini. The word *scapece* comes from a degeneration over the centuries of the name Apicius, the famous ancient Roman gastronome. Today, in the Naples area, it is used to describe food (mostly vegetables or fish) which is prepared in the same style.

This recipe is admittedly a lot of trouble but it is really worth sampling. Try it, for example, with plain roast lamb, a delicious variation on mint sauce.

ZUCCHINE TRIFOLATE ALL'AGLIO
Sautéed zucchini with garlic
In a frying pan, cook six medium-sized, cubed zucchini with four tablespoons of olive oil, one finely chopped garlic clove, a heaped tablespoon of chopped parsley, salt and milled black pepper. Turn them over often. Serve hot, warm or cold.

ZUCCHINE TRIFOLATE CON LA CIPOLLA
Zucchini sautéed with onions
In a heavy frying pan, sweat a sliced, medium-sized onion in one tablespoon of butter and two tablespoons of oil. When soft add six cubed, medium-sized zucchini. Season with salt and milled black pepper and flavour with fresh chopped tarragon. Cook gently until tender. Serve hot.

There are many recipes to be found in the **Antipasti** and **Soup** sections which are equally suitable as vegetable dishes:

Antipasti

CAPONATA ALLA SICILIANA Piquant-sweet egg-plants

CARCIOFI ALLA CONTADINA Artichokes country style

Note: artichokes prepared in this way are not really suitable as a vegetable accompaniment. They are more antipasto-like but may be served, together with the potatoes, as a vegetarian main course or perhaps as a side-dish.

CAROTE ALL'OLIO Carrots dressed with olive oil

These are very good as an antipasto, vegetables, side-dish or salad.

CAVOLFIORE ALL'OLIO Cauliflower dressed with olive oil

CIPOLLINE AL CURRY Glazed, curried button onions

These sweet and slightly curried button onions are more suitable served as an hors d'oeuvre or as a piquant side-dish. Or, served hot, they make an interesting accompaniment to a plain main course.

FUNGHI FRITTI TARTARE Mushrooms fried in batter

FUNGHI SOTT'OLIO Mushrooms in olive oil

These delicious mushrooms are certainly more of an hors d'oeuvre than a vegetable but they may also be served as a side-dish and will undoubtedly liven up any bland main course.

MELANZANE 'IMMAM BAYELDI' Baked savoury egg-plant.

Truly one of the greatest of all egg-plant dishes.

MELANZANE ALLA PARMIGIANA ALLA MINORESE Egg-plants 'Parmigiana', Minori style

MELANZANE SOTT'OLIO Egg-plants in olive oil

This is a great and very tasty way to prepare egg-plants and is, mostly, served as part of an hors d'oeuvre. They can also be good with bland main courses.

PEPERONATA Sautéed spicy peppers

One of the most well-known of all Neapolitan 'peperoni' (peppers) dishes. Not really a vegetable dish, unless the main course needs a 'zoom' in the direction of taste.

PEPERONI ARROSTITI Grilled peppers

PEPERONI RIPIENI ALL'AMALFITANA Peppers with savoury stuffing

RATATOUILLE ALLA NIZZARDA Sautéed, savoury vegetables

SCAROLA RIPIENA Stuffed escarole

ZUCCHINE RIPIENE Zucchini 'tragara' with savoury stuffing

Soup

CAVOLFIORE AL POMODORO Cauliflorets in tomato sauce

See Zuppa di cavolfiore petrit. Remember to put in less liquid when required as a vegetable.

CIANFOTTA Spicy, vegetable stew-soup

FAGIOLINI AL POMODORO French beans in tomato sauce

See Zuppa di fagiolini. When serving as a vegetable remember to drain off some of the liquid.

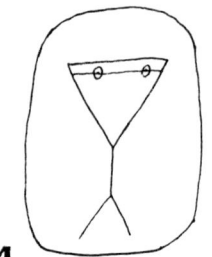

1

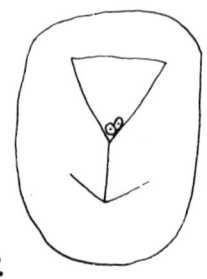

2

DOLCI
Desserts

Visitors returning from Italy often say that the dessert selections in Italian restaurants are limited in imagination, variety and quality – and I am forced to agree. A typical offering can be an amateurishly made Crostata (a sort of jam flan), Zuppa inglese (a travesty of the noble trifle), some soggy fruit salad, a slice of factory-made, synthetic, ice-cream cake or a so-called gelato which is to be doused in whisky, thus destroying both the ice-cream and the perfectly good whisky. Once these poor offerings have been considered and intelligently declined, one is forced then to turn to the unripe contents of the fruit basket. It constantly amazes me that the superb, Marsala-laden, delightfully creamy dessert, zabaglione, is hardly ever offered in restaurants in Italy; one would almost think that it has been officially disclaimed.

I know from my own experience that customers delight, especially if there are children, in drooling over a laden dessert trolley. And, if the presentation and the contents are bright and gorgeous looking, then tourists, foreign businessmen and even the domestic Italian customers themselves will be seduced into partaking. There is, however, one factor which may have a strong bearing on the scarcity of sweets and desserts in Italian restaurants and trattorie – bread. Wonderful, delicious, crusty Italian bread. Vast quantities of the substance are daily consumed all over the country. It would be unthinkable to serve a meal without bread. Thus, after having eaten a few slices of moist prosciutto (with bread) and a good minestrone (with bread), a main course (with bread to mop up the sauce), a little salad (with more bread) and a portion of cheese (with what else?), Italians may have neither the room nor the desire for a lavish sweet concoction.

Things are much the same in Italian homes. Even in today's swiftly changing times, despite what the elders say about the youngsters, the Italian woman is still a marvellously instinctive cook. But I doubt very much whether she, unlike her American or British counterpart who is so versatile in the preparation of desserts, can prepare much more than the sweetmeats, cakes or biscuits ceremoniously baked or fried in honour of the local patron saint's anniversary. It is just not the national habit.

On Sundays or special occasions, however, the Italian husband is very often dispatched to join the crowds of other husbands at the attractive laden counters of the local *pasticceria*. There, whilst leisurely sipping a glass of vermouth, he will make his difficult choice from the fantastic array of liqueur-drenched, decorated cakes, highly coloured mignon pastries, glazed almond-filled biscuits, petit fours of all sorts, chocolate shells with soft fillings and elaborately styled ice-cream confections which, when beautifully wrapped, will be carefully taken home. So I decided that it should be Sunday, holiday or feast day every day at my restaurants and hired the best pastrycooks in town!

ARANCII 'POSITANO'
Sliced oranges in caramel sauce

This orange dish is comparatively simple to prepare. It makes a refreshing end to a rich meal. The method of preparation is certainly of Turkish origin. In classical cuisine it is known as Oranges à l'orientale, but in order to give it local interest and to match up with Polish George's glorious mural of the Naples panorama, I decided to change the name to something more appropriate.

Remove the peel in long strips from four oranges with a sharp potato-peeler and cut them into a very fine julienne. Boil them for five minutes. Then drain, rinse and boil them once more. Boil a cup of water together with 225g (8 oz) of castor sugar until it becomes syrupy. Add the peel and continue to cook until the syrup begins to take colour. Allow to cool.

Meanwhile cut away the pith from the oranges with a sharp knife and slice the oranges very thinly. Chill them. Mask them with the syrup and pile the candied peel in tufts in the centre of each portion.

BANANE ALLA FIAMMA
Bananas flamed with Bacardi rum

Peel four large bananas and place them in a buttered dish. Sprinkle them liberally with brown sugar and grated coconut. Heat well through in a hot oven and then pass the bananas under a hot grill to allow the sugar to glaze. Spoon a generous amount of warmed Bacardi rum over them and flame. Serve the bananas while still alight, with a chilled Zabaglione al Marsala freddo (page 158) or cool, heavy cream.

COPPA 'CLEOPATRA'
Hazelnut ice-cream with stem ginger

Fill four glass or silver coupes with a good quality hazelnut ice-cream and sprinkle liberally with chopped, crystallized stem ginger. Mask with Caramel brandy sauce (page 160) and serve with crispy brandy snaps.

COPPA 'CLO-CLO'
Candied chestnuts with ice-cream

Quarter-fill four glass or silver coupes with chopped, candied marrons glacés. Sprinkle them with Maraschino and cover half with chocolate ice-cream and half with vanilla. Decorate with piped, whipped cream and finish by sprinkling with thin shavings of bitter chocolate.

COPPA ALLA GIACOMO
Ice-cream and fruit salad

Half-fill four glass or silver coupes with a good and varied fruit salad. Flavour it with Maraschino. Cover with a scoop each of lemon water-ice (or sherbert) and strawberry ice-cream. Decorate with piped, whipped cream and top with slices of orange and white grapes.

COPPA 'IMPERATORE'
Ice-cream and fresh peaches

Cover the bottoms of four glass or silver coupes with sponge fingers, soak them well with Marsala wine and cover with a good amount of peach or hazelnut ice-cream. Stand a fresh, poached, cold peach in each coupe. Mask with Melba sauce (page 163) and cover with chilled Zabaglione al Marsala freddo (page 158).

CREMA CARAMELLA
Cream caramel

Gently caramelize 100g (4 oz) of castor sugar in a saucepan. Do not allow it to burn. Pour a little into each of four individual custard moulds. Bring 280ml (10 fl oz) of milk containing 50g (2 oz) of sugar and half a vanilla pod or a strip of lemon peel to the boil. Remove the vanilla pod or peel. Beat two whole eggs and two extra yolks and, whisking continually, add the boiling milk very gradually without scrambling the eggs. Skim off the risen froth and strain the mixture into the moulds. Stand them in a shallow tin containing water and cover them with foil. Cook, or rather, let them set very gently in a moderate oven. Cool and chill thoroughly before serving.

The creams should be perfectly smooth all the way through without tiny bubbles or air-holes which would indicate that they have been cooked too quickly or in too hot an oven.

CRÈME BRÛLÉE
Burnt cream
Heat nearly to boiling point, stirring all the time, 570ml (20 fl oz) of cream (containing 50g (2 oz) of sugar and a vanilla pod) over a bain-marie. Remove the pod. Pour the hot cream gradually over four well-beaten egg yolks and blend it in smoothly. Return the mixture over the bain-marie and let it cook and thicken gently for five minutes. Do not allow it to boil. Pour into four small, individual soufflé moulds and leave to cool thoroughly. Sprinkle with a generous amount of brown sugar and caramelize under a hot grill. Decorate with toasted sliced almonds and serve slightly chilled.

CRÊPES SUZETTE
Orange and liqueur-glazed pancakes
Make 12 very, very thin, small pancakes with Sweet batter (page 163). Stack them and put to one side.

Rub 12 lumps of sugar on two oranges, impregnating the sugar with the orange zest. Melt the lumps in a frying pan—preferably copper—together with a strip each of lemon and orange peel. Remove the pan from the fire when the sugar is just about to take colour and add the juice of one and a half oranges and 25g (1 oz) of butter. Return the pan to the flame and dissolve the caramelizing sugar with the back of a spoon. Allow the mixture to bubble for a few minutes until it becomes quite syrupy. Remove the peel.

Quickly turn the pancakes over in the syrup and fold them into triangles. As they are prepared, push them to one side of the pan. Sprinkle them generously with Cointreau, a little castor sugar, a few drops of lemon juice and chopped, toasted hazelnuts. When the pancakes are nicely glazed, pour in a good amount of brandy. Pull the pan smartly across the fire: it will burst beautifully into a blaze of blue flame. Serve immediately while still alight.

FRAGOLE 'ROMANOFF'
Strawberries with port and cream sauce
Chill and macerate enough ripe strawberries for four people in a liberal amount of castor sugar and two liqueur glasses each of port and Cointreau for at least one hour. Drain and strain the liqueur. Whip 570ml (20 fl oz) of heavy cream until stiff and smoothly blended in the liqueur together with two tablespoons of Melba sauce (page 163) until it is evenly coloured. Cover the strawberries with the sauce. Serve chilled.

LAMPONI 'MIMOSA'
Raspberries in Grand Marnier sauce
Follow the same procedure as for Fragole 'Romanoff' (above) but substitute raspberries, Grand Marnier and brandy. Decorate the top with raspberries, some very thin slices of orange and dust lightly with powdered cinnamon. Serve well chilled.

LADY LEAH'S QUEEN PUDDING
Meringue sponge
Bring 570ml (20 fl oz) of milk containing a vanilla pod and 50g (2 oz) of butter to the boil. Pour it over five cups of fresh, white breadcrumbs mixed with two tablespoons of castor sugar. Allow this mixture to stand for ten minutes and then mix in four well-beaten egg yolks. Bake for 30 minutes in a buttered oven dish in a medium-hot oven. Remove, and spread two tablespoons of preserve on the top. Whisk four egg whites stiff, add a little sugar and whisk again briefly then pile it on top of the pudding. Return it to the oven and allow the meringue to set at a very low temperature for about 30 minutes.

MACEDONIA DI FRUTTA FRESCA
Fresh fruit salad

A few words of caution about fruit salads: beware of pallid gatherings of minutely cubed apple (mostly), pear (lots), brown, slimy slices of banana, cheered up with slivers of cheap, canned peach halves and plastic cherries. If those are the ingredients, then you can bet your life that the same small-minded, inefficient management has allowed them to macerate in a tepid, sugary liquid which, reacting to the almost certainly stuffy atmosphere, has fermented and transformed the unattractive combination into a limp, soggy, lightly bubbling, lukewarm yeast-tasting stew.

A really good, fresh, fruit salad simply has to be expensive. But, as I consider it to be one of the best ways to end a good meal, it's worth it! Choose from prickly pears, figs, lychee nuts, nectarines, mangoes, pineapple, Chinese gooseberries, melon, oranges, mandarins, plums, greengages, peaches, damsons, apples, pears, grapes (peeled and pipped), bananas (freshly cut), cherries (stoned), raspberries, strawberries, blackberries, loganberries (all added at the last moment) – and don't forget a few slivers of almonds.

Proportion the fruit carefully, do not let any one fruit predominate. Never, never cube – slice. Follow the contours of the fruit, halve or leave whole. Moisten the fruits liberally with a cold syrup made by boiling sugar and water together, flavoured with either Cointreau or Maraschino. Prepare the salad at the last possible moment. Chill for only 15 minutes so that the fruit retains its individual taste and remains either firm, moist or crisp.

MELANZANE AL CIOCCOLATO
Egg-plant with chocolate sauce

This dish originates from the fishing village of Maiori on the Amalfitan coast. The ancient sweet-sour technique of the Capri-Romans must have had some influence in its development. This, coupled with the vivid imagination of the people, helped to produce what was obviously a treat by ingeniously combining the locally grown egg-plant with the exotic chocolate bean from the New World.

Today Melanzane al cioccolato is only prepared on Amalfitan village feast days. But that is no reason why you should wait! So do try this strange and delicious dish.

Peel three medium-sized egg-plants and cut them into 6mm ($\frac{1}{4}$ in) slices. Fry them in hot olive oil until lightly coloured. Drain well. Dip in beaten egg and fry in oil once more until they are golden. Mix eight heaped tablespoons of dark cocoa powder with 570ml (20 fl oz) of boiling water. Sweeten with castor sugar and cool. Cover the bottom of a deep dish with a layer of fried egg-plant. Dust with castor sugar, a little powdered mixed spice and sprinkle them with dark Navy rum. Mask with some of the chocolate sauce. Continue to build up layers until all the egg-plant is used up. Decorate with silver confetti and sugared almonds. Serve well chilled.

MONTE BIANCO
Meringue with chestnut purée

Slit 900g (2 lb) of chestnuts all round and boil them in plain water for five minutes. Remove the peel and inner skin while they are still hot. Now simmer them in sweetened, vanilla-flavoured milk until they are soft.

Top four ready-made meringue bases with whipped cream. Rub the cooked chestnuts through a sieve and completely cover the cream with loose piles of purée. Dust lightly with confectioner's sugar and sprinkle with shavings of bitter chocolate.

MOUSSE AL CIOCCOLATO
Chocolate mousse

We once had a charming young Swedish-British-Spanish friend called Anne staying with us. Anne made very good chocolate mousse. Once I complimented her on a particularly successful one and asked which cognac she had included. In her inimitable way Anne answered brightly, if a little vaguely, that she had used 'some of that Neapolitan brandy'. I thought very hard. But I really could not imagine that the extremely wily and inventive Neapolitans could ever have reproduced even a passable imitation of cognac. As it turned out, Anne had misread the label. She had, as I suspected, used my precious Napoleon cognac.

Chop up 225g (8 oz) of dark and bitter good-quality chocolate. Melt it in half a cup of water containing two tablespoons of very strong made-up coffee and three tablespoons of ordinary brandy. Stir until smooth. Cool. Blend in four beaten egg yolks and evenly fold in four stiffly beaten egg whites. Pour into four individual coupes and chill well. Decorate with very thin shavings of bitter chocolate and thin slices of orange.

PÊCHES FLAMBÉES
Peaches flamed in kirsch

Maybe it was the thundery weather, or perhaps Tony had lost at the races. The fact was that the usually relaxed and expert feel was not evident on his station. This was probably due to the fact that the future Queen, Princess Elizabeth, was to be a guest at a small private dinner party at the club that evening. In any event it was plain to all that the service was not at all smooth.

This edgy feeling was contagious. It had transmitted itself to Mr Neri, the Restaurant Manager, who was feeling unsettled himself. But, in order to set a

good example all round and also to help calm Tony's nerves, he had decided to help him out by butting in imperiously and choosing to prepare personally the Pêches flambées in front of a customer's table.

Mr Neri liked to grasp every possible opportunity to demonstrate his skill at flambée cooking and this evening was no exception. But, although the setting-up ritual went well, the final glazing of the peaches did not, to the slightest degree, proceed in the usual manner. While suspiciously checking the contents of the kirsch bottle, Mr Neri, not noticing that the sugar had melted too quickly and had started to burn, lifted the fork from the pan. Suppressing a bleat of panic, he realized too late that it had welded itself firmly to the hardening syrup and the bright copper pan tilted forward dangerously. Mr Neri's frenzied contortions as he tried to correct the pan's insane angle only succeeded in tipping it the other way. This crazy see-saw movement went on for a few interminable seconds. With considerable embarrassment and very little patience, Mr Neri wrenched the toffee-topped fork free and overcame the problem by calling for a tablespoon, which is what he should have used in the first place. To his continuing discomfort, the spirit-lamp he was using began to splutter, spit and backfire in such a vicious way that even the dignified Mr Neri was compelled to back away hurriedly.

Muttering loudly that his staff did not look after their working equipment properly, he eventually changed the lamp for one in better running order and was able to complete the hot and syrupy dish successfully. Thankfully the pan burst beautifully into bright blue flames.

Unfortunately there was worse to come. Stout Mr Neri, now breathing heavily from his exertions, leant forward too sharply in order to serve the lady in the far corner and overbalanced badly. His outstretched arm, holding grimly onto the serving spoon, stiffened. The fiery peach zoomed away. It shot prematurely forward like a spirited comet, straight into the Christian Dior 'New Look' dress of the lady in the far corner. With a scream that startled the dance band, she stood up, all but overturned the table and, lifting her skirts high, tossed the peach directly back to a wildly side-stepping Mr Neri who, playing a defending backhand shot with the pan, dropped the rest of the contents onto the expensive carpet in a flaming pool of peaches, sauce and liqueur.

To prepare these Pêches flambées on calmer evenings, peel four firm but ripe peaches. Poach them in plain water and sugar syrup until barely tender. Do not over-cook them. Keep them warm.

In a copper pan melt 25g (1 oz) of castor sugar and allow it to take on the slightest colour over a low flame. Add the juice of one orange, four tablespoons of the poaching liquor and a strip of lemon peel. Dissolve the caramelizing sugar, moving it around with the back of a spoon. Now stir in two tablespoons of Melba sauce (page 163) and add the poached peaches.

Bring up the heat a little and, turning the peaches gently, glaze them in the syrupy sauce. Pour in a large wine glass of kirsch. Prick the peaches so that they absorb some of the flavours. Pull the pan sharply across the fire and stand well back while the whole lot bursts into beautiful blue flames.

Serve them while still alight, perhaps with a scoop of vanilla ice-cream.

PESCHE AL VINO
Peaches in wine

This is a simple dish of peaches and not a recipe at all. But they are so good, I just have to tell you how to prepare them. Peel and slice eight large, ripe and firm yellow peaches into segments. Sprinkle them generously with castor sugar. Drench them lavishly with ordinary red or white wine and leave to soak for at least two hours in the refrigerator. Serve them well chilled in tall glasses with plenty of the wine liquor. And if it isn't summer at the time, it certainly will seem like it!

PETITS POTS AU CHOCOLAT
Chocolate cream

That badly parked Mini-Minor outside my restaurant, the one with the darkly tinted windows (and probably about to be towed away) belongs to Lord Snowdon. If he is not in the restaurant with some professional photographer friends, he is most probably enjoying a tête-à-tête meal at his usual table at the far end with a very charming young lady – the one he adores so much and loves to escort, his very pretty little daughter, Lady Sarah. Whatever is on the dessert trolley, Lady Sarah likes one of these.

Over a bain-marie bring just to boiling point 570 (20 fl oz) of cream containing 75g (3 oz) of castor sugar, one dessertspoon of ground coffee, 50g (2 oz) of melted bitter chocolate and half a vanilla pod. Gradually add the hot mixture to a bowl containing four beaten egg yolks. Stir constantly. Strain and pour into individual pots. Stand them in a pan of water, cover with foil and place in a moderate oven for about 20 minutes or until the cream has set. Let them cool, and then chill in the refrigerator before serving.

RICOTTA AL CAFFE
Curd cheese with rum and coffee

Rub 225g (8 oz) of fresh Ricotta or similar curd cheese through a fine sieve. Mix in 125g (5 oz) of castor sugar, three tablespoons of dark Navy rum and two tablespoons of freshly roasted, finely ground coffee or a small cup of extremely strong made-up coffee. Stir until smooth. Pour into individual pots and chill well.

SALSA ALLO ZABAGLIONE
Whisked egg and Marsala sauce

I had heard about it, read about it, seen the place featured in movies and so always had a strong urge to visit it. I am talking of Sardi's, the fashionable showbiz restaurant that for years catered to all the great Broadway and Hollywood stars and pandered to their whims and fancies. It was the New York spot to be seen in. It was very smart – to be relegated to a less well-positioned table meant that the ever-vigilant management had heard on the grapevine that one's star was on the wane.

Sardi's has never been celebrated for the food it serves which, quite truthfully, is not over-imaginative. But, nevertheless, the restaurant does merit a visit if only for old times' sake.

I am sorry to say that of the food, I can only recall as being excellent a zabaglione sauce which was poured over a totally forgettable liqueur, sponge and ice-cream concoction. To make this sauce simply follow the instructions as given in the recipe for Zabaglione (page 158) and, when it is fairly cool, blend in smoothly a cup of fresh, heavy cream. Chill and serve as you would any other cold sweet sauce.

TARTE TATIN
Upside-down apple flan

Jacques Bourguillon is a very fine pastry-cook. While he was my Chef patissier, I used to ask him to prepare a quantity of these marvellous flans and time the baking of them so that they were sent out to the restaurant just as the lunch customers were thinking of their desserts.

Liberally butter a shallow round pie dish. Cover the bottom with a very thick layer of brown sugar. Fill the dish with overlapping slices of cooking-apples, add a couple of cloves and scatter generously with sultanas. Spread thinly with orange marmalade and dot with butter. Sprinkle with castor sugar. Cover with a Rich shortcrust pastry (page 164) and bake in a moderate oven for about 35 minutes. When the apples are cooked, cover the baking tin with a large dish and flip the flan over so that it emerges upside down. The top should be beautifully caramelized. If not, don't worry! It can happen to anyone. Just sprinkle more brown sugar over the apples and pass the flan under a hot grill for a few moments. Serve hot or warm. Pass lots of cool, fresh cream.

TIVOLINI
Rolled pancakes with hazelnut stuffing
Brown 450g (1 lb) of shelled hazelnuts for five minutes in the oven. Rub the nuts with a rough cloth to remove all the fine skin. Crush them with a rolling pin and blend smoothly with 100g (4 oz) each of castor sugar and vegetable margarine. Prepare eight very thin, sweet Pancakes (page 163), spread them with the hazelnut purée and roll lightly. Place them in an oven dish, and spread over more purée. Heat thoroughly in a moderate to hot oven until they are slightly crunchy on top. Serve hot.

TORTA ALLA RICOTTA
Italian cheesecake
Crush 325g (12 oz) of digestive biscuits and mix in two tablespoons of melted butter. Smooth and press this mixture lightly on the bottom of a round, well-buttered baking tin. Mix 450g (1 lb) of Italian Ricotta or fresh curd cheese with 100g (4 oz) of castor sugar, two tablespoons of heavy cream, two whole eggs and a little lemon juice. Beat this mixture until fluffy and turn it into the baking tin and bake in a moderate to hot oven for 20 minutes. Remove and let it cool.

Mix 140ml (5 fl oz) of sour cream with two tablespoons of castor sugar and sharpen the taste with a little lemon juice. Pour over the cooled flan. Return to a moderate oven for a further 20 minutes. Let it cool, cover with foil and chill well before serving.

ZABAGLIONE AL MARSALA
Whisked eggs with Marsala wine
This is unquestionably the most famous and well known of all Italian desserts. It originates from Piedmont and not, as many suppose, from Sicily. It is thought that the name zabaglione is a derivation of 'San Giovanni di Baylon' the patron saint of pastrycooks. The recipe dates back to the sixteenth century, when it included the overpowering ingredient of cinnamon.

Today's cookery writers do not always seem to agree on the exact ingredients or quantities. But this often happens with Italian recipes. They all, however, insist that zabaglione should always be whipped over a bain-marie. But even here they are not altogether right. It does not matter whether it is prepared over a bain-marie or directly over a flame. The essential thing is to whisk the egg-wine mixture smoothly and speedily and not to allow the eggs to settle, scramble or overcook.

I have never seen a professional restaurant pastrycook prepare zabaglione other than over direct heat. They all say, quite rightly, that, cooked over a bain-marie, the result is far too light and frothy and lacks the required body and consistency.

Place in a round-bottomed confectioner's bowl four fresh egg yolks and four half egg-shells each of castor sugar and Marsala wine. Whisk over heat (direct or indirect) quickly, smoothly and steadily until the mixture becomes thick and a little frothy. Serve quickly in long-stemmed glasses with finger sponge-biscuits.

ZABAGLIONE AL MARSALA FREDDO
Chilled zabaglione
It is not possible to make zabaglione and then cool and chill it for, in a short while, the Marsala will separate itself from the whisked egg and look a sorry sight. What you have to do instead is to fold into four quantities of whipped, slightly cooled zabaglione one cup of fresh, stiffly whipped cream. Chill and serve in long-stemmed glasses with finger sponge-biscuits.

SAUCES, STOCKS, ODDS & ENDS

AURORE SAUCE
Melt 25g (1 oz) of butter and, with a wooden spoon, smoothly stir in 25g (1 oz) of finely sieved flour until it takes on a light blonde colour. Gradually add 280ml (10 fl oz) of warm, strained Fish stock (page 162) and simmer for 15 minutes. Blend in one dessertspoon of tomato purée, two tablespoons of heavy cream and half a level teaspoon of sugar. Check the seasoning with salt and cayenne pepper. Continue to cook gently for a further five minutes. Remove from the stove and whisk in 25g (1 oz) of butter. The sauce should be pink, smooth and glossy.

This sauce is a perfectly acceptable substitute for Lobster sauce, as well as much more economical.

APRICOT SAUCE
Proceed as for Melba sauce (page 163) but use a fine quality apricot jam instead of the raspberry jam. A little dark Navy rum goes well here, too.

BAGNET 'D TOMATICHE
Pound half a clove of garlic to a paste. Add four tablespoons of olive oil, one tablespoon of vinegar, one tablespoon of tomato purée, one teaspoon of Dijon mustard, one teaspoon of castor sugar, a little salt and milled black pepper. Whisk briskly until well combined.

BARBECUE SAUCE
Put in a saucepan 450g (1 lb) of undrained, canned tomatoes, one tablespoon of tomato purée, six tablespoons of golden syrup, one small can of liquidized apricots, the juice of half a lemon, four crushed garlic cloves, three crushed chillies, two cloves, one dessertspoon of curry powder, one bay leaf, a dessertspoon of Worcester sauce, a teaspoon of English mustard, salt and milled black pepper. Bring to the boil and simmer until the sauce is thick. Strain and cool.

BÉARNAISE SAUCE
Put into an enamelled saucepan five tablespoons of vinegar with one finely chopped shallot, one dessertspoon of chopped fresh tarragon (or a level teaspoon of dried tarragon), salt and some crushed white peppercorns. Simmer until the liquid has reduced in quantity to three tablespoons. Strain and return to the saucepan. Blend in three lightly beaten egg yolks and 25g (1 oz) of melted butter. Place the pan over a container of hot, but not boiling, water. Beat smoothly and continually and add 75g (3 oz) of butter in small pieces, a little at a time, until the sauce thickens nicely. Check the seasoning. Stir in one teaspoon of very finely chopped blanched fresh tarragon or a little dried tarragon moistened with water.

BÉCHAMEL SAUCE
In a saucepan, blend 50g (2 oz) of melted butter with 50g (2 oz) of finely sieved flour. Mix well, cook gently but do not let it take colour. Slowly, stirring all the time, add 570ml (20 fl oz) of warm milk little by

little. Season with salt and white pepper. Let the sauce simmer for 20 minutes stirring all the time. It should be smooth, thick and glossy.

BEEF STOCK

Into a large saucepan put 570ml (20 fl oz) of water, 225g (8 oz) of beef shin-bone offcuts (or similar economical pieces), half a chopped onion, one sprig of parsley, one chopped celery stalk and the leaves, one chopped carrot, salt and white pepper. Bring to the boil and skim off the froth. Simmer for 30 minutes. Check the seasoning. Strain through fine muslin. Cool and skim off any remaining fat.

A plain beef cube dissolved in hot water will do for many of the recipes in this book. In either case be wary of over-seasoning your dishes as these stocks are already well seasoned.

BEER BATTER

Mix 150g (6 oz) of sieved flour, two tablespoons of beer, 140ml (5 fl oz) of water and a teaspoon of salt. Beat smoothly into a creamy consistency. Let it stand for an hour before using.

BEURRE MANIÉ

Work equal quantities of butter and sieved flour into small smooth balls. Use them for thickening sauces. Add them one at a time into the pan juices, gravies, stews etc., while swirling the pan over the stove, until the required consistency is obtained.

BLINIS

Combine 20g ($\frac{2}{3}$ oz) of fresh yeast in 570ml (20 fl oz) of warm milk. (If using dried yeast whisk two and a half level tablespoons of it with two-thirds of a level teaspoon of castor sugar in the warm milk.) Gradually add to 50g (2 oz) of sieved plain flour. Set aside in a warm place for two hours. Then add the yolks of four eggs, 225g (8 oz) of sieved plain flour, 280ml (10 fl oz) of warm milk and a pinch of salt. Mix thoroughly. At the last moment add four stiffly beaten egg whites and 140ml (5 fl oz) of whipped cream. Allow to stand for 30 minutes. Fry gently in butter as you would ordinary pancakes.

BRIOCHES

Sift together 225g (8 oz) of plain flour, a pinch of salt and 13g ($\frac{1}{2}$ oz) of castor sugar. Blend 13g ($\frac{1}{2}$ oz) of fresh yeast with 25ml (1 fl oz) of warm water and stir into the flour. (If using dried yeast whisk two level teaspoons of it with half a level teaspoon of castor sugar in the warm water. Leave until the yeast has dissolved and the mixture has become frothy.) Add two beaten eggs and 50g (2 oz) of melted butter. Work to a soft dough and then, on a lightly floured surface, knead well for about five minutes. Shape into a ball, place in a mixing bowl and cover with polythene or a damp cloth to prevent a skin from forming. Leave to rise at room temperature for one to one and a half hours. Grease twelve small brioche moulds or deep, fluted muffin tins.

Knead the dough well on a lightly floured surface. Divide into 12 pieces. Roll three-quarters of each part into a ball and place in the moulds. Press a hole in the centres as far as the tin base and place the remaining pieces, shaped as a knob, in each. Cover with polythene or a damp cloth and leave to rise, until light and puffy, at room temperature for an hour. Brush lightly with an egg glaze (a mixture of one egg, one tablespoon of water and a pinch of castor sugar) and bake in the centre of a very hot oven for 10 minutes.

CARAMEL BRANDY SAUCE

Bring 225g (8 oz) of castor sugar and half a cup of water to the boil. Let it simmer, watching its progress carefully, until it turns to a caramel-coloured syrup. Remove from the stove. Blend in half a cup of heavy cream and a small glass of brandy. Return to the stove and swirl the sauce until it has reheated. Serve hot or cold.

CHICKEN STOCK

Proceed in precisely the same manner as for Beef stock (page 160), but substitute a chopped raw chicken carcase, giblets, the winglets and the neck for the beef. Plain chicken cubes dissolved in boiling water may be successfully used for most of the recipes in this book. Do be careful with seasoning as these stocks are already well seasoned.

CHORON SAUCE

Make a Béarnaise sauce (page 159), but when adding the egg yolks, include one dessertspoon of tomato purée and a level teaspoon of sugar. Complete the sauce in the normal way.

COCKTAIL SAUCE

Mix one cup of mayonnaise with three tablespoons of tomato ketchup, one tablespoon of creamed horseradish, one tablespoon of brandy, a few dashes of Tabasco and Worcester sauce and half a cup of fresh heavy cream. Blend together smoothly.

CUMBERLAND SAUCE

Melt 225g (8 oz) of redcurrant jelly and add two tablespoons of finely julienned orange and lemon peel (without pith and previously blanched), one large wine glass of port, one dessertspoon of chopped blanched shallots, one teaspoon of English mustard and a few dashes of Worcester and Tabasco sauce. Simmer for 15 minutes. Thicken with a little arrowroot. Serve cold.

DIABLE SAUCE

In a saucepan, sweat two chopped shallots in butter until golden and soft. Pour in a cup of dry white wine and one tablespoon of vinegar. Boil and reduce by half. Add two teaspoons of tomato purée, one cup of Veal gravy (page 164), a few dashes of Worcester sauce, one bay leaf, a little thyme and abundant milled black pepper. Bring to the boil again and simmer for five minutes. Strain. Thicken the sauce with arrowroot or Beurre manié (page 160). Stir in a little chopped parsley. Serve hot.

FISH STOCK

Sauté in a large saucepan, all chopped, one medium-sized onion, half a leek, a carrot and a piece of celery in butter until soft but not coloured. Add 450g (1 lb) of bones and trimmings from any white fish (preferably those from a sole), two cups of dry white wine, 570ml (20 fl oz) of water, one bay leaf, one sprig of parsley, a tablespoon of peppercorns and season with salt. Bring to the boil. Skim off the risen froth and simmer for 30 minutes uncovered. Strain through fine muslin. Use when required.

FLAKY PASTRY

Sieve 225g (8 oz) of plain flour and a pinch of salt into a mixing bowl. Soften 150g (6 oz) of butter by working it with a knife blade on a plate. Divide this into four equal portions. Rub, using thumb and fingertips, one quarter of the softened butter into the flour, adding 280ml (10 fl oz) of cold water and the juice of half a lemon. Turn this elastic mixture onto a lightly floured surface and knead into a smooth dough. Allow to stand for 15 minutes.

Roll the dough into an oblong three times as long as it is wide. Distribute evenly another quarter of the butter in small knobs over the top two thirds of it. Fold the remaining third (which is not covered with butter) up, and the top third down. Turn it once to the right so that the folds are now at the sides. Using a rolling pin, seal the edges of the dough and roll out again. Repeat the procedure until all the butter has been added, allowing the dough to rest for 15 minutes between each turn. Leave to stand for 30 minutes before use.

GARLIC MAYONNAISE

Pound one large clove of garlic to a paste and blend smoothly into a quantity of mayonnaise.

GRIBICHE SAUCE

Work the hard-boiled yolks of two eggs into a smooth paste. Add one teaspoon of mixed Dijon and English mustards, six tablespoons of olive oil, two tablespoons of malt vinegar, a crushed garlic clove, salt and black pepper. Whisk smoothly together. Now add some finely chopped gherkins, chives, capers, hard-boiled egg whites, parsley, chervil and tarragon. Sweeten slightly with a little sugar. Let the sauce rest for a while to absorb the flavours, remove the garlic before serving.

HOLLANDAISE SAUCE

Boil two tablespoons each of malt vinegar and water with a pinch of salt and a little white pepper. Reduce it by half. Pour it into a bowl and allow to cool. Stand the bowl in a pan of water which is being kept hot over a low heat. Add three lightly-beaten egg yolks. Stir thoroughly. Whisking briskly, add 125g (5 oz) of soft butter cut into small pieces, a little at a time until the butter has been smoothly absorbed. The sauce should be thick enough to coat a spoon. Check the seasoning.

LOBSTER SAUCE

Cut open and clean a live (or cooked) lobster. Reserve the coral, liquid and creamy parts. Pound the lobster head and all the shell well and colour them slightly in a pan in butter. Flame with a small wine glass of brandy. Add and gently melt 125g (5 oz) of butter, a little anchovy essence and the reserved lobster parts. Season with salt and cayenne pepper. Stir well and strain the liquid butter through very fine muslin. Cool. Scrape away any bitty parts that may have collected at the bottom. Blend with two quantities of Aurore sauce (page 159) and with half a cup of heavy cream. Serve hot as required. The meat can be used in some of the recipes in the fish section.

MAYONNAISE

Do not use cold or chilled ingredients. In a china bowl blend two fresh egg yolks with half a teaspoon of salt and half a teaspoon of

Dijon mustard. Add 280ml (10 fl oz) of olive oil in a thin, constant drizzle, stirring all the time with a wooden spoon. When the oil is completely absorbed the eggs will have substantially increased in volume. Sharpen the taste with one and a half tablespoons of light malt vinegar. The sauce must be thick and glossy. It must not be kept in a metal container of any kind.

MELBA SAUCE

This is really nothing more than a purée of sweetened fresh raspberries. There are a few commercially bottled sauces available and they are very good. Nowadays it would seem an extravagance to purée perfectly good raspberries as an accompaniment to a dessert. So here is a good and useful restaurant tip. Merely dilute, with a little water, some good quality raspberry jam. Bring to the boil, simmer for a few minutes, strain and cool. Serve as required.

MORNAY SAUCE

Proceed as for an ordinary Béchamel sauce (page 159), but add one tablespoon each of finely grated Parmesan and Gruyère cheeses while the sauce is simmering. Finish by blending in two tablespoons of heavy cream.

PANCAKE BATTER
(SWEET AND SAVOURY)

Mix smoothly 100g (4 oz) of finely sifted flour with 280ml (10 fl oz) of mixed water and milk until a creamy consistency is reached. Add a pinch of salt, one dessertspoon of castor sugar and one whole beaten egg plus one egg yolk. Whisk well and stand for an hour before using. For a savoury pancake batter, merely omit the sugar.

PUFF PASTRY CRESCENTS

Sieve 225g (8 oz) of plain flour with a pinch of salt. Soften 225g (8 oz) of butter (preferably unsalted) by working it with a knife on a plate, then rub about 13g (½ oz) of it into the flour. Mix quickly to a soft elastic dough with 140ml (5 fl oz) of cold water and the juice of half a lemon. Turn out onto a lightly floured surface and knead lightly until smooth. Cover with polythene or a damp cloth and allow to stand for 30 minutes.

Roll the dough into an oblong about 12mm (½ in) thick and cover half of it—stopping 12mm (½ in) from the edge—with the remainder of the butter. Fold the other half of the dough over to cover it, and press the edges. Allow to stand for 15 minutes. Turn the pastry once to the right so that the fold is to the side, then roll out the strip three times as long as it is wide. Fold into three, seal the edges, leave the open edge facing the cook and roll again. Repeat the whole process twice more.

There are two ways to obtain the crescent shape. Roll out the dough thinly and cut into triangles with sides longer than the base; roll up each triangle, starting from the base and curl the ends round to form a crescent. Or, cut the thinly rolled pastry into circles which should then be rolled up; curl round the ends to form the crescent. Brush lightly with a glaze (a mixture of one beaten egg and a little milk).

RAVIGOTE SAUCE

Make a double amount of vinaigrette sauce with double the quantity of Dijon mustard and thicken it with the pounded yolks of two hard-boiled eggs. Mix in one dessertspoon each of finely chopped shallots, capers, gherkins and parsley. Flavour with a little chopped tarragon and chervil.

ROUILLE

Soak a slice of stale bread in fish soup (if you are making it) or in a fish stock and squeeze it out. Add it to three hot chillies, two large garlic cloves and a teaspoon of tomato purée. Pound them into a smooth paste. Blend in two tablespoons of olive oil, in a fine stream, stirring all the time. Dilute with half a cup of fish soup or fish stock. Serve cold.

This is usually spread onto slices of oven-toasted French bread and served with fish soups, stews or some grilled fish dishes.

SATÉ DIP
Mix thoroughly one tablespoon of crunchy peanut butter, five tablespoons of tomato ketchup, one teaspoon of curry powder, one dessertspoon of bottled Chinese chilli sauce, a few dashes of Worcester sauce, one teaspoon of horseradish sauce, half a teaspoon of sugar and one tablespoon of heavy cream.

PASTRY, PLAIN SHORTCRUST
Sieve 100g (4 oz) of plain flour and a pinch of salt into a mixing bowl. Cut 100g (4 oz) of butter into 12mm ($\frac{1}{2}$ in) cubes and, using the thumb and fingertips, rub lightly into the flour until the mixture looks crumbly. Add 30ml ($1\frac{1}{4}$ fl oz) of water a little at a time, mixing it in carefully until the mixture clings together in a ball. The dough should just hold together and should be pliable, not damp and sticky. Turn it onto a lightly floured surface and knead briefly until firm and smooth. Stand for at least 15 minutes before use.

RICH SHORTCRUST
Sieve 225g (8 oz) flour together with a pinch of salt. Cut 100g (4 oz) of butter into 12mm ($\frac{1}{2}$ in) cubes and rub into the flour, using thumb and fingertips, until mixture is crumbly. Sift and add 50g (2 oz) of icing sugar; mix two egg yolks and two tablespoons of water together and pour into the flour and mix quickly to a firm dough. Turn out onto a lightly floured surface and knead until smooth. Cover with polythene and chill for 30 minutes before using.

SIMPLE TOMATO SAUCE
In a saucepan, gently sauté a small, finely chopped onion with two crushed garlic cloves in four tablespoons of olive oil and a knob of butter until golden. Add 450g (1 lb) of roughly chopped, undrained, canned tomatoes, a small level teaspoon of castor sugar, salt and milled black pepper. Cover and cook for 15 minutes. Add six torn-up fresh basil leaves (or a pinch of dried), uncover and finish cooking for five more minutes. Remove the garlic Use as necessary either sieved or as it is.

TARTARE SAUCE
Put five tablespoons of mayonnaise in a bowl and smoothly mix in two teaspoons of Dijon mustard, one tablespoon of chopped parsley and one dessertspoon each of finely chopped gherkin, capers and spring onion. Flavour with a little chopped fresh tarragon and chervil.

VEAL GRAVY
Sauté in a large baking dish, all chopped, two large onions, two large carrots, a celery stalk and four slices of streaky bacon in pure lard until well coloured. Stir in 450g (1 lb) of veal bones and 450g (1 lb) of floured cheap veal offcuts. Brown quickly but thoroughly. Add two chopped ripe tomatoes, a bouquet garni, salt and milled black pepper. Cover with water. Cover the pan and cook in a moderate oven for at least three hours. Remove the meat and bones. Strain the remaining gravy, pressing out well. Let it stand and then skim off all the risen fat. The sauce should be thick enough to mask a spoon. If not, then thicken by swirling in an adequate amount of Beurre manié (page 160).

Any good gravy you have, strengthened with meat or vegetable cubes and thickened with beurre manié may, at a pinch, be successfully used.

VEGETABLE STOCK
Chop half a leek, one carrot, one celery stalk with the leaves, one medium-sized onion and one sprig of parsley. Place them in a saucepan with a piece of bay leaf, a

clove, salt and white pepper. Add 710ml (25 fl oz) of water. Bring to the boil. Skim off the risen froth. Simmer until the vegetables are tender and then strain through fine muslin. Use as necessary.

SALSA VERDE

Soak two tablespoons of fresh, white breadcrumbs in vinegar and then squeeze them out. Work one hard-boiled egg yolk to a paste, mix together with the bread and add four tablespoons of very finely chopped parsley, one finely chopped garlic clove and one teaspoon of chopped capers. Blend in one cup of olive oil. Season with salt and milled black pepper. If necessary, sharpen with a little more vinegar. Let this piquant sauce stand for at least one hour.

SAUCE AU VIN BLANC
White wine sauce

Make a Béchamel sauce (page 159) substituting a mixture of fish stock and white wine for the milk. Simmer for 20 minutes. Enrich with the yolk of an egg and half a cup of heavy cream. Season with salt and cayenne pepper and highlight with a few drops of lemon juice. The sauce should be thick and glossy. Take care that it does not curdle, stir it gently from time to time, and keep a watchful eye on it.

SAUCE AU VIN A L'ESTRAGON
White wine sauce with tarragon

Make a quantity of Sauce au vin blanc (above) with the addition of one tablespoon of fresh, chopped tarragon or a teaspoon of dried tarragon when the sauce is put on to simmer.

VINAIGRETTE SAUCE

Mix three tablespoons of fine olive oil with one tablespoon of light malt (or wine) vinegar together with one teaspoon of Dijon mustard, salt and milled black pepper. Whisk well to a creamy consistency. These quantities are sufficient for a salad for four people, provided that the salad is lightly but very thoroughly tossed. A little crushed garlic or sugar may be added and are, in fact, an improvement.

VOL-AU-VENT CASES

On a well-floured board roll 225g (8 oz) of Puff pastry (page 163) to about 6mm (¼ in) thickness. Stamp out 12 circles of pastry with a floured, plain 7½cm (3 in) round cutter. Place half on a greased baking tray. Brush with a glaze (a mixture of one beaten egg and a little milk). These will be the bases of the cases. With a smaller 5cm (2 in) plain cutter stamp out the centres of the remaining six. These will make the lids. Place them on a separate greased tray and brush with the glaze. Transfer the pastry rings onto the bases (take care not to pull them out of shape) and press to seal them together. Brush the tops with the glaze. Allow to stand for 20 minutes. Place towards the top of a very hot oven and bake for 20 minutes or until golden brown. Then reduce the oven temperature to hot and bake until cases are crisp. Scoop out any soft pastry inside. The pastry tops should then be baked for 10 minutes in a very hot oven.

FORMAGGI
Cheese

The mere mention of a cheese board to most Chefs de cuisine has almost the same effect as waving a red cloth in front of a bull. There is an awful lot of waste involved in the correct and appetizing presentation of cheese. Cut sides have to be continually trimmed to present a fresh look; small pieces are usually discarded instead of being profitably reused; waiters are often far too generous (thinking of the tip); customers are often too greedy (thinking of the bill); and lastly, cheese being out of sight of the kitchen is normally easy to pilfer. I doubt very much whether any restaurant in the world, including my own, ever made profits from the sale of cheese.

Parmigiano-Reggiano This is to Italian cooking the most important cheese of all. It is world famous and earns millions of lire in valuable foreign currency for Italy. The economics of the two producing centres, Parma and Reggio Emilia, are so highly geared to its production that some of the local banks even safe-keep mature cheeses in much the same way as they do gold.

The best Parmesan is known as Stravecchio. It is matured for not less than three years. It should be very dense, hard, of a definite pale straw yellowish colour and rich and mellow of flavour. Only buy the best quality or your carefully cooked dishes will be ruined. Watch out for some stores' habit when buying ready-grated Parmesan of mixing in the grated, musty, hard rind. This is a cheap trick and offenders should be denounced!

Apart from its wide use in cooking, Parmesan is also a wonderful cheese to eat on its own. Unfortunately, restaurants rarely offer it on their cheese boards. But do try a portion together with a luscious Comice pear.

Bel Paese I personally don't like it. I consider it to be a contrived cheese, dull of taste and with an elastic texture. However, such is the power of advertising that this is one of the first cheeses to spring to a waiter's mind when he is asked for advice. It is a mild soft cheese and can be used in cooking as a substitute for Mozzarella.

Fontina This is made in the beautiful region of the Valle d'Aosta and is one of the few classic cheeses in Italy protected by presidential decree. With its smooth tenderness and magnificent flavour, it is an appetizing and sensitive cheese. It cooks well and is, of course, essential to Fonduta, that superb cheese dish made of Fontina, butter, cream, eggs and topped with thin shavings of white Piedmontese truffles.

Brie One of the world's truly great cheeses. When I could find a good example, I used to present the whole round classic form; served from its straw bed, creamy soft to the touch and never runny, the freshly cut, gently bulging sides held back by thin marble strips. It deserves an honourable place in any selection.

Petit Suisse These attractively wrapped cheeses have a low fat content and a light, slightly creamy dryish taste. Petit

Suisse are eaten with thin crackers or dressed with olive oil and sprinkled with milled black pepper or chopped chives. They are also good when eaten with soft fruits or just fine castor sugar.

Taleggio This creamy semi-soft buttery cheese is from the Lombardy region originating from the province of Bergamo. When in peak condition it is a delicious cheese with a marvellous flavour somewhat reminiscent of the soft white parts of Gorgonzola but without such a powerful flavour.

Gorgonzola I am sorry to say that Gorgonzola is not as good as I remember it to be. I was introduced to that great cheese by my father who considered himself to be a connoisseur. And, judging from the fuss he made, I suppose he must have been. He permitted no one except himself to pass judgment or to purchase any quantity, however small, for his table. His weekly Gorgonzola purchase took the form of a studied and planned campaign. Once tasted, tested, savoured and convinced that the chosen form possessed all the correct properties, he reverently took it home, where it would be set before us.

Over the years I, too, became a fairly competent judge of Gorgonzola. The cheese that now reaches the table is a smooth, nicely piquant sort of old-style Gorgonzola and is known as Dolcelatte. It is very, very good.

Caciocavallo The word literally means 'cheese on horseback' and it is called this for no reason other than the fact that the fresh cheeses are tied in pairs and straddled over poles to be suspended and matured. Caciocavalli from the Naples-Amalfi area are usually pear-shaped, with thin, hard, smooth rinds. The cheese is pale yellow in colour when young and can be either sweet or very piquant – altogether an excellent old-fashioned kind of cheese with traditional qualities.

Ricotta A light, moist type of cottage-curd cheese, which should be made, delivered and eaten on the same day. It is extensively used in regional cooking all over Italy. To see it sold in the country on straw platters or wicker baskets brings back memories of the simple things and of how they used to be. There is a salty variety, but the unsalted kind is more generally used. Apart from its use in sweet or savoury cooking or baking, it is very good sweetened and flavoured with finely ground coffee or chocolate, spiked with rum or brandy and served chilled in little earthenware pots. It may be eaten slightly moistened with lemon juice or water and sprinkled with castor sugar. Or, of course, simply served as a cheese course and dressed with a little olive oil, salt and black pepper.

Gruyère Unfortunately no cheese board, especially a Swiss one, can be considered complete without the inclusion of this cheese. Gruyère is the one with few and small holes. Emmenthal is the other.

Mozzarella A Campanian soft cheese that should be made with buffalo milk. Current commercial production has become so highly industrialized that the end-product is almost laughable. So vague is the resemblance to the real thing that some firms do not even dare to call it by its proper name. When made with cows' milk, it should be known as Fior di latte.

I am sorry to say that I can detect very few virtues in Mozzarella. Some do say that it has certain dietetic properties. That may well be, but what more effective way to diet is there than abstinence?

Mozzarella is a white, slightly sour-tasting, rubbery cheese that should be made and eaten on the same day. Romans and Neapolitans today delight in stuffing Mozzarella morsels into the centre of some of their adored deep-fried delicacies such as croquettes known as *supplì*. The hot cheese forms long, thin, rubbery strands as it is pulled away from the mouth. These are known locally as 'telephone wires'. It is easy to see why those excitable, voluble southerners often give the impression to northern Italians of having their wires crossed!

Stilton One of the really great blue cheeses that compares favourably to any in the world. It should be treated with much respect and never sacrilegiously soaked with port, and never scooped out. Stilton, instead, should be cut into portions and savoured with a glass of fine port.

Cheddar When all is said and done, there is really no cheese in the world that can compare with a mature, tangy, real English Cheddar!

A NOTE ON ITALIAN WINES

It would be unthinkable in Italy to try to enjoy any meal, no matter how simple, without an accompanying glass or two of wine. There is no pomposity involved in Italian wine drinking. Generally speaking it is regarded as a convivial, joyous, everyday habit. Every honest Italian wine drinker will agree that their nationally produced wines are a pride unto themselves, that they should always be appreciated. But they will also tell you that they should never be taken deadly seriously.

Although Italians are very capable of understanding, approving and discussing the finer points of wine, they are not particularly overawed by the subject. A lighthearted approach has always been the order of the day. Lately, however, a disturbing tendency has been making itself felt all over the country. Various people, wine fanciers, interested groups, public relations or marketing set-ups, through the media of television, radio, books and articles are, almost desperately, trying to elevate Italian wines in general to the internationally agreed levels accorded for so long to some of the better wines produced in the classical wine regions of France.

This type of promotion, of course, is an attempt to clear the country's vast wine stocks caused by fantastic overproduction. But not only are they wrong and dishonest, they are attempting the impossible. It is like making absurd comparisons between Italian provincial or French bourgeois cooking with classical French haute cuisine. And they are not doing the hardworking Italian wine producer any favours by claiming standards that do not exist and could not be achieved anyway.

An initiate of Italian wines, bamboozled by these claims, could be easily deterred from drinking more of them once he discovers that the claimed virtues are more imagined than real.

At the risk of being hounded and forever banished across the Alps (in the direction of Burgundy I trust!) I must make a statement which is bound to displease many. In my opinion, born of years of practical experience, no classical Italian wine (white or red) exists at present which can be fairly ranked with any of the established vintage wines of France. Even over there only few are raised to those glorious heights. No wine in the world can ever hope to compare with such superlatives as La Tache, Grands Echezeaux, Bonnes Mares, the Romanées, Corton Charlemagne or any of the Crus Exceptionelles of Bordeaux.

It is, furthermore, my contention that no more than six classical Italian red wines (from a few carefully chosen producers) can be compared to French wines which have been officially graded as 'fine'. These are Brunello Biondi Santi from Montalcino, a couple of Barolos, Gattinaras, Spannas, Chianti Classici, and one Amarone. And believe me, having searched Italy and my conscience thoroughly, I cannot, for the life of me, enlarge on that seemingly puny list. So let's enjoy Italian wines and appreciate them for what they really are!

Having cast off any pretensions, you may now buy your Italian wine from a restaurant or wine dealer without any trepidation. Your choice will be a difficult one. There are so many of them! Barolo, Barbera, Barbaresco, Bardolino, Nebbiolo, Spanna, Valpolicella, Inferno, Cabernet, Lugana, Nuraghe, Soave, Frascati, Orvieto, Pinot Grigio, Verdicchio, Ravello. There isn't enough room to list them or even to begin to describe their varied properties. After all, Italy is the world's largest wine producer! But believe me, as long as you are satisfied (and this is important) that the wine you have chosen has been bottled in Italy and by a reputable wine house, you may be sure that it will be more than just good.

Please do not over-chill Italian white wines or any other for that matter. Do lay Italian red wines, which are suitable for aging, on their sides (label side up so that you always know where the sediment is) in a dark, ventilated, cool and quiet cellar or cupboard. Unfortunately, most Italian vintage wines available today do not contain as much of the natural deposit as would normally be necessary to assist proper maturing, which can only be completed in bottles. The deposit, instead, is sadly lost in those vast concrete and glass vats that save the producers and wine merchants so much money by way of bottle, cork, seal and storage charges.

Good, aged, vintage red wines should be stood upright for a least 24 hours before serving in order to let what sediment there is collect at the base and to allow them to adjust gradually to normal room temperature. Never serve aged wines in baskets or cradles for, despite careful handling, there is always a certain backwash. Instead, regardless of how mature or indeed, how modest they may be, do open all red wines at least an hour before serving them. And do get into the habit of decanting them. All of them, even the young ones! It is not a form of snobbery. Just good sense. The contact with the air can only do the wine good. It will revive the dormant properties, double their qualities and treble your pleasure. Finally, always serve your wines, all wines, in thin, clear, long-stemmed glasses of generous size; never overfill them, let the bouquet and fragrance be slowly released and properly savoured.

GLOSSARY

Beignet French for fritter. It describes any foodstuff (savoury or sweet) dipped in batter and fried in smoking-hot, deep fat.

Blanch A method of preparing food by plunging it into boiling water or bringing it to the boil with the water for various effects:
(a) It can soften, as in the case of the husks of shelled nuts;
(b) It is a method of partly cooking vegetables;
(c) Means that the peel of blanched vegetables and fruits are easier to remove;
(d) It can remove too strong a flavour;
(e) Some meats, mainly offal, previously soaked, are blanched in water which is gradually brought to the boil, in order to clean them and to harden the membranous skin to facilitate removal;
(f) To extract surplus fat.

Bouchée A small puff-pastry case to be filled with savoury or sweet stuffing. It is served as part of an hors d'oeuvre or as a garnish.

Canapés Rectangular (though shape does vary) slices of crustless bread, their size and thickness depending on the ingredients to be placed upon them. They can be either toasted or fried in oil or butter.

Cèpe French name for boletus. It is a wild, edible and delicious mushroom found in spring and autumn.

Chambéry Exceptionally fine dry white vermouth made in Chambéry, France.

Charcuterie French for the preparation of various meats, pork in particular, in different ways. It also means the shop where such meats can be bought.

Chef de Rang A restaurant waiter in charge of a group of tables (known as a station). It is he, together with the maître d'hôtel, who trains the younger waiters.

Chorizo Spanish garlic sausage. There are two types: one of pork, beef, garlic and peppers which is only used to enliven a stew; the other is eaten smoked or dried and is made with port, garlic and peppers.

Cocotte A deep round or oval dish with a tight-fitting lid and two side handles which can be made of iron, metal or pottery.

Commis Apprentice or assistant waiter.

Confectioner's Sugar Icing sugar.

Court Bouillon An aromatic liquid in which fish, and to a lesser extent meat and vegetables, can be poached. It is boiled up before the food to be poached is added. The ingredients of the court bouillon vary depending on the food to be cooked.

Croûte There are two main types of croûte:
(a) Bread (does not have to be stale) which is fried in butter, oil or lard and dried in the oven.
(b) A toasted breadcase made from stale bread which is cut as for a vol-au-vent, fried and drained; it is then filled with savoury mixtures.

Croûton Cubed, crustless, stale bread toasted, baked or fried (the latter is best) in butter, oil or lard until golden. Used for garnishing.

Dariole Mould A small cylindrical or cup-shaped mould for cooking pastries or vegetables to be served either hot, where they are to be used as a garnish (for example, Anna potatoes), or cold and set in aspic.

Deglaze Rinsing out the cooking pan with either stock, wine, sherry or water, and dissolving the pan residues in order to obtain a strongly flavoured base for the garnish or gravy for the dish.

Al Dente An Italian culinary term which means, literally, to the teeth. It usually refers to pasta which is cooked so that it is only just tender.

Entrecôte Beef steak cut from the top of the sirloin and ribs; (in French it means between the ribs).

Escalope Boneless slices of meat cut 10mm ($\frac{3}{8}$ in) thick and which are flattened to a thickness of 5mm ($\frac{1}{4}$ in). To ensure fineness and flatness it is cut across the grain from a solid piece of meat which contains no muscle separations.

Fondant French for melting, juicy, luscious, dissolving; also for sweetmeat. In culinary terms it is French for a very small croquette made from vegetable purées or custard filling mixed with grated cheese to taste, then quick-fried so as to remain soft and moist inside. It is served as an hors d'oeuvre.

Grappa A brandy made from the left-over skins of the pressed grapes.

Le gratin, au gratin, gratiné French culinary term for the thin crust formed on the surface of dishes when placed under a hot grill or salamander or in the oven. It can be thus 'browned' with butter, breadcrumbs or cheese.

Julienne This describes any food which is cut finely or coarsely into match-like shapes, as well as a soup of chopped vegetables cooked in meat broth.

Lardons Salt pork, streaky bacon and raw ham, cut into strips about 5mm ($\frac{1}{4}$ in) wide and 35mm ($1\frac{1}{2}$ in) long, though shapes and thickness vary.

Macerate Process of soaking foods (mostly fruits) in spirits or other sweet liquids for softening and flavouring.

Marinate To soak in a highly seasoned (usually lemon- or vinegar-based spices, herbs and vegetables) liquid preparation.

Mask To cover or coat a finished dish with sauce or thick gravy.

Meat glaze A strong meat stock which is reduced by boiling until it is syrupy. It sets like jelly.

Médaillons Any food which is cut in the shape of a medallion – either round or oval.

Mélanger French meaning to mix foods in a less vigorous way than when beating.

Meunière A method of cooking fish which involves seasoning, lightly flouring and frying in butter. Some lemon is squeezed on the cooked fish and the butter in which it has been cooked is poured over it.
Mignonette Pepper French term for a mixture of white and black pepper or coarsely ground black pepper.
Mostardi di cremona Fruits (pears, cherries, plums, greengages) preserved in sweet syrup with a strong mustard-seed flavour. Quite hot by Italian standards. Usually served with boiled meats. A speciality of Cremona, northern Italy.
Praires Large, cockle-like hard-shelled clams with a beautifully fluted shell. Eaten raw like an oyster or cooked like mussels. Similar to the Italian *vongole*. In the United States they are known as littlenecks or cherrystones.
Sauter, Sauté To brown and/or cook food, usually in a frying pan in a small quantity of butter and oil, oil or lard. In French *sauter* means 'to jump' which indicates that the food must be toasted in the fat (either shaken or turned with a fork) so that it does not stick or burn.
Sauteuse A special pan used for sautéeing food. It is like a frying pan but it is heavy and shallow, sides at least 50mm (2 in) deep with a thick base.
Strew To scatter or sprinkle over.
Sweat To draw the juices from food, usually vegetables. Before cooking they are gently cooked in a covered pan, in butter or oil or lard until moist and soft but not coloured.

WEIGHTS & MEASURES

Conversions from imperial to metric are only approximate as exact conversions are unwieldy for quick measurement.

IMPERIAL AND METRIC

Liquid measurements

Imperial Fluid ounces	Metric Litres	Millilitres
40 (2 pints)	1·14	1140
35	1	1000
26	¾	750
17½	½	500
9	¼	250
4½	⅛	125
4	1/10	100
2		50
1		25
1 cup	– 10½ fl oz	– 300ml
1 wine glass	– 7 fl oz	– 175ml
1 tablespoon	– ⅗ fl oz	– 15ml
1 dessertspoon	– ⅖ fl oz	– 10ml
1 teaspoon	– ⅕ fl oz	– 5ml

Solid measurements

Imperial ounces	Metric grammes	Imperial ounces	Metric grammes
16	450–500	7	200
15	425	6	175
14	400	5	150
13	375	4	125–100
12	350–325	3	75
11	300	2	50
10	275	1	25
9	250	½	12
8	250–225	¼	6

ENGLISH AND AMERICAN

Liquid measurements

English		American
2 pints–40 fl oz	–	2½ pints–5 cups
1 pint–20 fl oz	–	1¼ pints–2½ cups
½ pint–10 fl oz	–	1¼ cups
⅖ pint– 8 fl oz	–	1 cup
¼ pint–5 fl oz–1 gill	–	½ cup plus 2 tablespoons
2 fl oz–4 tablespoons	–	¼ cup
1 tablespoon–½ fl oz	–	½ fl oz

Solid measurements

English	American
8 oz butter or fat	1 cup (solidly packed)
2 oz butter or fat	¼ cup (4 tablespoons)
8 oz castor sugar	1 cup plus 3 tablespoons
2 oz castor sugar	4 tablespoons
1 lb plain flour, sieved	4½ cups cake flour, sieved
4 oz plain flour, sieved	1 cup plus 4 tablespoons
1 oz plain flour, sieved	4 tablespoons

OVEN TEMPERATURES

The table below is only an approximate guide and the suggested temperatures and timings are those appropriate to the oven of an average-sized domestic cooker.

°F	°C	Gas No	Oven Heat
225	110	¼	very cool
250	130	½	very cool
275	140	1	cool
300	150	2	slow
325	170	3	moderately slow
350	180	4	moderate
375	190	5	moderately hot
400	200	6	hot
425	220	7	very hot
450	230	8	very hot

INDEX

Alici in tortiera, 11
Anchovies (acciughe)
  baked savoury, 11
  with fried Mozzarella, 15–16
  with sautéed mushrooms, 140
  with thin spaghetti, 68
Animelle di vitello
  alla King, 105–6
  alla Normanna, 106
  'Victoria', 106
  vol-au-vent di, alla crema, 107
Anitra
  'Cesare Pizzala', 118
  alla conca d'oro, 118–20
  terrina d', 36–7
Antipasti, 11–38
Antipasto pasquale, 11–12
Apple
  with red cabbage, 136
  upside-down flan, 157–8
Arancii 'Positano', 152
Aringhe all'ubriaca, 12
Artichokes, globe
  country style, 14, 150
  fried, 134
  sautéed, 134–5
Artichoke hearts
  with fillets of sole, 89
  with fillet steak, 99
  stuffed with baked eggs, 52
Asparagus, fresh, 12
Astaco, 80–2
  coppa di, 17
  alla fra Diavolo, 79
  insalata di, 'Ofelia', 80
  maionese di, 'Patrizia', 80
  'à la nage', 79–80
Avgotarago, 13
Avocado:
  and smoked salmon mousse, 26
  soup, chilled, 40
  stuffed with chicken and crab, 32; with shrimp and ham, 31; with tuna fish, 31

Baccalà
  con le patate, 80
  zuppa di, con le patate, 48
Bacon
  and eggs, with macaroni, 65
  with French beans, 138
  and raw spinach salad, 148
  with sautéed Brussels sprouts, 135
  with scallops, 84
Bananas
  with fillets of sole, 88–9
  flamed with Bacardi rum, 152
Barchettine di scampi, 12
Beans, broad
  with pasta, 64
  sautéed, 138
Beans, French
  with bacon, 138
  crisp, fried, 138
  sautéed, with garlic, 137–8
  soup, 45
Beans, haricot (Italian cannellini)
  with braised ox-tail, 98–9
  with pasta, 64
  with sage, 137
  soup: with escarole, 45; Minori style, 45; Neapolitan cream of, 40; and rice, 44
Beef, 95, 96–105
  in Bollito misto, 96–7
  braised: with beer, 98; ox-tail with haricot beans, 98–9; in red wine and onions, Genoa style, 98; with vegetables, Florentine style, 105
  broth, 39–40
  and chicken broth, 40
  fillet steak: with artichokes and truffles, 99; stuffed with oysters, 99
  fillet strips in paprika and cream sauce, 99
  Florentine T-bone, 96
  marrow, with sirloin steak, 100
  médaillons, 102–3
  patty, 102
  Pickwick pudding, 103–4
  raw: dressed fillet of, 14–15; spicy, chopped, 99
  rehashed: with potatoes, 102; with tomatoes, 102
  salted, smoke-cured, 13
  sirloin steak: with beef marrow, 100; chopped, with pine nuts and sultanas, 102; with endives and grapes, 101; with mushrooms and herbs, 99–100; with pepper sauce, 100; with Roquefort butter, 101; with tomato and oregano, 100; with whisky sauce, 100
  steak Diane, 104–5
  stew, with Cabernet wine, 104
  stock, 160
  thinly beaten, grilled, 103
Beer
  batter, 20, 160
  beef braised with, 98
Beetroot
  and baked onion salad, 137
  cold soup (Bortsch), 39
Beignets
  di cavolfiore, 135
  di cozze, 12–13, 94
Beurre manié, 160
Bigos alla Polacca, 13
Bistecca alla Fiorentina, 96
Blinis, 160
Bollito misto all'Italiana, 96–7
Bortsch fredda, 39
Bottarga, 13
Brains, calves'
  with black butter sauce, 107
  fried in savoury butter, 107
Brasato di manzo, alla Genovese, 98
Bresaola della Valtellina, 13
Brioches, 160
  filled with seafood, 80–1
Broccoli leaves, 134
Brodo (broth)
  di manzo, 39–40
  di pollo, 40
  di pollo e manzo, 40
Brussels sprouts
  sautéed with bacon, 135
  sautéed with garlic, 135–6
Bucatini all'amatriciana, 56
Butter
  black butter sauce, 107
  Roquefort, with sirloin steak, 101
  savoury, with deep-fried sole, 90

Cabbage (cavolo)
  casserole, with partridge, 131
  Lombardy style, 136
  and pork, Polish style, 13
  and pork ribs casserole, 116
Cabbage, red
  with apples and wine, 136
  with sautéed pork chops, 116
  with venison cutlets, 129–30
Calamari, 81–2
Calves' feet salad, 26–7
Calzoncini al curry, 13–14
Cannelloni
  al forno, 56–7
  alla Sorrentina, 57
Canoncei alla botticino, 57
Capers, 93, 112
Caponata alla Siciliana, 14, 150
Caprioli
  con cavoli rossi, 129–30
  al pepe, 129
Carbonata alla fiamminga, 98
Carciofi
  alla Appiana, 134
  alla 'Cesare', 134–5
  alla contadina, 14, 150
  sauté di, e patate, 135
Carpaccio, 14–15
Carré d'agnello alla Ligure, 115
Carrots
  cream sauce, 135
  dressed with olive oil, 14, 150
  Vichy style, 135
Carrozzella alla lucania, 15–16
Casoncei alla botticino, 57
Casseola alla Milanese, 116
Cauliflower (cavolfiore)
  with cheese, 135
  dressed with olive oil, 16, 150
  fritters, 135
  with pasta, 63
  with Sara's pasta, 63–4
  soup, 44, 150
Cavolini di Bruxelles, 135–6
Celery
  braised in butter, 147
  fritters, 147
  with Parmesan cheese, 147–8
Cervella di vitello
  al burro nero, 107
  alla Monteverde, 107
Cetriolo alla crema, 136
Cheese, 166–8
  with cauliflower, 135

Cheese (contd)
  Mozzarella, 14–15, 23–4, 26, 167
  Parmesan, 54, 138, 147–8, 166
  Ricotta, 58, 157, 167
  Roquefort butter, 101
  sauce, 91
Cheesecake, Italian, 158
Chestnut(s)
  candied, with ice-cream, 152
  purée, with meringue, 154
  with honeyed duckling, 118–20
Chicken, 96, 120–9
  avocado with crabmeat, 32
  and beef broth, 40
  in Bollito misto, 96–7
  with brandy and tarragon, 126–8
  breast, rolled and stuffed, 122–4
  broth, 40; with whisked eggs, 44
  casseroled, lemon-flavoured, 124
  with cream sauce, 124, 125–6
  and cream soup, 41–2
  croquettes, 120–1
  curried, with egg-plant, 128–9
  escalope with egg-plant, 129
  left-over, fried in batter, 121
  leg, braised, stuffed, 121
  mayonnaise, 122
  omelette with crabmeat and, 50
  pancakes on spinach, 120
  pie, English, 120
  in red wine sauce, 124–5
  salad, 122
  sautéed, 125
  Southern Italian fried, 121
  split: grilled and flamed, 128; sautéed, 124
  with whisky and cream, 128
Chicken liver(s)
  pâté, 29
  skewered, grilled, 121
Chicken stock, 46–7, 161
Chick-peas with flat pasta, 59–60
Chocolate
  cream, 157
  mousse, 154–5
  sauce, 154
Chowder 'King Bomba', 44–5
Cianfotta, 40, 150
Cima di vitello alla Genovese, 113
Cime di broccoli, 134
Cime di rape, 147
Cipolline al curry, 16, 150
Clam
  sauce, red and white, 61
  sautéed, Alexandria style, 93
  soup, 48
Cocktail
  crabmeat, 17
  lobster, 17
  Pacific seafood, 18
  seafood, Amalfi style, 16–17
Coda di bue con fagioli, 98–9
Coppa
  di astaco, 17
  alla caprese, 17
  'Cleopatra', 152
  'Clo-Clo', 152
  alla Giacomo, 152

'Imperatore', 152
Costata di maiale, 116
Coste di maiale, 17–18
Cotechino con lenticchie, 117
Coupe 'Pacifico', 18
Crab claws, deep-fried, 32, 94
Crabmeat
  avocado with chicken and, 32
  cocktail, 17
  croquettes, 18, 94
  omelette with chicken and, 50
  scalloped, 83
Crema see also Soup
  di fagioli, 40
  fredda di pera avocado, 40
  di patate e porri, 40–1
  di semolina, 41
  Senegalese fredda, 41–2
Crème brulée, 153
Crêpes
  all' formaggio, 57
  Suzette, 153
Crespelle di pollo, 120
Crochette
  di granchio, 18
  di patate, 143
  di pollo, 120
Crostone di scampi 'Rothschild', 18–19, 94
Croûte(s)
  landaise, 19–20
  with savoury egg filling, 50–1
  scampi-filled, 18–19, 94
Cucumbers in cream sauce, 136
Curry, curried dishes
  chicken, with egg plant, 128–9
  chicken and cream soup, 41–2
  glazed button onions with, 16
  puffs, 13–14, 39
  scampi, 86

Duck, 96
  in port and cream sauce, 118
  with oranges, 118–20
  terrine of, 36–7
Dumplings
  delicate soup, 43
  potato, with tomato sauce, 58
  spinach, with butter sauce, 66

Egg-plant(s)
  baked savoury, 24–5, 150
  caviar, 16
  with chicken escalope, 129
  with chocolate sauce, 154
  cooked as mushrooms, 141–2
  with curried chicken, 128–9
  with fillet of sole, 88–9
  fried, 141
  in olive oil, 25, 150
  'Parmigiana', 25, 150
  piquant-sweet, 14, 150
  with ribbed pasta, 67
  Salerno style, 141
  sandwiched, fried, 142
  with savoury, baked pasta, 71–2
Egg(s), 49–52 see also Omelettes
  and bacon, with macaroni, 65

baked: peasant style, 51; southern style, 50; on stuffed artichoke hearts, 52
cooked as tripe, 51–2
poached: the bishop's way, 52; in croûtes, 50–1
Endives
  Belgian: in cream sauce, 136; sautéed in butter, 136
  with sirloin steak and grapes, 101
Escarole
  with bean soup, 45
  with pine nuts and sultanas, 147
  stuffed, 35, 150

Fagiano all'Italiana, 130
Faraona, 130–1
Fave stufate, 138
Fegatino di pollo alla Siracusa, 121
Fegato di vitello, 108
Fennel (finocchi)
  fried, 138
  grilled sea bass flavoured with, 91
  with Parmesan cheese, 138
  salad, raw, 138
  sautéed in butter, 138
  seeds, with black olives, 37
Fettuccine, 55
  alla panna, 57–8
  con piselli e prosciutto, 58
Filetto
  all Boston, 99
  alla Massena, 99
  alla Strogonoff, 99
  'Tartare', 99
Fish, 77–94 see also Seafood
  soup, 48, 93–4
  soup sauce, 59
  stock, 162
Foie gras, 20
  with calves' kidneys, 109–10
  au gratin, 19–20
Fracosta
  alla Boscaiola, 99–100
  alla fiamma, 100
  al midollo, 100
  al pepe nero, 100
  alla pizzaiola, 100–1
  al Roquefort, 101
  alla vignaia, 101
Fragole 'Romanoff', 153
Frittata
  alla campagnola, 49
  di cipolle, 49–50
  di spaghetti, 50
Fritters (fritelle)
  cauliflower, 135
  celery, 147
  mussel, 12–13, 94
  potato, 143
  rice, 73, 125–6
  zucchini-flower, 148
Fritto
  misto alla Lombarda, 101
  misto 'Baia bella', grande, 82–3
  di pollo, 121; rifatto, 121
Frogs' legs, sautéed, 20–1
Fruit salad, 152, 154

173

Gambe di rane pontina, 20–1
Garlic mayonnaise, 162
Gazpacho, 42
Giambonett di pollo, 121
Gnocchi
    di patate al pomodoro, 58
    di semolina 'Sara', 76
Grapefruit 'Van de Hum', 33
Grapes
    with chicken, cream and rice, 124
    with sirloin steak and endives, 101
Guinea fowl, 96
    roasted, 130
    with sour cream sauce, 130–1

Ham, 35
    avocado with shrimp and, 31
    with noodles and peas, 58
    Parma and Turkey escalope, 124
    with peas, 146
    raw, cured, 33–4
Herrings, soused, 12

'Kebab' di maiale, 117
Kidneys, calves'
    with foie gras, 109–10
    with red wine sauce, 110
    sautéed with onions, 109
Kipper pâté, 29

Lady Leah's Queen Pudding, 153
Lamb, 96, 113–16
    casserole, 113–14; Roman style, 114–15; cutlets: baked, 115; grilled, 116; rib of, 115
    skewered, Italo-Greek style, 116
Lamponi 'Mimosa', 153
Lasagne
    pasticciate alla Minorese, 58–9
    alla vincigras, 59
Lattuga Romana alla Cinese, 141
Leek(s), 147
    with butter sauce, 146
    flan, 37
    and potato soup, 40–1
Lentil(s)
    with boiled Italian sausage, 117
    soup, thick, 46
Lettuce
    Romaine: in Caesar salad, 140; Chinese style, 141
    and truffle salad, 140
Linguine
    e ceci, 59–60
    'Joni James', 60–1
    al lardo e basilico, 61
    al sugo di pesce, 59
    alle vongole, 61; in bianco, 61
Liver, calves'
    sautéed, 108
Lobster, 78–80
    cocktail, 17
    hot, devilled, 79
    mayonnaise, special, 80
    salad, 80
    sauce, 83, 106, 162
    with sole and cheese sauce, 91
Lumache farcite al forno, 24

Macaroni (maccheroni)
    with bacon and eggs, 65
    baked, savoury, 65–6
    with egg-plant, 71–2
    with four cheeses, 62
    with Italian sausage, 63
    with Neapolitan meat sauce, 62–3
    with onion sauce, 61
    stuffed and baked, 62
    with zucchini, 66
Macedonia di frutta, 154
Manicotti al forno, 62
Mayonnaise (maionese), 162–3
    chicken, 123
    garlic, 162
    lobster, 80
Meatballs, 69, 118
Medaglioni di manzo, 102–3
Melon, seasonal, 25–6
Meringue
    with chestnut purée, 154
    sponge, 153
Merluzzo affumicato, 29, 36, 83
Mezzani
    al ragù Napoletano, 62–3
    con la salsiccia, 63, 118
Minestra
    di Lilli, 42
    maritata, 42
Minestrina di Sara 'frettolosa', 43
Minestrone
    alla 'Luisa', 43
    con la zucca, 43
Monte Bianco, 154
Moules 'Ravigote', 26
Mousse
    avocado and smoked salmon, 26
    chocolate, 154–5
    smoked haddock, 29
Mozzarella, 167–8
    fried sandwich, 26
    fried, with anchovies, 15–16
    salad, 23–4
Mullet
    grey, roe, (Bottarga), 13
    red, with tomato and herbs, 92
Mushroom(s), 138–40
    fried in batter, 20, 150
    in olive oil, 20, 150
    risotto, 74–5
    sauce, with egg noodles, 70–1
Mussel(s)
    chowder 'King Bomba', 44–5
    fritters, 12–13, 94
    gratinéed, 82
    with ribbed pasta, 66
    salad, piquant, 26
    soup, Amalfi style, 44, 94

Nervetti all'insalata, 26–7
Nodino di vitello
    alla buona donna, 108
    alla Sassi, 108
Noodles
    in cream sauce, 57–8
    egg: in Bolognese meat sauce, 70;
    with mushroom sauce, 70–1
    with peas and ham, 58

thin, with seafood sauce, 71

Octopus salad, 33, 94
Olives, black
    with fennel seeds, 37
    with turbot, 93
Omelette
    Arnold Bennett, 50
    country-style, 49
    onion, 49–50
    of smoked haddock, 50
    soufflé 'Trianon', 50
    spaghetti, 50
    stuffed with chicken and crabmeat, 50
Onion(s)
    baked, 136; and beetroot, 137
    button, glazed, curried, 16, 150
    au gratin, 111, 137
    omelette, 49–50
    sauce, with macaroni, 61–2
    with sautéed calves' kidneys, 109
    with sautéed calves' liver, 108
    soup, 46–7
    with tripe and tomato, 105
Oranges
    with honey duckling, 118–20
    sliced, in caramel sauce, 152
Osso Bucho alla Milanese, 109
Oysters (ostriche), 27–8
    baked with spinach, 28
    fillet steak stuffed with, 99
    in white wine sauce, 28

Padelle reali
    'Buona Mamma', 83–4
    'Donna Luisa', 28–9, 94
    'Letizia', 84
Paillard di manzo, 103
Palline di rita, 43
Pancakes
    batter for, 163
    blinis, 160
    with cheese stuffing, 57
    chicken, on spinach, 120
    crêpes Suzette, 153
    rolled, with hazelnut stuffing, 158
    Swiss potato, 144
Pappardelle all papalina, 55–6, 63
Partridge and cabbage casserole, 131
Pasta, 53–72
    fresh, home-made, 55–6
Pastry, 16–25
Pâté
    chicken-liver, 29
    country-style, 29
    de foie gras, 19–20
    kipper, 29
    smoked haddock, 29
Peaches (pesche)
    flamed in kirsch, 155–6
    and ice-cream, 152
    in wine, 156–7
Peas (piselli)
    with ham, 146
    with noodles and ham, 58
    with pasta, 65
    with risotto and ham, 75

Penne
   alla carbonara, 65
   pasticciate al forno, 65–6
   con le zucchine, 66
Peppers
   gratinéed, 145–6
   grilled, 30–1, 150
   sautéed spicy, 30, 150
   with savoury stuffing, 31, 150
   with veal scaloppines, 109
Pernice con cavoli, 131
Petits pots au chocolat, 157
Petti di tacchino all'Emiliana, 124
Petto di pollo sorpresa, 122–4
Pheasant, Italian style, 130
Piccatine di vitello
   alla Minorese, 109
   'Palazzo di Cristallo', 109
Pickwick pudding, 103–4
Piede di maiale 'Gribiche', 32
Pigs' trotters, 32
Pike quenelles with wine tarragon sauce, 35–6, 94
Pilaff, rice, 73
   à la grecque, 73
Pinze di granchi fritte, 32, 94
Pizza, 32–3
Polenta (maize flower), 72
   layered and baked, 73
Polipo alla luciana, 33, 94
Pollastrino in Tegame, 124
Polpettine di manzo al sugo, 69, 118
Pompelmo Van der Hum, 33
Pork, 96, 116–18 see also Sausages
   barbecued kebabs, 117
   barbecued spare ribs, 17–18, 118
   and cabbage, Polish style, 13
   chops, with red cabbage, 116
   cooked with milk, 117
   produce, 35
   ribs and cabbage casserole, 116
   skewered, Malayan style, 117
Potatoes (papate), 142–5
   with baked lamb cutlets, 115
   cake, savoury, 143, 144–5
   croquettes, 143
   dumplings, with tomato sauce, 58
   farmer's wife style, 143
   with fillets of sole, 89
   fondant, 143–4
   fritters, 143
   with globe-artichokes, 135
   hot-pot, 145
   and leek soup, 40–1
   pancakes, Swiss, 144
   with pasta, 64–5
   with rehashed boiled beef, 102
   salad, hot or cold, 143
   with salt-cod, 80
   and salt-cod soup, 48
   sliced, baked savoury, 144
   white pizzaiola style, 144
Prawns, Dublin Bay, 86
Pumpkin
   with pasta, 65
   with vegetable soup, 43

Quails, split cooked, 132

Ragù alla Bolognese, 70
Raspberries in Grand Marnier, 153
Ratatouille alla Nizzarda, 34, 150
Ravioli alla Fiorentina, 66
Rice (riso), 73–6 see also Risotto
   baked savoury, 73
   and bean soup, 44
   fritters, 73, 125–6
   pilaff, 73; alla greca, 73
   truffled, with chicken and cream sauce, 124
Ricotta al caffè, 157
Rigatoni
   alle cozze, 66
   con le melanzane, 67
   al tonno, 67
Risotto
   Friday's, 75–6
   with ham and peas, 75
   Milanese, 75
   mushroom, 74–5
   seafood, 74
   white, 73–4
Ristretto alla madrilena in gelatina, 44
Roesti, 144
Rotolo di fiorella, 67–8
Rouille, 163–4

Salad(s), 140
   baked onion and beetroot, 137
   Caesar, Mayfair style, 140
   calves' feet, 26–7
   chicken, 140
   chick-pea, 140
   lettuce and truffle, 140
   lobster, 80
   Mozzarella, 23–4
   Niçoise, 21
   octopus, 33, 94
   piquant mussel, 26
   potato, hot or cold, 143
   raw fennel, 138
   raw spinach and bacon, 148
   scampi, 21, 94
   sea bass, 23, 94
   Sinatra's seafood, 21–3
   spaghetti, 68–9
   tomato, 146
Salami and pork produce, 35
Salmon with champagne, 84–5
Salt-cod
   and potato soup, 48
   with potatoes, 80
Saté alla Malesiana, 117
Saté dip, 164
Sauce(s), 159–65
   Aurore, 83, 106, 159
   bagnet'd Tomatiche, 159
   barbecue, 159
   béarnaise, 159
   béchamel, 159–60
   Bolognese meat sauce, 70
   butter, 57, 66, 146; black, 107
   champagne, 84–5
   cheese, 91, 111–12
   Choron, 161
   clam, red and white, 61
   cocktail, 161
   cream, 57–8, 72, 86, 99, 109–10, 118, 124, 125–6, 128, 135, 136, 147, 153
   Cumberland, 161
   diable, 161
   fish soup, 59
   Gribiche, 32, 162
   hollandaise, 93, 147, 162
   lobster, 83, 106, 162
   mornay, 120, 163
   mushroom, 70–1
   Neapolitan meat, 62–3
   onion, 61–2
   pepper, 100
   piquant, 56, 69, 104
   ragù alla Bolognese, 70
   ravigote, 163
   salsa verde, 165
   seafood, 71
   shellfish, 75–6
   sour cream, 130–1
   tartare, 164
   tarragon, 126–8
   tomato, 58, 63, 69, 71–2, 76, 164
   truffle, 102–3
   tuna fish, 113
   vinaigrette, 147, 165
   whisky, 100, 128
   wine: red, 110, 124–5; white, 28, 35–6, 89–90, 165
Sauces, sweet
   apricot, 159
   caramel, 152
   caramel brandy, 160
   chocolate, 154
   Grand Marnier, 153
   melba, 163
   zabaglione, 157
Sausage(s), Italian
   boiled, with lentils, 117
   cotechino, 97
   with macaroni, 63, 118
   pork, with lentils, 117
Scallops
   with mushrooms, bacon and tomato, 84
   sautéed, 28–9, 94
   in wine sauce, 83–4
Scaloppa di vitello
   farcita, 110
   alla 'Orloff', 111
   'Savoiarda', 111–12
   alla Valdostana, 112
   al limone e capperi, 112
   alla Partenopea, 112
Scampi, 85–8
   with brandy and herbs, 86
   with calves' sweetbreads, 107
   with Chambéry, 87–8
   with cream sauce, 86
   croûte filled with, 18–19, 94
   curried, 86
   salad, 21, 94
   savoury, deep-fried, 86
   skewered: with bacon, 87;
   with mint, 87
   spicy, chilli-hot, 87

175

Scampi (contd)
  in whisky, 87
  zucchini stuffed with, 12
Scottaditi sacromonte, 116
Sea bass, 91
  baked stuffed, 91
  with fresh mint, 91–2
  grilled fennel-flavoured, 91
  salad, 23, 94
Seafood see also Fish
  cocktail, Amalfi style, 16–17
  crisply fried, 82–3
  Friday's risotto, 75–6
  hot brioche filled with, 80–1
  Pacific cocktail, 18
  risotto, 74
  salad, Sinatra's, 21–3
  sauce, with thin noodles, 71
Semolina
  'hangover' soup, 41
  pasticciata al forno, 76
  patties with tomato and basil, 76
Smoked haddock
  Monte Carlo, 83
  mousse, 29
  mousseline, 36
  omelette, 50
Smoked salmon, 34–5
  and avocado mousse, 26
Snails, baked stuffed, 24
Soffietti di luccio alla
  serpentaria, 35–6, 94
Sole (sogliole), 88–91
  cooked with dry vermouth, 90–1
  deep-fried, 90
  fillets of, 88
  au gratin, with parsley and
    garlic, 90
  with lobster and cheese sauce, 91
  with mushroom and wine, 89–90
  with tomato and mushroom, 89
  with tomatoes and herbs, 90
Soufflé di taglioni, 68
Soups, 39–48 see also Brodo;
    Crema; Zuppa
  dumplings, 43
  fish, 48, 59, 93–4
Sovrana di pollo
  'Belgravia', 128
  'Marc Antonio', 128–9
  alla Vesuvio, 129
Spaghetti
  cart-drivers', 68
  fisherman's, 69
  with meatballs, 69
  omelette, 50
  with piquant sauce, 69;
    Roman style, 56
  salad, 68–9
  thin, with anchovies, 68
  with tomato and basil, 69
Spezzatino al Cabernet, 104
Spiedini d'agnello, 116
Spinach (spinaci)
  baked with oysters, 28
  with chicken pancakes and
    mornay sauce, 148
  dumplings, with butter sauce, 66

  with Italian sausages, 117
  with lemon dressing, 148
  with Parmesan cheese, 148
  and pasta roll, 67–8
  with pine nuts and sultanas, 148
  raw, and bacon salad, 148
  soup, 42, 47, 48
  in stuffed pasta with cream, 72
Spuma di merluzzo affumicato, 36
Squid
  with flat pasta, 60–1
  piquant sautéed, Napoli style, 81
  stuffed, braised, 81–2
Storione affumicato, 36
Stracciatella alla casalinga, 44
Stracotto alla Fiorentina, 105
Strawberries with port and cream
    sauce, 153
Sturgeon, smoked, 36
Sweetbreads, calves'
  with calvados, 106
  creamed, 105–6;
  in vol-au-vent, 107
  with scampi and lobster, 106

Tagliatelle, 55
  alla Bolognese, 70
  con funghi, 70–1
Tagliolini
  alla Franco, 71
  soufflé di, 68
Tarte tatin, 157–8
Tenerone di vitello alla
    rustica, 112–13
Timballo di maccheroni, 71–2
Tivolini, 158
Tomato(es)
  baked, 146
  consommé, jellied, 44
  alla crema, 146
  with garlic and herbs, 146
  with mushrooms and herbs, 140
  with rehashed boiled beef, 102
  salad, 146
  sauce, 58, 63, 69, 71–2, 76, 164
  soup, iced piquant, 42
  with zucchini, 149
Tongue, with veal escalope, 112
Torta
  di patate, 144
  di porri, 37
  alla Ricotta, 158
Tortellini alla panna, 72
Tortiera di patate, 145
Triglia alla Livornese, 92
Tripe, with tomato and onions, 105
Truffles, 133
  with fillet steak, 99
  and lettuce salad, 140
  with rice and chicken, 124
  sauce, 102–3
Tuna fish
  avocado stuffed with, 31
  with ribbed pasta, 67
  salted, dried, 13
  sauce, 113
Turbot
  braised with wine, 92

  with olives and capers, 93
  poached, 92–3
Turkey escalope stuffed with
    Parma ham, 124
Turnip tops, 147

Ulive nere al finocchio, 37

Veal, 95–6, 105–13 see also Brains;
    Kidneys; Liver; Sweetbreads
  in bollito misto, 96–7
  braised breast of, 112–13
  braised shin of, 109
  chops, 108
  cold: sliced, with tuna fish sauce,
    113; with savoury stuffing, 113
  cutlets, Milanese style, 107–8
  escalope: with onion, 111;
    stuffed, 110; with tongue and
    cheese, 112; with wine, cream
    and cheese sauce, 111–12
  gravy, 164
  sautéed in white wine, 110
  scaloppines: with brandy and
    cream sauce, 109; with fresh
    peppers, 109; with lemon and
    capers, 112; with tomato and
    cheese, 112
Vegetable stock, 164–5
Venison
  cutlets with red cabbage, 129–30
  with pepper sauce, 129
Vol-au-vent, 107, 165

Wines, Italian, 168–9

Zabaglione al Marsala, 158
  freddo, 158
  sauce, 157
Zucchini
  crisply fried, 149
  with macaroni, 66
  poached, 128
  sautéed: with garlic, 149; with
    onions, 149
  with savoury stuffing, 38, 150
  stuffed with scampi, 12
  sweet and sour, 149
  with tomatoes and herbs, 149
Zucchini-flower
  fritters, 148
  soup, 48
Zuppa
  di baccala con le patate, 48
  di cavolfiore 'petrit', 44, 50
  di cozze: all'Amalfitana, 44, 94;
    'Chowder', 44–5
  di fagioli: alla Minorese, 45;
    con scarola 45
  di faglioni, 45, 150
  forte o soffritto, 45–6
  di lenticchie, 46
  di pesche, 48, 93–4
  dei ronchi, 46–7
  rustica, 47
  di sciurilli 'agnese', 48
  di spinaci, 48
  di Vongole, 48

EA